GUNS
OF
TEXAS

By Carroll C. Holloway
edited by Michelle M. Haas

Copano Bay Press
2014

Originally published in 1951
under the title *Texas Gun Lore*.

ISBN: 978-1-941324-04-2

CONTENTS

— Introduction —

Our historians, all good factual reporters, hesitate to comment on the events they record.

Hundreds of years in the future, historians writing of American social and economic progress, will describe the marvelous development of the highway system during the first half of the twentieth century. Because they cannot cite "volume and page" in proof, they will not mention that our progress in road building was due to the invention of the automobile and motor truck.

In the past, historians have recorded events but frequently have withheld reasons. There was a Dark Age, followed by a brighter age. There was a feudal system in which a noble landowner owned his serfs as surely as he owned his castle. The Magna Carta was inoperative, and there were no Bills of Right. The common man had no liberties and received no consideration. History tells us of this, and also of the newer and better order.

Why did men acquire rights? How was the foundation of liberty and democracy laid? An invention is the answer to these questions also—the invention of the gun!

In feudal times, a ruler might maintain a dozen armored knights riding on armored horses. This force insured the authority and right to total rule within the district.

The serfs were powerless, and hence were slaves. They could acquire no armor, nor any skill at swordplay. They were cattle. It was unnecessary to solicit their goodwill, their hatred was harmless. Their opinions were of no consequence.

But the gun changed the thought of both serf and nobleman. An uncouth lowborn, with small training in the art of arms, could destroy, with a gun, the best armor that money could buy. And inside the armor would die a knight who had spent his life acquiring the art of sword, shield and lance.

The Emperor formerly occupied his throne and defended his empire with the consent and help of his warlords, his feudal nobility. In case of war, the king called together his chiefs, who brought their knights for the impending battle of plumes and armor. Except for porters and lackeys, they desired the aid of no common citizens.

But after the gun, the king needed the common man for his armies. The plumed knight was no longer reliable. The citizen assumed a new value, his good will became important. Thus were the rights of the common man acknowledged. Thus was laid the cornerstone of equality and democracy.

Texas historians mutter in their beards over the absence of a Spanish rush to Texas. It is lamented that this great land lay two hundred years after discovery without development. The answer is that guns, then, were insufficiently developed.

A small European army could not defeat a large savage force. Armies transported to distant lands necessarily remained small, until the time of other inventions. So history marked time, awaiting material development. The gun, like most inventions, was a long time aborning. Events, the results of its inventions, could not outstrip the development of the gun.

American historians gleefully report the Battle of New Orleans, where the Americans won by killing and wounding 3,336 British, with the loss of only eight Americans killed, and thirteen wounded. We are to assume, possibly, that some supernatural power enabled "our side" to win so decisively, as a reward for being ever right. The answer, again, is firearms. The British were using short range muskets of poor accuracy. The Americans were equipped with finer rifles than the Europeans suspected were in existence. At a range which was deadly for the rifles, the smoothbore muskets were almost harmless.

The story of firearms has never been attempted by any writer who excluded history. History should not be written excluding firearms. The two are irrevocably intertwined. Development in one surely means development in the other.

Because we object to omissions of past histories, we shall offer this supplement. This book is not a history of Texas. Our pen is not equal to the power and color, the drama, adventure and sweeping action of the history of the Lone Star State. This is written, rather, as a story of guns, and the part they played in making that history.

Neither is this a technical catalog for the gun expert. To that large class of gun scholars who require ballistic tables with their cereal; maybe you will not like us. Nevertheless, we promise to furnish you a few items hitherto unpublished.

We do not view a gun with the gun scholar's eyes. He sees the patent dates, the perfection of manufacture. He rates the efficiency in foot pounds per second, and in the quality of engineering design. To him the gun is a thermodynamic machine which is clever or inefficient.

Not so with us. A gun or pistol is a tool. Tools are dedicated to practical use by man. When we see guns, we see the men who made them, and the men who used them. A sveltely checkered quail gun, with its proudly burnished barrel, holds beauty. But even more beautiful is the vision which it connotes: soft, light boots with their earthy smell, stylish dogs quartering the field, or drumming wings whirring through the yellow and scarlet leaves.

By all means, give the gun its associations. Alone, it is a cold machine, a thing of wood and metal. Clothed with rich garments of dreams, it cannot be cold. For it is filled with vibrant life, energy and adventure. The gun takes these things from the men who use it, cherish it and possibly live by it.

So we shall not be ballistically technical, but shall try to be instructive. This shall be a story of the Texas tradition of the gun.

PART I –
THE FIRELOCK

— Early Firearms —

Mists of antiquity veil the invention and earliest use of firearms. The many translations of old papers confuse, rather than prove the date, location and use of the first guns and pistols.

The word gun is derived from the old word, "gonne," which was a contraction of the word "mangonel." Mangonels were great stone-throwing catapults employed in the siege warfare of early European history.

Gunpowder was known to the Arabs in 846. Spain used gunpowder in pyrotechnic displays, a hundred years before it became known in the remainder of Europe.

A few crude firearms were used to throw their flashing thunderbolts against an enemy prior to 1340. These weapons may not have fired a missile. It is possible that they depended on the noise and flame-lined smoke frightening the opposition. It is recorded that men were only slightly less intimidated than were the horses, which were stampeded out of control.

Cannon definitely were in use in 1339. English ships were equipped with cannon by 1345. Firearms were used in the Battle of Crecy in 1346. The early English guns came from France and Belgium, as England had no gunmakers. The first guns made in England were fabricated about 1350.

Bell makers, the most skillful of early metalworkers, were the first gun founders. The metal utilized in bell founding was the best and purest metal available. This was the metal employed in the first gun manufacturing.

Early small arms were the demihague, culverin or hand cannon. They consisted merely of a barrel equipped with a touch hole, and a handle of varied design. They were loaded like ancient cannon, and fired the same way—with a slow burning match applied at the touch hole, while the piece was pointed in the right general direction.

By 1450, matchlock guns came into use. They were the first guns carrying the components of "lock, stock and barrel."

Matchlock stocks were first shaped to hook over the shoulder of the shooter. Later, they were shaped to fit against the shoulder, as do modern guns. On military guns, these stocks were plain and inexpensive, while guns fabricated for rich noblemen were often decorated with the finest examples of wood carving, sculptured metal, pearl inlays and even precious jewels. These guns were such works of art that some have been preserved, in admiration of their artistry, after their usefulness disappeared.

The lock, action or working mechanism, on the matchlock was simply a lever which pivoted on a pin. To one end of the lever was fixed a holder for the match. The match was a long fuse, or wick, which burned very slowly, lasting possibly two hours after ignition. After taking aim, the shooter used one finger to press the lever, forcing the burning match to the touch hole. Of course, the match had to be shifted in the holder as the fire consumed it. Also, the clinging ash had to be removed, so that the live coal came to the touch hole. Ash from the match was apt to contaminate the weak gunpowder to the extent of a misfire.

Improved matchlocks boasted a serpentine. This serpentine was a lever, as described above, and added the trigger feature. The serpentine was shaped like the letter S, pivoting on a pin in the center. The match was fixed to the top of the S, the lower curve of the S serving as a trigger. Later, a spring was added which held the match away from the touch hole. Trigger pressure overcame this spring pressure to effect fire.

A still later improvement removed the touch hole from the top of the barrel, and installed it in the sidewall. Then, a flashpan and cover were built around the touch hole. After the shooter poured powder down the barrel and seated the ball, he opened the cover of the flashpan and placed in it a small quantity of priming powder. When he pulled the trigger, the serpentine pushed the pan cover away and rammed the burning match into the powder in the flashpan. The resulting flash set off the main charge in the barrel through the touch hole, or vent.

If guns have developed considerably, so has the propelling charge used in them. The early gunpowder was dangerous, but only at short range. Armored soldiers could be killed, a circumstance which revolutionized warfare, but the armor was soft iron, and the range had to be favorable.

The orders, "ready, aim, fire," of those days were: "take forth your match, blow off your coal; cock your match, try your match. Guard, blow and open your pan; present arms; give fire!" Following orders in the military manual were: "Dismount your musket, uncock your match, return your match, clear your pan, prime your pan, shut your pan. Cast off your loose powder, blow off your loose powder; open your charge, charge your musket. Draw forth your scouring stick (ramrod), put in your bullet and ram home; withdraw your scouring stick, return your scouring stick." The gun was then reloaded. Long lines of soldiers loading and giving fire to the rhythmical orders, was a sight which inspired many battle paintings. One file advanced to fire; the other file fell back to reload. The uniforms were bright and colorful.

Concealment was undesirable; the opposing lines were forced to approach quite closely. Their lack of range and the inaccuracy of their firearms dictated this mode of warfare. The reader will recall that this system of massed men advancing to battle, with their drums rolling, persisted after the development of the rifle rendered such tactics obsolete.

A skillful gunner could load his weapon within the time it takes to tell of it, but even so, shots delivered in battle were painfully spaced. Rain, or even fog, incapacitated the musquet, or arquebus. Neither were they effective at night, as the burning matches revealed the number and location of the gun bearers to the enemy.

The invention of the wheel lock, which occurred in Germany about 1517, was one of the most important steps in the progress of firearms. In the wheel lock, or firelock, as it was called at that time, the serpentine became the cock. The cock was a lever pivoted on one end, and equipped with jaws on the other end. Into these adjustable jaws was placed a piece of flint, or a piece of pyrites.

The other important component of the ignition system of the wheel lock was the wheel and the spring which motivated it. Previous to firing, this wheel had to be wound with a key, in the manner of a child's toy of today. Pressing the trigger released the spring, resulting in the rapid rotation of the wheel, which had a serrated perimeter. This rough rim of the wheel rubbed the flint, or pyrites, held by the cock, and sparks were produced which ignited the priming charge which, in turn, ignited the main charge of powder.

If the Spanish did not invent the wheel lock, they acquired use of it very shortly. The firelocks were common equipment with the Spanish soldiery sent to America in 1528, only eleven years after the German claim to invention.

The advantages of the new wheel lock over the old matchlock are readily apparent. Dampness did not extinguish the match; the gunner was able to conceal himself from game or foe. Pistols, after the invention of the wheel lock, could be primed and wound up, spanned was the term for the winding, and carried in the sash, ready for instant use. These were the advantages.

The disadvantages were almost as great. The wheel locks had too much mechanism that was made of soft iron, and soon wore to uselessness. Where the matchlock was ultrasimple, the wheel lock was so complicated that only a highly skilled gunsmith could effect repairs. The cost of the wheel lock was its greatest disadvantage. Armies retained their pikemen, bowmen, etc., equipping only companies with firearms with which to combat armored horses and men.

The wheel lock was the gun first brought to Texas by the Spanish explorers. If their early explorations and attempts at colonization in this land of fierce Indians failed, such failure was due to the underdevelopment of their arms. Progress in Texas simply had to await better guns.

— Explorers —

Alonzo Alvarez de Pineda, a Spaniard, may have brought the first gun to Texas in 1519. He shall get small credit from us, for he was never sure he had been in Texas. Little was known of the immense continents of the Western hemisphere, so we must not harshly judge Pineda, who had no accurate maps or instruments.

The fact is, nearly all the early explorers who entered Texas were lost. The vast, uncharted plains and forests of Texas only added to their bewilderment and hardships.

Cabeza de Vaca, another Spanish explorer, entered Texas in 1528. His expedition was trying to reach Mexico, where there were Spanish settlements. The expedition had been badly beaten in a campaign in Florida, and having lost their ships, they constructed crude boats for the coastal journey.

These boats were unequal to the Texas Gulf storms, and the Spaniards were shipwrecked near Galveston Island. Having lost most of their weapons and courage, they were enslaved or killed by the Indians. De Vaca and two companions finally reached Mexico after six years among the Indians. As de Vaca was quite a journalist, his expedition became important by reason of his vivid records.

Francisco Vasquez de Coronado entered Texas in 1540. He was well equipped and better still, he was not lost. His retinue consisted of three hundred armored horsemen, seventy foot soldiers, more than a thousand Indian porters, adequate livestock and supplies. This expedition successfully mapped large areas.

In 1542, Ferdinand de Soto's expedition entered Texas from the East. But alas, they were lost, and soon turned back to the Mississippi River.

Rene Robert Cavalier de La Salle, the famous French explorer, landed on Texan shores in 1685. He, too, was lost, having mistaken Matagorda Bay for the Mississippi River.

La Salle attempted to found a colony in Texas. His attempt was unsuccessful, and he was shot to death by one of his men, after claiming Texas for France. His advent is important only because it stirred the Spanish to action.

The Spanish had long looked on Texas as their exclusive territory by virtue of their rather unsuccessful explorations. Because they did not possess superiority of arms, they had considered occupation of this broad territory unfeasible. The Indians had literally taken the pants off of the early Spaniards in Texas.

De Vaca recommended that guns should be withdrawn from service against the Indians, although he admitted that Spanish crossbowmen stood little chance against the savage archers.

The Spanish were so overawed by the proficiency at arms of the red men that their reports on the Indians make interesting reading. De Vaca, in describing a fight with the Indians in July, 1528, said:

> Their bows are as thick as one's arm, eleven to twelve hand-spans in length, which they shoot at two hundred paces with so much sureness that they miss nothing. In this conflict some of our men were wounded, for the good armor they wore was of no use. There were men that day who swore that they had seen two oaks, each as thick as a man's lower leg, pierced entirely through by Indian arrows. I, myself, have seen an arrow buried in a poplar stump a good half a foot.

De Soto recorded that the Indians shot six or seven arrows while a Spaniard was loading his musket. He elaborated:

> One shaft penetrated a horse's breast, and lodged in his bowels. A test was made; a coat of mail worth a hundred and fifty ducats was fitted on a basket, and a captive Indian was permitted to fire on it at a hundred and fifty paces. The coat was broken. Then a second coat was placed over the first. The Indian's arrow penetrated them both with enough force to kill a man.

De Soto and his men abandoned their coats of mail, and substituted clothes heavily padded with wadded cloth. He explained:

> The Indian's bows were made of hardwood (Osage orange or bois d'arc) with a string of deergut or deerskin; the arrows were of reed, feathered, and pointed with snake teeth, fish bone or flint. Some had no point but the sharpened reed, and these would split on the chain mesh of the armor and inflict a deep, double wound.

Had the Indians been half as good as the Spanish reported, the white men would have been outgunned.

The Indian tribes of Texas were quite diverse in their culture and warlike tendencies. In the eastern portion, there were the Tejas, from whom Texas got her name. The fierce Comanches were on the northern plains. In the western mountains lived the Apaches, while the gulf coast afforded the cannibalistic Karankawas and Attacapas (attacapa means man-eater).

Of these tribes, only the Tejas could be encroached upon by the white men. They were naturally friendly, and their political organization was too weak for the strongest defense.

The coast Indians were considered the lowest in the social order because of their man-eating proclivities. They acquired this practice from the Spaniards.

As the white men were apt to overlook the finer points in Indian character and culture, but adopt his evils—smoking, painting the body, scalping, etc.—the Indians were prone to overlook the white man's culture but adopt his evils—drunkenness, burning at the stake and cannibalism.

The Indians of the Texas coast were not cannibals when de Vaca arrived. Some Spaniards in de Vaca's expedition, marooned in the winter of 1528, ate one another in an extremity of privation. The Indians were indignant and angry on discovering this, and turned from friendly relations to enemies of the remaining Spaniards. This is recorded in de Vaca's journal.

In 1719, a Frenchman, Simars de Belle-Isle, reported that this same tribe had turned to cannibalism, eating their dead enemies amid wild celebration. Cabeza de Vaca never saw any cannibalism during his long association with the coastal tribes, but the Attacapas and the Karankawas stand convicted by many later reports. The Spanish evidently planted this root of social decay among the Indians.

Part II -
The Flintlock

— Development of the Gun —

About the middle of the sixteenth century there came another development in the progress of firearms. The snaphaunce was invented.

As with other early gun inventions, there is considerable controversy over the time and place of this development. Some authorities claim the snaphaunce was invented in Germany, while others claim it was invented in Holland. Still others claim Belgium as the seat of this development. But another school gives Spain the credit, explaining that the Low Countries acquired knowledge of this gun through a Spanish invasion of Flanders. It may have been developed in all of these places independently, and in other localities also.

We have seen that the early matchlock was simple, inexpensive and easily repaired. The wheel lock was more or less weatherproof, less dangerous, and offered a quality of concealment to the gunbearer not attainable with the matchlock. Each of the old types, however, contained such inherent weaknesses, that it is probable that gunmakers of all countries strove for a weapon combining the merits of the two old types, while eliminating their chief faults. Hence, it is not unlikely that arms experts in more than one country conceived the idea of the snaphaunce.

The snaphaunce, also called snapharmce and snaphance, was an improvement in the method of ignition. The main powder charge was augmented by a priming charge placed in the flashpan. Over the flashpan was a cover, arranged to slide back and forth, covering or exposing the priming charge. A piece of steel, called the hen, or battrie, or frizzen, pivoted from the lockplate, normally standing more or less erect. The hen was connected to the flashpan cover by a link.

The cock, somewhat similar to the hammer on a modern gun, afforded adjustable jaws into which was affixed a piece of flint.

When the piece was cocked and the trigger pulled, the cock descended and the flint struck the steel hen a smart blow, creating sparks. The hen sprang backward under this impact, which uncovered the flashpan, allowing the sparks to fall into the priming charge.

This mechanism was so simple and effective that it spelled doom to the preceding forms of ignition. It also rendered obsolete the pikemen, crossbowmen and broadswordsmen. The gun and pistol had come into their own at last.

A later improvement simplified the pan cover by making it an integral part with the hen. The cover then exposed the priming charge by opening, as does a cigar box, rather than by sliding backward. Modern experts term the latter "flint-lock," and the earlier type with the sliding pan cover is de-scribed as "snaphaunce." They were both flintlocks, and the accepted designation is a matter of descriptive convenience.

With the advent of the flintlock, the hen came to be called the "frizzen" to the almost complete disuse of the other des-ignations.

As the ramrod was carried in a slot under the barrel of the gun, or pistol, the gunner now carried only his powder, ball and patching, with an extra flint or two. A flint was apt to last from twenty to fifty shots, so a huntsman on a short trip might carry only a bag of premolded balls with a supply of powder carried in a metal flask, or a powder horn.

Metal powder flasks, with their measuring devices on their spouts, are far more popular with collectors today, than they were with the practical users of yesteryear. Many gun experts of that day held the flasks to be a curse and abomination.

Frequently, after a shot, fire lingered in the barrel of the gun. It might be a faulty grain of powder, it might be a smol-dering thread of patching. When the flask was upended in the muzzle of such a barrel, the entire flask might ignite and explode.

Most gunners preferred to measure their own powder into their hand, replacing their powder magazine in their belt or pouch, before moving the powder charge to the gun muzzle.

Powder containers made from cattle or buffalo horns were favored by Americans.

The Spanish version of the flintlock is called the miquelet. Its ignition system does not vary from the European system. The difference is mechanical. The main spring is outside the lockplate and exposed. The piece is held at cock, or half-cock, by a movable cleat protruding through the lockplate, and engaging the forward end of the cock.

Why the Spanish adhered to this system of lock construction is not known. It was more unsightly than the European system, and as exposed parts are more apt to be broken than covered parts, it would seem to offer several disadvantages, with superiority nowhere.

Our theory is that the Spanish were the true inventors of the flintlock system, and the European method of lock construction was an improvement on the Spanish discovery.

Texas was the meeting place of the miquelets, carried by the Spaniards of 1820, and the American flintlocks, carried by the backwoodsmen who pushed westward from the American frontier. This culminated in the Texas War of Independence, or the Texas Revolution, as it more often is called.

— SPANISH COLONIZATION —

For many years after the Spaniards discovered Texas, they remembered it only with distaste. Exploration had revealed the absence of gold and jewels. The new country could yield only hides and pelts to the mother country. The inhabitants were fierce and warlike. As they could not be subjected easily, major efforts were not considered worthwhile.

However, since firearms had advanced in effectiveness, the Spanish believed that they could cope with the Texas savages if such course became desirable.

The church solicited the government's aid in establishing missions and presidios in the territory. The churchmen believed the Indians were amenable to Christian religion. But the government demurred. They had had all the contact with these savages that they cared for.

At last, the French who owned Louisiana, spurred the Spanish to action. The Frenchman, La Salle, was active in Texas in 1685. A French settlement called Fort Saint Louis was established on the Lavaca River. Another small trading post, Nassonite, was established in what is now Red River County. A third, Carlorette, was located far up the Red River in north central Texas. The latter was abandoned in 1762, and since has been known locally by the misleading name of "Old Spanish Fort."

The Spanish government, fearful of the French encroachment, decided to cooperate with the church, and establish missions.

There was no agreed boundary between Texas and Louisiana, but the Spanish sought to occupy to the Red River, as the French were just across this stream.

In 1689, a Spanish expedition left Mexico to capture the French Fort Saint Louis. Upon arriving at the fort, the Spanish discovered that the French already had abandoned their post on the Lavaca.

In 1690, Father Massanet with three priests, accompanied by a strong military escort under de Leon, arrived among the Tejas Indians in east Texas. There they established the first mission in Texas, San Francisco de los Tejas. It was located about four miles from the Neches River, near the present village of Weches, in Houston County. The traveling public may be interested to know that this old mission, situated in a beautiful national forest, has been historically restored.

Results did not justify expectations at the new mission. The Indians were quite different from the Aztecs and Pueblos, with whom the missions had dealt successfully. These latter tribes were more civilized, enjoyed permanent homes and farms, and were amenable to the encroachment and teachings of the whites. Contrarily, the Texas Indians were more nomadic, warlike and independent.

Neither was there complete harmony between the religious and military factions. The soldiers fraternized with the Indian women, drank and gambled and generally set an example for the Indians which was deplored by Father Massanet. Possibly, personalities and jealousy entered into the picture.

On the other hand, de Leon pointed out that no colonization was possible among these Indians without compelling their fear and respect with a gun.

Father Massanet prevailed, and all the soldiers, except three, were withdrawn. In 1693 Father Massanet agreed that the missions could be sustained only by force of arms. He had learned the difficult way. On October 25, 1693, the Spaniards fired their mission, and fled before the rampaging Indians.

In 1716 the Spanish began a chain of missions in east Texas. San Francisco de los Neches was built near the site of the first mission. Nuestra Senora de la Guadalupe was located near what became Nacogdoches. Nuestra Senora de los Dolores was established near the present city of San Augustine. San Jose de Nazones, La Purisima Concepcion and San Miguel Cuellar de los Adaes were built nearby.

In 1718, the presidio of San Antonio de Bejar was established at what became San Antonio. Its chapel, the Alamo, was to become the chief Texas shrine. San Antonio was established as a sort of way-station on the long road from Mexico to east Texas.

The presidio established by the Spanish at the site of the old French fort, Saint Louis, was called Santa Maria de Loreto de la Bahia Espiritu Santa. If the missions were perpetually short of supplies, they were long on names. This presidio, built in 1722, became known simply as La Bahia.

French traders continued to slip into Texas and trade with the Indians, despite the Spanish strong points. As the French offered the Indians guns which were superior to the Spanish arms, these traders were well received by the savages.

From 1720 to 1770, the Spanish were busy establishing missions or presidios wherever the French influence was growing too powerful. Other Spanish settlements established in this half-century include El Paso and San Saba.

Due to the scarcity of troops, the difficulty of supplying these distant points, continued friction between the religious and military leaders, poor organization and administration, most of these Spanish colonies soon were abandoned.

At one time, Spanish strength was so feeble that when seven armed Frenchmen approached Los Adaes, the French perceived that the capture of the place would be easy. After the capture had been effected, it was discovered that there were only two Spaniards present, one soldier and one priest.

The Spanish soldier escaped and spread the alarm to the other missions. The French, with heavy forces, were attacking, he told them. The misinformed and frightened Spaniards then abandoned their other missions in this region. This incident occurred in 1719, and the Spanish did not occupy their posts until two years later. The new garrisons were more capable, with one boasting six brass cannon and a hundred soldiers.

After Spanish efforts to deal peaceably with the Indians had failed, it was recognized that no position could be maintained in Texas except by force of arms. Even this failed miserably on several occasions.

In 1759, the Comanches began raiding some of the missions and driving off cattle and horses. After one particularly vicious raid, in which nineteen Spaniards were slain, the Spaniards determined to retaliate.

Parilla led a force of three hundred and thirty-eight men to attack the Indians in their own country. But the Comanches, who served as a barrier to white encroachment for two centuries, were equal to the occasion. The Spanish suffered a stinging and humiliating defeat.

In 1803, when Napoleon sold Louisiana to the United States, Americans and Spanish disputed, almost to the verge of war, over the western boundary of Louisiana. The disagreement was ended in 1806 by the Neutral Ground Treaty. By the terms of this agreement, Spanish Texas should not reach east of the Sabine River, and American Louisiana should not extend westward from a torturous negotiated boundary somewhat east of the Sabine. This Neutral Strip, lying adjacent to and east of the Sabine, became the refuge of the worst element on the North American continent. The pirates, murderers, counterfeiters and escaped convicts who assembled in this lawless sanctuary, were to play a part in the later history of Texas.

Spanish rule in Texas was nearly at an end. Spain, in 1812, was rent terribly by internal revolutions. By 1821, when Mexico rebelled against the mother country, Spain could do little to preserve its Western empire. Almost without bloodshed, Mexico won her independence.

What had the Spanish accomplished in Texas? Almost nothing. After one hundred and thirty-one years of colonial endeavor, the civilized population of Texas was about seven thousand. There were few towns, and these were very small. There were no schools or roads. There were no seaports, public buildings or trade.

The Spaniards bequeathed Texas a host of place names, herds of wild cattle and horses, and a land system dating from the Dark Ages. From Spain, Texas has a few examples of majestic architecture. It is not much. But remember, if Spain gave Texas little, Texas gave Spain even less.

Texas was a cruel land filled with savages. These Indians did not react favorably to the mission system. They never honored a peace treaty for long. They not only held the pitifully few Spaniards by the throat, they kept more numerous and better armed Americans at arms length, on the same ground, at a later date.

Texas could not be profitable until the Indians could be restrained. The Comanches and Apaches could not be controlled until the advent of repeating firearms. The flintlock simply was not good enough.

— American Colonization —

It is very likely that the first Americans entered Texas for hunting and adventure, although other reasons will be discussed later.

The guns used by the huntsmen were the long-barreled backwoodsman's rifle that was developed in Pennsylvania and New England. The type is known at present as the "Kentucky rifle."

These rifles were usually single shot, although some double-barrel specimens are in evidence. The caliber varied widely, ranging from .28 to .56. They were full stocked and carried a wooden ramrod underneath the barrel. The sights were of iron and the barrels rifted, although they shot a spherical bullet.

The lockplate was usually signed by some well-known American maker (the guns were all handmade), but a number of gunmakers purchased their locks in England and fitted them to American stocks and barrels.

The ignition system was flintlock, as described in a previous chapter. Most rifles were equipped with double set triggers to insure accuracy. Due to the tediousness of reloading, accuracy was essential.

A large number of Kentucky rifle makers, when they had mastered the intricacies of gun-building, were tempted to ornament those long, graceful, well-stocked and efficient guns as a sort of crowning glory to a well completed job. It is impressive how seldom the early, authentic Texas gun is found bearing these ornaments. Whether the Texas-bound man was reluctant to pay for this finery, whether he hesitated to make his gun more desirable to the Indians, or whether he begrudged carrying the extra weight of those brass inlays is not known. Possibly, he merely was unpretentious, and selected his gun only from the utilitarian viewpoint.

His knife was the Bowie type, carried in a sheath at his belt. His pistols, if any, were usually holstered on his saddle. They, like his rifle, were handmade by a competent gunsmith, and were usually plain also. Their grips were wooden, with the butt curving slightly back toward the front. This was before the day of the bone-handled pistols, or Mexican carved ivory grips affixed to the "Western" shaped butt.

American arms smiths whose long rifles were brought to Texas and saw extensive service in hunting, beef-shooting and warfare were Armstrong of Pennsylvania, Astol of New Orleans, Baker of Pennsylvania, Bartlett of New York, Bean of Tennessee, Beck of Pennsylvania, Best of Pennsylvania, Boone of Pennsylvania, Charrier of Maryland, Constable of Pennsylvania, Coons of Pennsylvania, Crandall of New York, Goetz of Pennsylvania, Golcher of Pennsylvania, Huntington of Pennsylvania, Jennings of New York, Miller, Morrison and Pennebecker, all of Pennsylvania, and Remington of New York. Tubbs, Woods and other gunmakers helped arm these men bound for Texas.

Makers of pistols, single shot or double barreled, were Cherington, Cooper, Deringer, Golcher, Henry, Kunz, Moll and Shuler of Pennsylvania, McKim of Maryland, Jennings of New York, and French of Massachusetts.

The above list is necessarily incomplete. The origin of these weapons is diverse, as settlers journeyed to Texas from all of the old American States. The number of Pennsylvania-made guns far overbalances the number of immigrants from that state, and would indicate that Pennsylvania might justly claim the title of "Armorer to young America."

Horse pistols were prevalent in early Texas. These weapons were long, heavy, of .69 caliber, smooth bored, single shot flintlock pistols. The cheapness of these weapons, and the prevalence of travel by horseback in Texas, are the chief reasons for their popularity. They were usually carried by pairs in saddle holsters. Prominent makers of horse pistols were S. North, Waters, Deringer, Evans, the Harpers Ferry Aresnal, R. Johnson and Aston.

One favorite pastime of Western settlers was beef-shooting. Contestants paid twenty-five cents each for a shot, until enough chances had been sold to pay for a steer.

Each contestant furnished his target, a board with an X drawn in the center. Two judges were selected. One by one, the contestants placed their targets against a tree, and fired from a deadline. After each shot, the judges took charge of the target, marking the name of the shooter on it.

When the firing was done, the judges withdrew and measured the targets. The marksman who cut the center of his X, or came closest, was the winner, and received the hide and tallow of the beef.

Second place was awarded his choice of the hindquarters, with third place taking the other. Fourth and fifth prizes were the two fore-quarters of the beef, and sixth prize was the lead embedded in the tree, which might weigh several pounds. As each contestant could buy several chances, one man might win more than one prize. David Crockett once won the first five prizes in a shoot, thus winning the entire beef.

Shooting accuracy was much more difficult to achieve with the flintlocks than with later guns, due to the longer interval between the trigger pull and the explosion. In an indictment of the flintlock gun for its slow firing qualities, an old pioneer told this story:

He fired his ancient flintlock rifle, from rest, at an old turkey gobbler standing on a stump. At the moment he pulled the trigger, the old gobbler flew away, but while his gun sputtered and finally gave fire, a young gobbler lighted on the same stump, and was killed.

However, the flintlocks were not as slow as this narrative indicates. Flintlock fowling pieces were used for quail, duck and other forms of wing shooting by rich sportsmen. The amount of lead, the allowance in aim ahead of the flying target, was so great and uncertain that the poor "meat-getter" refused to gamble on wing-shooting.

Various historians deny that the first Americans entered Texas for the hunting. They seek a reason more burdened with politics and intrigue. Our conception of the pioneer is that he cared little for conniving.

One idea advanced is that the American government planned to rob Spain of Texas, and encouraged American citizens to infiltrate the land for future ulterior motives. There is no evidence to corroborate this theory, but a number of facts tend to refute it. The American government was to buy Florida. It had bought Louisiana, and it is probable that if the U. S. had desired Texas at that time, an effort to purchase it would have been made. The Americans felt no need for more territory; they had recently doubled the size of their country by the acquisition of Louisiana. Most convincing, however, is the fact that the U. S. rejected a Texian request for annexation in 1837.

Another theory advanced for the entry of Americans into Texas is that slaveholding states wished to expand the area of slave territory for obvious reasons. But there was no reason for the slave states to be concerned over the implied issue in 1820. Had they been concerned, there was more land at their disposal than they could develop in years.

The French, from Louisiana, had been visiting Texas regularly since La Salle claimed this land for France in 1685. When the United States acquired Louisiana and Anglo-Americans began mingling with the French, it was only natural for some Americans to accompany the French traders on their expeditions.

East Texas was a hunter's paradise. The country was like a park, beautiful green glades scattered among the tall, virgin forests. Underbrush did not appear until the virgin forest had been cut away. Deer, turkey and bear were bountiful, as were wild hogs, wild cattle and a great assortment of small game.

David Crockett has told of killing more than a dozen bear on a single hunt in east Texas. These were plentiful until around 1850, and the deer and turkey survived much longer.

On the plains, west of the timber belt, there roamed the buffalo and large herds of wild horses. These horses were the magnet which attracted some of the earlier Americans. Groups would assemble, usually ten to twenty men, and journey into Texas to capture horses, which they drove to Louisiana for sale. These horses were sold at a comparatively low price, but as several hundred might be procured on each trip, the business attracted a considerable number of pioneers.

About eighty-five American families had made their home, illegally, in Texas by 1820. These were Indian traders, wild horse hunters, or farmers who acquired no title to the land they developed. A number of Americans bought land from Mexican titleholders, and settled around Nacogdoches and San Augustine.

The renegades from the Neutral Ground were spilling into Texas. The East Texas boundary was so far from the Spanish base of operation, and the Spanish garrisons were so small, there was little fear of authority. Occasionally, however, Spanish soldiery gobbled up a group of trespassers. These rare incidents served to generate a hatred for the Spanish, rather than act as a deterrent for further encroachment. And thus northeast Texas became Americanized from 1800 to 1836.

Southeast Texas colonization passed through two phases. Pirates controlled the first, and empresarios motivated the second. Jean Lafitte, a pirate of commendable organizational and administrative talents, established a fort on the Brazos River in 1818. Later, he occupied Galveston Island, and his hijacking and slave-trading business was so great that hundreds were employed in furnishing an outlet for this nefarious business.

When the Spaniards failed in their efforts to settle Mexicans in Texas, they determined that the country must be settled at any cost. Following this decision, Moses Austin was able to secure a contract to bring several hundred Americans into south Texas. But Austin died, and the Mexicans won their independence from Spain. Stephen F. Austin, the son of Moses, with the help of the Baron de

Bastrop, secured a confirmation of the old land colony contract, and brought in the first aggregation of colonists at the dawning of 1822.

At this time, there were but four towns in Texas: Nacogdoches, San Antonio, La Bahia and a small town which later would be called El Paso.

Austin not only brought in 1,200 families on his various contracts, he also brought in a class of people who were urgently needed in Texas. His colonials were of good character, and some of them had substantial means. Excellent examples are Josiah H. Bell, a member of Austin's first colony, who attained fame and wealth in Texas, and Jared E. Groce, who came to Austin's colony in 1822 with fifty wagon loads of supplies and ninety slaves. Groce received ten leagues of land, about seventy square miles.

Other empresarios also were busy. Eighteen grants for colonies were made between 1825 and 1832, predominantly in south Texas. The civilized population of Texas increased from 7,000 in 1810 to 21,000 in 1834. The settlements assumed the rough shape of a reversed letter L sprawled on the map. Beginning at Red River and extending down the eastern boundary to the Gulf, thence turning southwestward with the shoreline to Corpus Christi Bay. Each arm of the L was approximately one hundred miles broad.

This pattern of settlement was the result of several contributory causes. "Wood and water" has been mentioned most often. River transportation was a big factor. The most obvious reason was the Indian situation. The settlements gravitated toward the spots of least Indian resistance.

In northeast Texas the Caddos were fierce but numerically small and beset by other enemies. In central east Texas were the Tejas combine, the only Indian group in Texas inclined toward friendliness. Along the coast were the Karankawas and Attacapas, fierce and cruel, but numerically small, and badly scattered.

Restraining the settled belt was that large portion of Texas occupied by the Apaches, the Wacos and the Comanches, all of them brave, numerous, politically welded by able leaders, and determined to yield to no one.

Trade was developing, roads, or "traces," were being laid out. The communication of trade and mail with the United States was by road from Nacogdoches to Natchitoches, La., and from Galveston, Velasco and other ports to New Orleans by water.

Nacogdoches was still the largest town, with 3,500 population. It afforded a school, as did San Augustine, Jonesborough and Brazoria in east Texas, and San Antonio in southwest Texas.

These newfangled cap and ball guns were coming to Texas with great rapidity now. The flintlock period was ending. The percussion period was on.

Part III -
Cap & Ball

— Revolution! —

In 1807, Alexander Forsyth, a Presbyterian minister in Aberdeenshire, Scotland, secured a British patent on an improvement in firearm ignition that was of the greatest importance. Although his patent was for a new type of gun lock, the explosive force it utilized is the important thing.

The French chemist Berthollet had developed the old idea of potassium chlorate, or one of the fulminates, and abandoned it as too dangerous. Forsyth conceived the idea of using the fulminates for priming firearms. After some experimentation he and a London gunsmith formed a partnership and began manufacturing the new locks.

In their system the priming hole was enclosed, and a small amount of the fulminate powder, fed from a magazine, was struck by a firing pin propelled by a hammer, similar to the hammer on a modern gun. This priming powder detonated violently and set off the main charge. The main charge and ball had to be loaded from the muzzle, with a ramrod, as before. But the new primer was a success by 1809. It eliminated the flint and steel, was not affected by dampness and permitted less gas loss through the priming hole.

In 1814, Captain Joshua Shaw, a Philadelphian, applied for a patent on a percussion cap. This little gadget was shaped like a hat with little or no brim. It was made of iron, and the top of it contained a small quantity of fulminate of mercury. The cap was placed over the priming hole, or vent, and was crushed when the hammer fell on it, the resulting fire running through the vent to set off the main charge. This iron cap was not altogether successful, and the patent was not granted.

Shaw experimented with other metals, pewter and copper. He learned in 1816 that copper was the answer, but he did not get his patent until 1822.

This perfected the percussion caplock which was in general use until the early eighteen seventies. Although the U. S. government did not have any percussion guns made until 1842, its armories did begin altering flintlock guns and pistols to the caplock about 1825.

By 1836 there were a large number of the converted guns in Texas. It has been estimated by various methods that about half the guns in use in Texas in 1836 were altered from flintlock to caplock. The Mexican army retained the flintlock. These were the weapons, then, of the Texas Revolution.

Before embarking on a study of this conflict, we must remark on the extreme self-reliance, or rampant individualism, as it has been called, which prevailed among the Texians. For years past, most of them had been accustomed to no laws or law enforcement worthy of the name. Neither had they been afforded any protection physically or economically.

The pioneer and his family settled in a strange and savage land, miles from their nearest neighbors. When Indians went on the warpath, the settler rarely went to a blockhouse for protection. The distance was too great, the population too scattered. He and his family fought off the savages until dark and then hid in a thicket until the Indians departed. These colonials knew none of the security which accrued from a closely knit colony in other lands, where the strong helped the weak, where food could be rationed to prevent direst hunger. In Texas it was every man for himself. A man had to be endowed with an unusual amount of self-sufficiency to embark on a project so daring as moving his family to the Texas of that day. This bump of self-reliance grew until it became a vice.

Until the catastrophe of Civil War swept across the land in 1861, and welded Texans into some semblance of amenability, the Texas man was a law unto himself. He could not be disciplined, he would not take orders. He valued his own judgement and opinions above those of any other man. He understood little of teamwork. He had no knowledge of strategy. When he saw an enemy, he or the enemy died. Without constantly bearing this in mind, it is difficult to understand the military fiascoes of Texas forces when one remembers the courage and proven fighting ability of the Texians taking part.

Pressure had been building up between the Texians and the Mexicans for some time. Diverse language and customs, and basic differences in their conception of democratic government were important factors of friction. Since Mexico had won her independence from Spain, her government had been unstable. Dictators had become tyrannical, Mexican laws had been changeable and partly unjust. To the credit of Mexico, let us add that they could not have enacted laws that would have pleased the Texians. As Mexico was pervaded with a spirit of revolution, the Texians naturally were imbued with their share. Before the actual war for independence occurred, various local revolutions broke out, but Texians generally displayed their loyalty to Mexico by helping subdue these outbreaks.

While the U. S. is not believed guilty of coveting Mexican holdings in 1800, it is almost certain that by 1836 the American government was seriously conniving to acquire Texas. Unofficial offers of purchase had been made. Rumors that the U. S. intended to seize Texas caused Mexican fear and distrust of the Texians, a condition which was reflected in more harsh measures. Mexico refused to grant land which would pay for the beginnings of an educational system in Texas. Texians desired to become a separate state within Mexico, rather than a territory of the State of Coahuila. The Mexicans refused this request also.

The thorn which festered the largest sore was the law that denied entry of any more immigrants from the United States. This act struck at the very future of the development of Texas. With no more immigration, how could Texas grow? If Texas did not grow how could the pioneer's land increase in value? This act brought rioting, and the Texians captured Velasco.

Mexico was too involved in Civil War to notice. But in 1835 Santa Anna had consolidated his position as an absolute dictator in all Mexico, except Texas. He sent General Cos with four hundred men to San Antonio. The Texians, as ever, were self-reliant. They defied the Mexican garrisons in Texas that sought to disarm the settlers.

The Texian sense of assurance was enhanced through knowledge that their firearms were superior to those of the Mexican army. A Mexican force of eighty men tried to capture a cannon in Gonzales defended by one hundred and eighty Texians. The Mexicans were scattered.

Sam Houston wrote to friends in the United States, "If volunteers from the United States will join their brethren in this section, they will receive liberal bounties of land. We have millions of acres of our best lands unappropriated. Let each man come with a good rifle and one hundred rounds of ammunition."

The Mexican garrisons assembled at San Antonio under General Cos and the Texians confronted them. On December 4, 1835 Ben Milam asked for volunteers to attack the strongly fortified Mexicans. The attack was made the next day and after a six day battle, General Cos and eleven hundred men surrendered. All prisoners were released under parole not again to fight the Texians. They promptly broke this pledge.

The Texians set up a provisional government. Henry Smith was named governor, James W. Robinson, lieutenant governor, Sam Houston, major general of the army. A three-man commission, Stephen F. Austin, B. T. Archer, and William H. Wharton, was sent to the United States to borrow money, procure warships, provisions and arms. It was suggested that they borrow one hundred thousand dollars in New Orleans. They borrowed two hundred and fifty thousand there by January 10, 1836, and were promised fifteen hundred armed men from New Orleans within a short time.

This help was needed. The lack of discipline in the Texian army was having its effect. Houston ordered a withdrawal of his army from the western sector to east Texas. He further ordered scattered commands to assemble for the retreat. He directed a scorched earth policy in order that the Mexican army, operating far from their base, would have trouble following the Texians. When Houston burned one Texian town the population became so hostile that the scorched earth policy was abandoned. Thereafter the Mexicans burned the towns after pillaging.

Part of the Texian army, under Frank Johnson, decided to invade Mexico without the consent of the Texian government, and took the gulf coast route. Four hundred men, under Colonel Fannin, decided to garrison and hold Goliad. Part of the Texians went home after the capture of San Antonio and the retirement of General Cos. Colonel William B. Travis, with one hundred and fifty men, including Davy Crockett, Jim Bowie, and others of that ilk, decided to hold San Antonio against all comers. Houston managed to control a part of the army.

On February 23, 1836, Santa Anna arrived at San Antonio with about four thousand men, and surrounded the Alamo, where the Texians were fortified. The Texians held a conference and decided not to abandon the fort. They sent a summons for help, declaring they would never surrender or retreat. No doubt, they believed the Texian army would unite and make San Antonio the battleground that should decide the outcome of the war immediately. Thirty-two men came to their aid.

While the one hundred and eighty-two Texians were beleaguered in the Alamo, a Texian convention assembled on March 2, 1836 at Washington on the Brazos, and declared Texas a free and independent republic. The men in the Alamo never learned of this. Four days later Santa Anna sent three thousand men to storm the Alamo, which they accomplished in one hour. None of the Texians survived except a lady, the wife of Lieutenant Dickinson.

The Mexicans suffered two hundred and eighty-eight casualties in the assault and many more from the Texian sniping during the eleven day siege. The Texians had given a good account of themselves. They had displayed fanatical bravery. They accomplished no more than any other "lost cause," and they would have, undoubtedly, been worth more to their country had they abandoned the Alamo and joined Houston.

A Mexican army under Urrea swept up Fannin and his four hundred men who had remained at Goliad in disobedience of orders. Fannin surrendered his command as prisoners of war, but the Mexicans violated the terms of surrender, lined up the men before firing squads and murdered all except twenty-seven Texians who escaped by running.

Following these incidents, some of the Texians went home to move their families out of the Mexican line of march, but most of the militia or armed men joined Houston in his retreat. At the Colorado River, the men voted to stand and fight. Houston prevailed on them to continue the retreat. Santa Anna pursued Houston's army of about eight hundred men with a Mexican column of about fifteen hundred men. Two other columns were sweeping Texas, burning and pillaging behind the fleeing population.

When the Texas army reached the San Jacinto River, near Houston, the time for battle had arrived. The Mexicans were far from their base of operation. Should the Texians lose the battle, refuge for the survivors was near, in the United States.

"Remember the Alamo, remember Goliad," cried the Texians on April 20, 1836, as they attacked the Mexican army. General Houston had but one company of cavalry, one battery of two cannon, and four companies of infantry but so vicious was the charge of the Texians that the Mexicans failed to put up a fight. It was not a battle, it was a slaughter. Eight hundred Texians killed six hundred and thirty Mexicans, and captured seven hundred prisoners. Houston's killed and wounded amounted to only twenty-five.

How can a fight like this be explained? Fog and superior arms. The morning was damp and foggy. General Cos, he of the parole, had just joined Santa Anna, bringing four hundred Mexican reinforcements. The Texians were approaching also across the open plain but due to a fog, the Mexicans were unaware of their close proximity. When the fog lifted, the Texians attacked.

The Mexicans, using flintlock guns, were handicapped by many misfires. The flint, striking a wet frizzen, produced no sparks. Many Texians had the new caplock guns and pistols, which were unimpaired by moisture. Only the almost complete failure of Mexican arms could account for the fact that only two Texians were killed, the other twenty-three casualties being wounds, partly inflicted by swords and bayonets.

When the Mexican prisoners were being rounded up, Santa Anna was discovered among them. To save his life, the Mexican dictator agreed at the treaty of Velasco, in May 1836, to end the war upon Texas, to aid in gaining recognition of her independence, and an agreement on boundaries.

So ended Mexican rule north of the Rio Grande. So ended the career of the flintlock method of gun ignition which had served the civilized world for nearly three hundred years.

— Republic —

Probably no nation populated almost entirely by fighting men, ever had so inglorious a record at arms as did Texas in her Republic years, 1836-1846.

President Lamar wished to open a trade route from Austin to Santa Fe. The latter city was east of the Rio Grande, and consequently a part of Texas as defined by the Mexican treaty. As Santa Fe was a populous place—old, cultured and wealthy—Lamar wanted to bring it and its surrounding territory into association with Texas. Santa Fe, being almost entirely Mexican, had never relinquished allegiance to Mexico, and refused to deal with Texians. Her main commerce, outside of Mexico, was with St. Louis in the United States. Mr. Lamar considered that a trade route to Santa Fe would be the entering wedge of his campaign to peaceably alienate the city from Mexico. Texas had won Santa Fe and the eastern half of what is now New Mexico as the spoils of war; the problem was to possess them.

A large expedition was determined upon. It was to blaze a trail for commerce, and prove Texian good-fellowship when it reached Santa Fe. It should be a friendly mission, but as it must pass through the heart of the Apache country, it must be well armed.

The expedition left Austin June 30, 1841. An advance guard of eighty soldiers was followed by supply wagons and beef cattle for food. One company of soldiers looked after these supplies. Three companies of soldiers brought up the rear. One cannon was carried along. About fifty governmental officials made the trip, and about two hundred and seventy citizens, merchants and traders, were allowed to accompany the expedition. General McLeod was in command. The party made slow progress, for the group was unwieldy. Too, reports of Indian war parties caused frequent delays while extensive scouting took place.

In the country which is now New Mexico, the expedition lost their way, ran out of food and were reduced to eating snakes, lizards or whatever the arid land could yield them. The expedition divided into foraging parties, seeking ranches where sheep or cattle might be procured.

The Mexicans whom they encountered spread an alarm, and the Mexican governor, Armijo, believed the Texians had come to sack and burn Santa Fe. He quickly assembled large bodies of armed men and captured the Texian scouting parties which accepted capture with relief.

Merchants of the expedition saw their goods looted by the Mexicans. All of the Texians, except a few who were killed, were marched twelve hundred miles to Mexico City. They were released in the summer of 1842.

The sequel to the above ill-starred expedition was the equally impotent Snively expedition of 1843. Armijo, governor of Santa Fe, was to accompany a rich supply train from St. Louis to Santa Fe. This caravan was scheduled to cross a portion of Texas. A group of north Texas citizens organized near Denison in the last week of April, 1843, under the leadership of Colonel Jacob Snively. Their purpose was to capture Armijo and the wagon train. The party consisted of one hundred ninety of the most prominent men in that section. That the motive was reprisal, rather than the suggested motive of looting the Mexican train, is almost certain from a perusal of the roster of names enrolled. The fact that the expedition was sanctioned by the Texian government further indicates this was no wildcat project of irresponsible outlaws.

Upon reaching the Arkansas River, the Texian expedition established camp about eight miles off the Santa Fe-St. Louis road. Scouts and local traders and trappers advised Snively that six hundred Mexican troops were on hand to escort the Mexican train across Texian territory. On June 20th, a detachment of these Mexican troops met a Texian patrol, and seventeen Mexicans were killed and eighty captured without Texian loss. Four days later, several hundred Indians appeared. When they observed the strength of the Texians, the Indians withdrew without offering fight.

After the Texians had spent a month in camp, scouts reported no evidence of the Mexican train's approach. Two days later, seventy of the impatient Texians, tired of waiting, went home. The proclivity of the men to go home whenever it suited their personal convenience handicapped many Texian enterprises, yet it never occurred to these individualists that such practice should not be condoned.

When the Mexican caravan appeared, it was being escorted by Captain Cook of the U. S. Army, with one hundred ninety dragoons and a field battery. Captain Cook led his detachment across the U. S. boundary into Texas and captured a Texian patrol, which refused to fire on the Americans. Forty-two Texians were disarmed and sent to St. Louis. The American government later apologized for this breach of boundary, and paid for the confiscated arms.

The Mexican train crossed into Texas on July 6th. Dissension broke out among the ranks of the Texians. One faction wanted to attack. The other faction doubted if the remaining seventy-eight Texians could conquer the Mexican train with its five hundred armed guards. Colonel Snively resigned his command, and the men selected C. A. Warfield to lead them. Warfield was to lead the attack on the Mexicans on July 13th. At the last moment, he also decided that the Mexicans were too strong for his remnant command. Snively again was given command. The Texians were now subjected to two bitter Indian attacks, but managed to beat the Indians off, though they lost horses to the red raiders. After three months, the Texians limped home without having accomplished anything.

In 1842, a Mexican army suddenly appeared outside San Antonio and demanded that city's surrender. As the city was defended only by Captain Jack Hays and four or five Rangers, it quickly capitulated. Two days later, as Texian militia began swarming from the hinterland, the Mexicans retreated into Mexico as quietly and suddenly as they had appeared.

Six months later, another Mexican army under General Woll captured San Antonio with considerable Texian loss of life. Shortly after, General Woll also abandoned Texas and moved south of the Rio Grande. These hit and run invasions rankled in the hearts of the Texians. They determined to retaliate with an invasion of Mexico.

On November 25th, 1842, General Alexander Somervell, commanding 1,200 Texians, moved toward the Rio Grande. At Laredo, on the border, the Texians dallied awhile, and three-fourths of the entire force, including the commander, went home. The remaining three hundred stubbornly elected to continue the invasion, although the Mexicans were massed to halt a much superior force.

Crossing the river into Mexico, the Texians attacked the town of Mier. After savage fighting, the remaining one hundred seventy-six Texians surrendered to the Mexicans. Santa Anna decreed that one of each ten prisoners should die. Decimating was an old Mexican method of punishment; it had been practiced many times before. The Texians probably expected it when they surrendered, although glowing promises had been tendered them. Seventeen black beans were shaken up in a jar of one hundred fifty-nine white beans. Each prisoner drew a bean from the covered jar. Those drawing the black beans died before a firing squad. The remainder were imprisoned for long years.

In northeast Texas a dark red blot was growing on the map. The numerous thieves, murderers and rogues of the Neutral Ground had settled in large numbers around Shelbyville, county seat of Shelby County. Seldom has fiction created such large scale organized crime as existed in Shelby County Texas in 1839. Texas money was counterfeited in Louisiana. Money of the United States was counterfeited in Shelbyville. Horses were stolen in the United States and sold in Texas. One of the famous roads of Texas, Trammel's Trace, which later became the county line dividing Panola and Rusk counties, was laid out by thieves who drove fine horses, stolen in Missouri, to Texas, where they were destined to upbreed the Spanish mustang.

Smuggling was rampant. Slaves were stolen in both Texas and the United States, and sold in the other country. Land certificates were counterfeited and sold until the title on practically all land in that district was clouded. The brotherhood of crime acquired control of the county politics. The officers of the law, even the courts, paid allegiance to the brotherhood.

This state of affairs rendered Shelby County almost untenable to the honest pioneer who had his money and his labor invested in the county for the purpose of rearing his children and growing up with the land. This condition had been growing worse since its inception in 1824, until 1839.

Bill George, with brotherhood affiliation, bought a slave from Joseph Goodbread in 1839, and paid for it with a counterfeit land certificate. It happened that a member of the land commission from Austin was in town, and Goodbread asked the commissioner to check the certificate. When the certificate was revealed as fraudulent, Goodbread demanded restitution of George.

Charles W. Jackson, a steamboat ex-captain, was a gunman who worked in the interest of the combine. He was asked to look after Mr. Goodbread, who refused to be sensible and swallow his loss with the customary sheepish grace. Jackson pistoled Goodbread to death on the main street of Shelbyville.

The anti-combine crowd had enough. They began organizing under the leadership of Goodbread's friends. By bringing considerable pressure to bear, they were able to have Jackson tried for murder in Marshall, the county seat of Harrison County, rather than in the controlled courts of Shelbyville.

They made a poor choice. In Harrison County there had been killings in the courthouse, in the city hall, in the main hotel, brothers had killed brothers, fathers had killed sons, and sons had killed fathers. There have been dozens of "difficulties," with acquittal for all. Probably it doesn't deserve to be singled out from the other 253 counties on this score. All of them seemed to relish an occasional good killing. Be that as it may. A special term of District Court convened in Marshall, and the trial of Jackson got under way. The people of Harrison County took sides on the issue. Many determined men of both sides came from Shelby County for the trial, and near-violence was easily discernible.

Finally, Judge John M. Hansford was forced to adjourn court and flee for his life. In his order to the Sheriff of Harrison County, he wrote: "…being unwilling to risk my person in the courthouse any longer where I am surrounded by bravoes and hired assassins, and no longer free to preside as an impartial judge…" After Judge Hansford fled, he was followed and killed.

After Jackson returned to Shelbyville, he organized about thirty hard cases into a body with the announced intention of combatting crime. This body recognized the failure of established agencies to preserve law and order, and they ostensibly intended to supplant the corrupt courts. The group actually was intended to serve as a bodyguard for Jackson. They called themselves the "Regulators." Night riders soon burned the homes of James Strickland and the McFadden brothers, all close friends of Joseph Goodbread.

Other friends of Goodbread organized a band called the "Moderators," with the avowed purpose of ending night riding depredations. Edward Merchant was elected leader of the Moderators. Shortly after the formation of the Moderators. Charley Jackson was dry-gulched.

The Regulators then chose Matt Moorman, or Matt Norman, as he has been called, as their leader. A campaign was begun which resulted in the capture and hanging of Jackson's alleged slayers. Moorman took over Shelbyville with his armed men, established headquarters there, dismissed courts and officers of the law. After a desultory guerrilla warfare, the Moderators ceased resistance, and Moorman ruled as dictator.

However, Moorman could not stand prosperity. He singled out twenty-five of the leading citizens of Shelby County and ordered them from the county immediately. Their alternative was death. This action caused the revival of the Moderators, some sixty-five in number, under the leadership of Colonel Cravens. Where the feud had been confined to an occasional killing or house burning, it now entered an armed camp phase.

Practically every man in Shelby County became embroiled on one side or the other. Two companies of Regulators, under Captains Davidson and Boulware, came from Harrison County, which county also had its Moderators. San Augustine County was swept into the maelstrom.

The fortunes of war varied from 1840 until 1844. First one side, then the other, achieved temporary ascendency. Shelby County, the battlefield, reached a deplorable condition under this state of anarchy. Fields were unworked, stock was untended. Every house became a fort, blocked up at night, and with armed guards. During this reign of terror, men were shot from ambush, prisoners were taken only to be murdered, homes and barns were burned. Both sides were equally culpable.

The Regulators built a palisade fort four miles north of Shelbyville. Ephriam Daggett commanded the garrison, which consisted of nearly three hundred men. In 1841, Ned Merchant with about two hundred Moderators attacked it, and the first large scale battle of the Regulator-Moderator war was fought. The fight was a fierce standoff. The Moderators retired when it became apparent that they lacked the strength to capture the fortification. Soon after, the Regulators abandoned their fort to concentrate their forces in another fort they had constructed a mile south of Shelbyville. This second fort had also been assaulted.

Various battles of more or less magnitude were fought over the entire county. The Battle of Cedar Yard, and the Battle of Hilliard Springs are the most noteworthy. In the surrounding counties the war was taking a foothold by following the pattern of early Shelbyville guerrilla warfare. Men were killed in Marion, Harrison, Panola, Sabine and San Augustine counties. Many of these murders were for personal reasons, and the Regulator War merely served as a cloak for the lawlessness.

By 1843 so many prominent men, citizens who had had a large hand in founding the Republic, were being slain that the climax was evident. Captain Davidson of Marshall was killed. Captain John M. Bradley, a very prominent man in Nacogdoches, was killed at San Augustine by the Regulators. The fact that Bradley was killed at church on Sunday morning, in a community at peace, and that Bradley's wife was on her husband's arm when he was slain, created an unusually unfavorable national reaction.

On March 3, 1843, Senator Robert Potter, a signer of the Texas Declaration of Independence, and a former Secretary of the Texas Navy, was slain at his home on Caddo Lake. Captain Willian Pickney Rose, the "Lion of the Lake," led a force of sixteen men which surrounded the Potter home at midnight.

At daybreak, Hesekiah George left the house, which was located high on the bluff of Potter's Point, to reconnoiter. Rose fired on him with both barrels of a shotgun loaded with pistol balls. Although practically all of the charge took effect, George survived. He was known as "Rose's lead mine" thereafter.

Potter, having been warned, ran from his house and dived from a bluff into Caddo Lake, where he hoped to evade his ambushers by swimming under water. John W. Scott, one of Rose's men, was armed with a long barrel, match target Kentucky rifle. Scott watched the water carefully and finally glimpsed a portion of Potter's head. One shot took Potter's life.

Attempts were made all day to recover Potter's body. The following day, Mrs. Potter had a cannon, which muzzled over the lake, discharge a heavy load. The concussion caused Potter's body to rise from the depths of the dark water, and he was buried on Potter's Point.

On August 14, 1844, near Shelbyville, was fought the last battle of the Regulator-Moderator war. About 600 men participated and another standoff resulted. The following day, somewhat belatedly, it would seem, President Sam Houston took measures to halt the strife. Five hundred copies of a presidential proclamation were printed and distributed throughout Shelby County:

> Proclamation: Executive Department, San Augustine, August 15, 1844
>
> It having been represented to me that there exists in the county of Shelby a state of anarchy and misrule, that parties are arrayed against each other in hostile attitude contrary to law and order; now therefore, be it known that I, Sam Houston, President of the Republic of Texas, to the end that hostilities may cease and good order prevail, command all citizens engaged therein to lay down their arms and retire to their respective homes. Given under my hand and seal the day and year above written.
>
> Sam Houston.

Houston, with one eye on Shelbyville, where a fight to the death was forming, hastened to call up six hundred militia from the nearest counties not involved. General Travis G. Broocks was given command. Colonel Alexander Horton, Marshal of the Republic, was handed warrants for the arrest of the ten leading men of each faction.

General James Smith and the first company of militia to arrive at Shelbyville found themselves making a climactic entrance, of the stage or screen variety. Several hundred Moderators were drawn up in assault formation, and were on the verge of attacking the fort manned by practically the entire force of Regulators.

The militia came up in the rear of the Moderators and Smith called upon them to lay down their arms and surrender. The Moderators readily complied. The Regulators, perceiving the trend of events, quietly evacuated their fort and slipped away.

After Marshal Horton had arrested Colonel Cravens, Sheriff Llewellyn, Judge Hicks and seven other leaders of the Moderators, a call was sent to the Regulators for them to send in ten of their leaders for trial. Forthwith, nine leaders of the Regulators came in and surrendered. Moorman did not voluntarily surrender, but Horton caught him in an intoxicated condition at Hilliard Springs.

District Court was convened in Shelbyville under charge of President Sam Houston. Judge Ochiltree, a brilliant jurist, was named to preside. Resolutions were drawn up by D. S. Kaufman, pledging all adherents to disavow the names of Regulators and Moderators and to stop all hostility. The leaders of each side signed. Although hatred remained, and an occasional quarrel and fight ensued, the dreaded words and the entire subject were avoided by the entire county for fifty years.

When the Mexican War broke out on the border, Shelby County furnished two companies of enlisted men. Ex-Moderators went to one company, and ex-Regulators gravitated to the other company. Army commanders shrewdly placed these companies in the line, side by side, where each tried unsuccessfully to outdo the other. This circumstance forced a reluctant respect, each for the other. Sharing dangers and privations so far from the home they both loved also formed a bond between them. When the Mexican War was over, the veterans led the movement of consolidation, forgiving and forgetting.

— Texas Arms —

In addition to the Mexican border which posed a constant threat, the Republic of Texas had a seacoast of some three hundred sixty miles which could not be left unguarded. More urgently in need of defense were five hundred miles of western frontier, each mile of which was in constant danger of Indian attack.

The defense of the Mexican border was simplified by a cushion of one hundred twenty miles of semiarid land situated between the Rio Grande River and populated areas. County militia, subject to instant call, was deemed sufficiently strong and mobile to cope with any thrust from that quarter. This defense scheme failed in 1842, due to inferior scouting. However, it had been demonstrated that the plan would work. When the Mexican invaders suddenly withdrew from San Antonio, the Texians had amassed a force of 3,000 men, and were on the verge of counterattacking.

Possibility of attack from the sea was believed limited to Mexico alone. Naval plans were formulated on the basis that Texas had only this single enemy. Fortunately, Mexico was not a strong maritime nation. But the Mexican navy preyed on shipping along the Texian coast. The peace treaty between Texas and Mexico was taken even less seriously at sea than on land.

Texas had a few small ships which had been used during the revolution, and these formed a stop-gap navy until ships could be procured. The first Congress of Texas, in 1837, provided for a small fleet of good quality. The new ships were not placed in service until 1839.

The old vessels on hand were not quite of the quality suggested by the name of the flagship, *Invincible*. Before the new ships could be activated, the old ones had disappeared from the seas. Some, including the *Invincible*, were captured by the Mexicans. The others were lost in gulf storms.

The new navy consisted of one steamship of war, and six smaller sailing vessels of various weights and armaments. Commodore Edward Ward Moore commanded.

The new fleet was equipped in Baltimore. Moore had considerable freedom in outfitting his ships. One of his purchases was three hundred Colt revolvers, a new invention which is described below. Mr. Colt had made one sale to militia officers in South Carolina which numbered seventy-five revolvers. Otherwise, his weapon had been unfavorably received. His gratitude to the Texian Navy well may be imagined. In later years, Commodore Moore proved zealous in giving Colt testimonials for sales purposes.

Discipline in the Texas Navy was poor. Moore disobeyed the commander-in-chief consistently. His men, in turn, disobeyed him. There was a mutiny and resulting hangings.

But the navy got results. Commodore Moore put the Mexicans on the defensive. In a battle off Campeche, on May 16th, 1843, the Texian Navy worked itself out of a job. On that date the *Austin*, six hundred tons, and the *Wharton*, four hundred tons, attacked the Mexican fleet and chased it into demoralization. Neither side lost ships, but both factions suffered heavy shipboard damage and a high rate of casualties. That ended the Mexican naval threat.

The Colt revolver of 1851 commemorates this naval action by displaying on its cylinder an engraved picture of the battle, and the words "Engaged 16 May 1843." Some arms students protest that the picture depicts the U.S.S. *Mississippi* in battle. They fail to explain why the *Mississippi* in the engraving was flying the Texian flag so proudly and prominently. Samuel Colt was friendly and grateful to a number of Texians, as we shall see later. It is not strange he should so honor a Texian victory.

But let us return to the defense problems of Texas. Where the militia and the navy were deemed adequate to deal with the Mexicans, the more constant threat of Indians demanded a standing army.

Congress authorized fifteen companies of infantry, each company consisting of fifty-six men. Eleven companies of cavalry supplemented them. These troops were intended to protect the long flank of Texas which was exposed to the Comanches and Apaches. Actually, the army often had far more men than were authorized. Single men coming from the States wanted to serve a short term in the army until they could orient themselves and decide upon a business and a location which would best suit their needs. On one occasion President Houston visited a large army camp and issued several hundred furloughs to soldiers, in the absence of the commanding officer. Houston hoped many of them would not return; the army needed a reduction in size for reasons of economy.

Let us add that this camp was not on the frontier at the time of Houston's visit, so the men were not actively engaged. Too often the army was not on the frontier when it should have been. Many of the officers preferred their fighting in the grog shops.

Most of the army recruits were forced to furnish their own rifles. Texas was long on riflemen, but short on rifles and cash with which to purchase them. The only important purchase of rifles by Texas on record was the contract of April 3, 1840, with Tryon, Son and Co., of Philadelphia. Mirabeau Bonaparte Lamar had succeeded Houston as President of Texas in 1838. The new president discarded Houston's policy of small armies and rigid national economy.

The lack of money at that time did not worry Lamar; the country basically was worth millions, and the president did not shun a modest debt. During this administration, Texas spent possibly eight or ten times as much money on military matters as had been spent during Houston's administration.

The Tryon, Son & Co. contract was for 1,500 Mississippi type rifles. The so called Mississippi rifle received this appellation in the U. S. Army. After a Mississippi regiment had been issued this new style percussion rifle, the other regiments began clamoring for "rifles like those Mississippians." These guns also have been called "Yerger," "Jager," and "Harpers Ferry" rifles. Their caliber was .54, the barrel length was thirty-three inches. The rifle delivered to Texas was not equipped to receive a bayonet, nor did it have the U.S. proofmark on the barrel. It used a round bullet of one-half ounce weight, and the rifling was one turn in six feet. Its total length was four feet, one inch, considerably more convenient than the extremely long guns then prevalent.

The new gun carried a double barrel-band in front and one single barrel-band in the rear. The ramrod was iron. A large patch box was inlaid in the stock. The rear strap swivel was attached to the forepart of the trigger guard. The forward strap swivel was attached to the long front barrel-band.

The lockplate carried a serial number stamped on the forward end. In the center of the lockplate was stamped a Lone Star in a circle. Outside this circle, and enclosed by yet a larger circle, was stamped the words "Republic of Texas." At the rear of the lockplate was stamped "Tryon," and the date. The dates ranged from 1842 to 1846, denoting a four year delivery of some nine hundred guns. Approximately six hundred guns of the 1,500 gun contract were never delivered to Texas. It is said that the U. S. Army got them in late 1846 for use in the Mexican War.

The rate of survival of these nine hundred guns is very low. This is understandable, as they served through the Texas Indian Wars, the Mexican War and the Civil War. Most of the few which survived these wars, were ruined by later owners, who reamed their barrels to convert them into cheap shotguns.

Another type of weapon which became popular in Texas during her republic days was the duelling pistol. Prior to the Texas Revolution, few duels were recorded. That of John A.

Wharton and W. T. Austin, famous leaders of the country, was the most noted of Colonial days. After the Revolution, duelling was practiced entirely too frequently. Texas army regulations forbade duelling, but the regulation was not enforced. The commandants fought, the officers fought and even the enlisted men fought. Texas is probably the only nation where officers and enlisted men openly engaged in duels with one another.

Houston, the capital until 1839, had a regularly recognized duelling field. Sam Houston, in whose honor the city was named, was challenged to duel five times during his first presidential term.

Texians not only fought with pistols, they engaged in so many brutal and freakish types of duels that General Zachary Taylor, the Texas-hater, remarked, "Texians are neither cowards nor gentlemen!" Helena duels were popular. In this form of mayhem the principals each had one wrist bound to the wrist of his adversary. Each free hand contained a Bowie knife. The thong was not removed from their wrists until one man was helpless. Formal duels were fought with rifles at close range, with shotguns as closer range, and with Bowie knives not in the Helena tradition.

In a formal duel in Panola County, then a part of Shelby County, Henry Strickland, called "Bully of Teneha," was crippled horribly by "Riproaring Jim" Forsyth, who was described as a very resolute man. Forsyth cut the flesh from Strickland's arms, "trimming his marble" as it was called in cultured circles, and when Strickland turned to flee, Forsyth cut one shoulder blade in two. The Forsyths have been "very resolute" even to the present.

Rifles at twenty yards at six in the morning were the terms of the Laurens-Goodrich meeting of June 25, 1837. Laurens was unjustly forced into this duel and was killed when he received the ball through both thighs. Dr. Goodrich was killed later in San Antonio.

It was customary to turn a profile to the opponent in a pistol duel, thus affording a smaller target. The smooth-bored pistols, not too heavily charged, most often failed to shoot through a man. Mr. Laurens should have altered his stance when facing a heavy rifle. His wound may have been less severe had he been shot through from front to back.

The circumstances of the Laurens-Goodrich duel were such that they furnished all the required examples of the evils of duelling. This duel was cited most often during the campaign to end duelling in Texas. Senator Francis Moore led the fight which finally led to the passage of the stringent anti-duelling law in 1840. Ninety-nine years later, publicly elected officials were compelled to swear they had never acted in a duel before they were allowed to assume office.

Informal duels were not frowned upon then, and though they are deplored now, the survivor was rarely punished. In 1841, Charles Hooten of England reported in his book, "Human life in Texas is held at the least possible value." Charles Gillet, in Houston in 1843, said, "Go through this land and point me to a single town which has not been the scene of some deadly affray. Tell me of an instance where the murderer has been made to suffer...Men walk the streets with deadly weapons...and murderous intentions. When one has fallen, how often is heard the comment, 'It is alright. He should have been killed long ago.'"

About ten men were legally executed during the days of the Republic. But this was for horse stealing. Smaller crimes were punished by whipping or branding. There were few prisons, consequently there were few prison sentences.

Nearly three of every four cases tried in the courts of the Republic were for assault and battery (fist-fighting), assault with intent to kill, or murder. Fist-fighting usually brought a fine of five dollars. Combat with weapons was usually excused, as now, on the grounds of self-defense, or honor, and the case was dismissed. Drunkenness and gambling were prevalent, and there were many indictments and few convictions for these offenses.

Fighting was not confined to the ignorant lower classes. J. Pinckney Henderson, the first governor of Texas, killed a man in San Augustine. At least five fights occurred in the Texas Congress. Canings, shooting scrapes, fist fights and formal duels were common at the Capital. Once Congress recessed to watch a fight between A. C. Horton and Judge Edwin Waller.

Analysts of the times attribute the Texian proclivity for fighting and mayhem to five reasons: The end of the war with Mexico was uncertain, and war spirit still ran high. The organs of legal authority were in their formative years, and needed time to develop. There were no bars to immigration, and many criminals entered Texas. The natural aggressiveness and rampant individualism of the pioneers produced fighting as a natural by-product. The weak and timid never started to Texas, or soon turned back. The custom of wearing Bowie knives and pistols as ordinary apparel may have contributed to the frequency of combats.

Texas was a great meeting ground for the various types of duelling pistols. A stream of immigrants from the United States came well equipped with arms, furnishing a source of American made duelling pistols. Many immigrants from Germany brought or imported German duelling pistols. The Kuchenreiters and Jungs, master builders of German duelling sets, are frequently found in old Texas families. Whether more Kuchenreiters or Jungs were used, or whether the German families merely take better care of their antiques, is not known.

England and France were great friends of the Texas Republic. Texas competed with neither of them in trade. Texas did furnish both of them raw products, cotton, sugar and hides. Also, both European nations looked to Texas to stop the western expansion of the United States. As a result of these European trading contacts, English and French duelling sets came to Texas. The English makers, Richards, Manton, Wogdon, Van Wart, Forsyth, Williams, Egg and others had their signatures on Texas-used duellers.

The French masters, Boutet, LePage and Renette are seldom found, though other French makers are. Possibly the gentlemen of Paris, with their idea of sculptured art on pistols, had trouble selling their high priced products to a people who bought duelling pistols to use, and not to admire in a drawing room.

William Ransom Hogan, in his social and economic study of Texas, says, "The Republic of Texas in the early eighteen forties was virtually impoverished…What, then, held it together? Like frontiersmen everywhere, most of them were people of unhesitant faith, and their materialism was always tinged with visions of things hoped for in a world that was not only competitive but adventurous and quickly changing. Even new inventions, such as the Colt revolver, were reaching the frontier more rapidly than in an earlier day."

Admittedly this Colt revolver was a large factor in the hope of Texas. How their hearts went out to this multiple shot weapon! With its help, the pioneers visioned victory over the stubborn Comanches and Apaches. At last, they visioned peace in which to expand their ranges and granges, to enjoy constructive progress rather than a constant fight for life.

Samuel Colt, as a boy, conceived the idea of a revolver, and secured patents in the United States covering the most essential functions on February 25, 1836. Of course his revolvers were not the first ones. They were the first ones widely utilized, hence the first successful ones. Mr. Colt hastened to patent his invention in all other nations that afforded patent offices. After the Texas Patent Office opened, in 1839, Colt went to Texas. He found a strange, raw land, bursting its seams with growth. Land speculation was rife, and he bought a large tract in his name, and another in the name of his brother James.

The capitol had just been moved from Houston to Austin. Six months before, there had been no town of Austin. Five commissioners had met, selected the townsite on the Colorado River, and had it surveyed into lots and streets. Workmen brought lumber from Bastrop and began erecting the public buildings. An auction was held and lots sold to citizens.

Public buildings were of frame construction. A few were built of logs. Many hotels and taverns were erected immediately, mostly of frame construction. Business houses and residences, likewise, were wooden. Dozens of tents served as temporary shelters while all available carpenters worked long hours to construct more stable structures. The city was built almost overnight to receive the governmental administration, the archives and the Congress, which was to convene in November. The population of Austin in its first year was 1,500. This set a pattern that was to be duplicated in the West many times, when the discovery of gold, or the extension of a railroad, motivated a boomtown.

Mr. Samuel Colt did not care to go to Austin. The road was long and rugged. That would not have detained him, possibly, but in Galveston he acquired the details of the Texas patent laws. The Texas Patent Law, of January 28, 1839, provided that any citizen of Texas, or any alien who declared his intention to become such citizen, might obtain a patent for a term of fourteen years by complying with certain regulations. Another section of the act declared a patent could not be issued on an invention which had enjoyed two years prior use in Texas or abroad.

Colt had no intention of becoming a citizen of Texas, although he had bought land there. This purchase was made because the land was very good and very cheap. Also, Colt recognized that his invention had been in public use for two years. On the other hand, shrewd Yankee that he was, he realized that he needed no patent in Texas. The patent would have afforded protection for only fourteen years, and Sam Colt was industrialist enough to see that Texas was more than fourteen years away from manufacturing revolvers. It is almost certain that Colt was not among the Americans who had patent requests in Texas refused them, rumors to the contrary.

Colt's revolver, like most other inventions, did not emerge letter perfect at the first production. There were changes in design necessary before the ultimate in achievement could be obtained. Although Colt's firearm, compared to other pistols of that day, was a marvel, it did not achieve instant success.

The Colt factory at Paterson, New Jersey, had gotten into production very late in 1836 or early in 1837. Sales had not been good. No army or navy of the world had been interested until the Texas Navy purchased three hundred revolvers in 1839. Mr. Colt had made a number of voyages for the purpose of promoting sales.

As was usual with Colt, when he landed in Galveston, he had a supply of samples with him. Upon reaching his decision regarding his patent application, his thoughts turned to sales. Mr. S. M. Swenson, a Galveston merchant and friend of Colt, was moving his business and home to the new boomtown of Austin. Mr. Colt begged him to deliver a few revolvers into proper hands in Austin. Accordingly, four Colt revolvers were turned over to John Coffee "Jack" Hays in Austin by Mr. Swenson, with the compliments of Sam Colt. These revolvers were the "large size" caliber .36, with flared grips. Later they became known as Texas Patersons to differentiate them from other Colt models.

The Texas Patersons had no attached rammers, were finished in dark blue except the hammers, which were case-hardened. The seven and one-half inch barrels were grooved with eleven bands with a slow right hand twist, although they shot a round ball. The grips were plain walnut. The trigger was concealed, springing out from the frame only when the piece was cocked. The cylinder was chambered for five shots, and bore a stamped decoration, a scene depicting a stage coach holdup. A separate rammer, extra cylinder with identical serial number, bullet mold and a powder and ball flask accompanied each revolver.

Jack Hays presented a pair of the revolvers to Rip Ford. Other Ranger officers joined Hays and Ford in test firing the new weapons. All were enthusiastic over the Colts. Imagine being able to fire five shots from horseback without being forced to halt and load! This revolver was the answer to the Rangers' prayers.

As the revolvers were received in late 1839, they were not tested thoroughly enough to justify ordering a supply until 1840. The order was effected, however, and the revolvers arrived from the factory before the end of the year. The exact number purchased on this original purchase order is not known. It has been described simply as enough to equip a company of Rangers. As pistols were issued in pairs, and a company nominally consisted of fifty-six men, probably the order was one hundred and twelve revolvers.

In the spring of 1841 the new weapons got their baptism of fire. Victoria and Linnville were raided by Comanches on August 5, 1840. Both towns were pillaged and burned, twenty-one whites were killed and many were wounded. Several thousand head of horses, mules and cattle were stolen.

Sam Houston ordered Jack Hays to recruit and ready a company of Rangers to assist in protecting the settlements from the savages. This company was issued the new Colt five-shooters. This company of Rangers consisted of such men as Big Foot Wallace, Sam Walker, Sam Luckey, Ben Highsmith, Kit Ackland, Ed Gillespie, P. H. Bell, Ben McCulloch and others almost as famous.

In Bandera County there is the deep mountain pass named for General Bandera of the Spanish army, who fought a bloody battle with the Indians there in 1733. Into this pass rode Captain Jack Hays with his illustrious band of Indian fighters and scouts—only to be completely ambushed by a large force of Indians!

The Texians, surprised nearly to demoralization, hurriedly dismounted and sought shelter in the rocks and brush. The Indians, observing that the whites were badly outnumbered and somewhat uncertain, boldly charged. Of course, the Indians knew nothing of the repeating pistols. Highsmith was administering water to Sam Luckey, who was critically wounded at the first savage volley. The others fired rapidly with great effect. The Comanche chief wounded Ackland and then attempted to ride over him. Ackland shot the chief from his horse with a revolver. Both wounded men closed in embrace, each armed with a knife. Wallowing in blood and dirt, Ackland killed the chief.

The continued volley of the whites was beyond the comprehension of the Indians, and their charge was beaten back. The battle began at eleven in the morning and lasted for hours. Finally the Indians withdrew from gun range. The Rangers took their five dead and numerous wounded and withdrew to the south end of the Pass, where they cared for their casualties and buried their dead.

After the Rangers withdrew, the Indians gathered their dead and wounded and repaired to the north end of the Pass. There they buried their chief and numerous other dead. Many horses were killed in the battle. Their bones lay bleaching in the Pass for many years, a reminder of this grim struggle in the newly green brush of a Texas mountain pass.

The new revolvers did not win the battle, but they earned the Texans a standoff under very unfavorable conditions. Due to the element of surprise, the Rangers failed to capitalize fully on their new weapons. Before acquiring the revolvers, the Rangers always dismounted to fight; they were unable to reload while mounted. Upon being so completely surprised in this battle, they instinctively followed the old strategy of dismounting.

In some quarters the Rangers are given credit for introducing Colonel Colt to the Indians in 1839, on which occasion the Rangers enjoyed signal success. The records, however, show only five fights with the Indians in 1839, and the Indians won four of these. Colonel Burleson won the fifth, commanding two companies of the standing army. There is no evidence that Colt revolvers participated in any of these battles.

In October of 1840, John H. Moore and ninety men got the drop on a band of Comanches and killed one hundred and thirty of them. Also in 1840 Major Howard had a skirmish with Indians at Georgetown, near Austin, and the Indians lost seven dead to the Rangers.

The testimonials given by appreciative Texians to Samuel Colt, for advertising purposes, date the use of Colt revolvers by the Texas Ranger Force as 1839. That is correct. The Rangers had four of them that year. The first general issue was in 1840. The first important use of revolvers was as described above, in 1841. John Salmon, "Rip" Ford, who received one of the first two pair received by the Rangers, is authority for the above statements.

The oft-told fight in which Jack Hays chased the Indians and slaughtered so many, was the Nueces Canyon fight of 1844. On this occasion, Hays and fourteen men, nearly all of whom had been in the Bandera Pass fight, were on a scout. Noah Cherry was up a bee tree trying to obtain honey, when he spied several hundred Indians coming. The Rangers were each armed with two Colts and a rifle. Some of these arms had formerly been used by the Texas Navy, and recently had been reissued to the Rangers.

When the Indians came up and prepared to charge, the Rangers had formulated their plans and had mounted. The strategy was to countercharge. So dismayed were the Indians that the small band of whites were charging, instead of fleeing for their lives, that the Indian force became separated. Under the constant drumming of the revolvers, the Indians became demoralized, split up into smaller groups and began running for their lives. Hays chased them and killed an estimated hundred. The number of the Indian losses has been placed at various figures by various writers. This tends to discredit the accomplishment. Of course, no one knows the actual Indian loss.

These Indians had not fought against revolvers before. They believed that the whites were at their mercy after the first Ranger volley. As the pistols continued flashing, the Indians were said to have dropped their spears and shields while dodging. Years later, the chief of this group was captured. He said he received five pistol wounds in this battle, and that his warriors had died for a hundred miles along his retreat. Hays and his company of Rangers later scored thirty

Indians in a Gillespie County fight. The battlefield did not cover as large an area, so the dead were counted; no estimate was necessary.

Still later, in 1845, Hays counted fifteen dead Indians in the fight at Enchanted Rock. Captain Warfield and fifteen men, armed with revolvers, attacked an Indian raiding party of sixteen on the Cibolo in 1845. None of the Indians escaped, all being slain within a half-mile of running fight.

The following testimonial is reproduced since many Colt fans will find it interesting. Also, it reveals some of the problems and methods of Indian fighting.

Washington, D. C.
Feb. 26, 1850

Sir,

Being requested to give our opinion relative to the merits of your justly celebrated repeating pistols, we do so with much pleasure, as we know their efficiency from long experience, and deem them to be the greatest improvement in small arms of the age.

We have been familiar with the use of your effective invention on the frontiers of Texas since 1839, and we do unhesitatingly affirm that they give the combatant greater confidence and spirit of defiance in those hand-to-hand struggles with the prairie Indians than any other arm now in use. Those prairie tribes ride with boldness and wonderful skill and are perhaps unsurpassed as irregular cavalry. They are so dexterous in the use of the bow that a single Indian, at full speed, is capable of keeping an arrow constantly in the air between himself and the enemy; therefore to encounter such an expert antagonist with any certainty of doing good execution requires an impetuous charge, skillful horsemanship and a rapid discharge of shots, such as only can be delivered with your six-shooter.

They are the only weapon which has enabled the experienced frontiersman to defeat the mounted Indian in his own peculiar mode of warfare. In these encounters which, though soon over, require a steady nerve, the greatest possible precision and celerity of movement, there is no time to reload firearms, even were it possible to do so and manage your horse in the midst of a quick and wily enemy, ever on the watch, and ready to lance the first man who may lose the least control of his animal.

In this description of service, the revolver asserts its great and unquestionable superiority over all weapons. We state, and with entire assurance of the fact that your six-shooter is the arm which has rendered the name of Texas Ranger a check and terror to hostile bands of our frontier Indians. With the citizens of Texas they are considered unparalleled in the force and accuracy of their shooting and are esteemed an invaluable weapon in offensive operations against those marauding tribes which depredate upon our frontier settlements.

As for the difficulty in keeping those pistols in order, which is sometimes raised as an objection, we have never discovered any. Those instruments can only become unfit for service in the hands of men who never possessed the proper pride of a soldier, or where discipline must be most egregiously neglected.

> With great respect,
> your obedient servants,
>
> G. T. Howard
> Late Major Texas Regiment
>
> I. S. Sutton
> Late Captain Texas Rangers

If the first paragraphs are slightly colored, the last paragraph is flagrantly untrue. However, the letter was written in 1850 and by then, the Colt revolver was easy to maintain, though the revolvers used by Howard and Sutton in Texas certainly were not.

Rip Ford has written better praise of the 1847 and 1848 model Colts. He said (not in a testimonial) that the revolver would outshoot the Mississippi rifle, as to range and accuracy. When Texas desired revolvers for Civil War use, it follows that the Colt 1848 Dragoon model was specified as a pattern for type.

The first revolver had many faults: it was fragile and hard to repair, it did not shoot hard enough (its range and shocking power were poor), the lack of an integrated rammer was a defect, and the trigger was unsatisfactory. Still, Texas had found a weapon with which Comanches might be defeated.

But Texas found it too late. Samuel Colt and his Patent Firearms company had gone out of business in 1842, due to lack of sales! The winning weapon was no longer available.

— Statehood —

Most Texians had their origin in the United States, and they never lost their filial devotion to their Mother Country. It is true that after the United States rejected Texas' request for annexation in 1837, Texas toyed with the idea of remaining a separate republic. However, the vacant lands of the country had to be settled by Americans to satisfy the Texians, who wanted no more Europeans or Mexicans. If the population necessarily must be American, why not make Texas American, reasoned the voters. Another powerful influence in the determination of annexation were the relatives most Texians left back in Virginia, Massachusetts or Alabama.

The United States became an ardent suitor. She wooed Texas with every blandishment. Suddenly the United States had realized that Texas was turning more and more to England and France for trade, financial backing and cultural contacts. She realized that Texas blocked her path to the Pacific. Suddenly she wanted Texas intensely, even should the union mean war with Mexico. In 1845 the United States Congress and President Polk accepted Texas as a sister state, and on February 16, 1846, Texas state officials replaced Texas national officials.

"The Republic of Texas is no more!" said President Anson Jones, as he hauled down the Texas flag and raised the flag of the United States. The men who watched this exchange of flags, with tears streaming down their cheeks, had faced death to establish the Republic of Texas. They had fought and bled for the flag they removed, so that the flag of another

nation might fly in its place. No other compliment so high
has ever been paid a nation as was paid the United States of
America by Texas on February 16, 1846.

The terms of annexation were: 1. The state of Texas to
be formed subject to all boundary adjustments; 2. Texas
should cede the United States all forts, docks, navy yards
and other edifices pertaining to public defense; 3. Texas
should retain all public funds and moneys due her; 4. Texas
should retain all unappropriated lands lying within her lim-
its; 5. Texas should pay off her debts and liabilities; 6. new
states of convenient size, not exceeding four in number, in
addition to the state of Texas, might, if desired by Texas, be
formed from the territory of Texas, such states lying south
of the Missouri Compromise Line might be slave states,
those lying north of said line must be free states.

This agreement gave Texas two concessions which she felt
were indubitably hers in any event. The American government has welched on both. First, all that part of Texas lying
south of the Compromise line might be slaveholding. It
was evident in less than a dozen years after the treaty of annexation, that this provision would be violated. Second, the
boundaries of Texas as defined by Congress extended into
the Gulf three leagues. The United States government accepted this boundary. The American government had apologized to Texas for Captain Cook and his dragoons crossing
this boundary. The war with Mexico was fought to defend
this definition of the boundary. The United States bought
the northern sector of territory lying within this boundary
from Texas for ten million dollars, ample recognition that
the boundary was accepted. Yet, the tedious tidelands dispute is over the southeast portion of this same boundary.
The federal government intends to appropriate tidelands
expressly retained by Texas in her treaty of annexation.

In 1845 when annexation was certain, General Zachary
Taylor moved an American army to the Nueces River in Tex-
as. On March 8, 1846, Taylor began moving his army from
Corpus Christi to the Rio Grande. This was to effect posses-

sion of the boundary claimed by Texas under her treaty with Mexico.

Mexico, however, had repudiated Santa Anna's treaty and claimed the Nueces River to be the proper boundary. On April 11, 1846, Mexican General Ampudia arrived at Matamoros with an army, and ordered Taylor to retire from the Rio Grande. Paredes, President of Mexico, declared war on the United States April 23, 1846.

An undecisive battle was fought between Taylor and the Mexicans at Palo Alto, on the Texas side of the river, on May 8th, and an American victory was won the next day at Resaca de la Palma. The invasion of Mexico began on May 18th.

The Texan part in this war attracted adverse notice. Texas enthusiasm was commendable, as the Texans had been yearning for another chance to fight the Mexicans. Governor Henderson left the executive chair to command volunteers. Eight thousand and eighteen Texans volunteered, which was good representation from a population of 102,000. Large numbers of Texans were used for scouting. They understood Mexican fighting, many spoke the language of the enemy. The Texans should have been very valuable to General Taylor.

Unfortunately, they seemed to have given the good general more trouble than he experienced from the Mexicans. They engaged in raids without authority, they foraged, plundered, deserted and returned at will, captured towns and executed prisoners against orders. To many Texans it was an expedition of personal revenge. The bodies of the members of the Mier Expedition who had drawn black beans and had been executed, were exhumed and returned to Texas. Many Mexicans who had been connected with the Goliad Massacre and other outrages, were personally sought out and killed.

The Texans were too numerous to control or punish. They comprised more than one-third of his entire army. Taylor conceived a bitter hatred of Texas and Texans. One phase of Texan performance won Taylor's respect. The Texas

Rangers had been incorporated into the U. S. Army. Many Rangers were armed with the Texas Paterson five-shooting revolvers. These men were very effective.

The Mexican light cavalry, the Rancheros, were extremely bothersome. Taylor's men were partly equipped with cap-lock guns, but mostly they fought with the outmoded flint-lock weapons. Against the dashing Rancheros, the Americans did not fare so well. The Texas Rangers, however, were as light and mobile as the Mexican best. The five-shooters rendered the Texans better armed. Taylor was forced to believe that the ordnance department had erred in rejecting Sam Colt's revolver. This error he proposed to correct.

Ranger Captain Samuel Walker, an educated ex-Mary-lander and an arms expert, was chosen to return to the United States and negotiate a contract with Colt for 1,000 revolvers. Walker had, from experience with the first model revolver, very definite ideas on the improvements which should be embodied in the new military revolver.

Imagine Samuel Colt's reaction. He had headed a $300,000 firm for seven years. During this time he had been well-equipped to care for large orders, indeed, he had worked like a Trojan to procure them. But his efforts were of no avail. The company was bankrupt, the machinery had been sold for a pittance. Colt was now engaged in another type of business. Fortunately, he retained his patents.

Then suddenly, he was asked to redesign his revolver and deliver 1,000 on a rush order, while a war killed good men for the lack of suitable equipment. Colt pursued the only course available to him. He sought out Eli Whitney, of cotton gin fame, and the two made a deal. Whitney would manufacture the revolvers, but Colt could expect little more than the ownership of the machine tools after the contract was complete. Whitney got the cash, Colt received the tools.

Sam Walker and Sam Colt worked out the design details, and Walker rushed back to the front where he was killed in action seven months later, in October of 1847. The new Colt revolvers, called the Whitneyville Walker model, arrived at the front only two or three months before the end of the war. Their importance lies, not in Mexican war accomplishments, but rather because they inaugurated a period of perfected handgun manufacture. Revolvers henceforth would give a performance not too incongruous when compared with our modern handguns. These Walker model Colts are important to the collector because they are the most expensive scrap-iron on the market, worth only a little less than four hundred dollars a pound.

The Walker Colts are .44 caliber six-shooters. They fire either a round or conical ball. The conical ball weighs one-half ounce, the same weight utilized by the old .54 caliber horse pistols. The round ball weighs one-third ounce. These revolvers have ample shocking power and are capable of good penetration. Where the Rangers formerly were forced to ride into close quarters and "powder burn" the enemy with their smaller five-shooters, they enjoyed a weapon of good range in the new revolver.

The new model was large, sturdy and heavy. The rammer was attached and more convenient. The tricky and fragile folding trigger was dispensed with, and a conventional trigger in a square-backed brass trigger guard replaced it. The revolver weighed four pounds, nine ounces unloaded, probably the heaviest pistol produced in two hundred years. The barrel was nine inches long, rifled with seven grooves to the right at the rate of one turn in three feet. The grips were plain, black walnut; the grip strap was iron.

The new revolver had only one fault. The rammer catch was a failure. It consisted of a small, fragile spring located so as to engage a slot in the rammer. Its design necessitated its absorbing stresses of a cantilever nature which were beyond its inherent strength. This fault was easily remedied by placing a more positive acting catch at the fore-end of the rammer.

The 1848 model Colt Dragoon corrected this rammer latch trouble. Also, the cylinder was shortened and the barrel length was reduced from nine to seven and one-half inches.

There were other slight modifications, mostly to facilitate manufacturing processes.

The advent of the 1848 model found Colt in his new factory at Hartford, Connecticut. His revolver had achieved recognition at last. He had a new U. S. Army contract; he was not to falter again.

It might be timely to insert here a brief biography of Samuel H. Walker, the man whose personal experience and sound arms judgment enabled Colt to dissever his revolver from its glaring faults in a single redesign. Walker was born in Maryland about 1810. He served in the Indian campaigns of Georgia and Florida, and went to Texas in 1836. He participated in the Mier Expedition, and was commissioned lieutenant in the Texas Rangers under John Coffee Hays. During the Mexican War, Walker commanded a company of scouts, called "Spys," which rendered excellent service. Walker distinguished himself signally in the Battle of Palo Alto. He was promoted to lieutenant colonel of Hays' Second Regiment, and was killed at Huamantla, Mexico, in October, 1847, by a sharpshooter hidden in the steeple of a church. His remains were returned to Texas, and he was buried in San Antonio.

After the Mexican War ended on February 2, 1848, the U.S. Army established a chain of forts along the Rio Grande River. They were: Fort Brown, Camp Ringgold, Fort McIntosh, Fort Duncan, Camp San Elizaro and Fort Bliss. The first was located near the mouth of the river, and the last named being near Franklin (later renamed El Paso) in the westernmost corner of the State.

Along the Indian frontier was another chain of forts: Fort Inge near Uvalde, Fort Lincoln near Medina, Fort Marion Scott near Fredericksburg, Fort Croghan near Burnet, Fort Gates near Gatesville, Fort Graham near Hillsboro, and Fort Worth.

As the expanding settlements reached westward, this retaining wall of forts necessarily had to be moved along with the frontier.

The next line of defenses consisted of Fort Clark, near Brackettville, Fort Terrett in Sutton County, Fort Mason where General Robert E. Lee served as a young officer, Fort McKavett in Menard County, Camp Colorado in Coleman County, Fort Chadbourne near Bronte, Fort Phantom Hill near Anson, Camp Cooper in Throckmorton County and Fort Belknap near Newcastle. These forts were erected and occupied in 1851 and 1852.

Later forts were Fort Hudson, established 1854 on Devils River; Fort Lancaster, 1854, near Sheffield; Camp Verde, 1856, near Bandera; Fort Davis, 1854; Fort Stockton, 1859; Camp Quitman, 1858; Fort Concho, 1867; Fort Griffin, 1867 and Fort Richardson, 1866. Fort Elliott was established as late as 1875, near Mobeetie.

While the U. S. Army never distinguished itself for Indian action in Texas, there were reasonable excuses. Probably the army brass thought Texans, like the populace in a great many places, wanted only the payroll, beef and corn contracts, and other commercial advantages which attended an army post. No doubt, these were as welcome to Texans as to any others, but Texans wanted and needed protection from a numerous and bravely fighting foe— the Comanche.

The above outlined forts, when plotted on a map, reveal considerable strategy in location. The garrisons of these forts were frequently infantry, sometimes augmented by cavalry. The raiding Indians thought little of passing within a few miles of an army post. The soldiers, while campaigning, were burdened with baggage and accoutrements. They were clumsy and slow, and their weapons, while never better than the Indian arms, were frequently inferior.

The posts were valuable beyond their cost however, even though they did not accomplish their purpose fully. They furnished havens for refugees fleeing from Indian raids; they resulted in a network of roads, or trails; they furnished escort to stagecoaches in periods of stress, and best of all, they formed hubs around which were built wheels of towns, commerce and communication. Without the aid of army forts, the Comanche dominance would have been expelled more slowly, the building of the West could not have come with such a rush.

The population of Texas increased from 102,000 in 1846 to 421,000 in 1860, including slaves and "civilized" Mexicans and Indians.

Part IV -
Civil War

— Secession —

The Civil War, or War of Secession, was precipitated by the slavery question, but the different ideologies which were involved are with us yet. To what extent should federal power prevail over state's rights?

Southern states maintained that each state was a sovereign government (this idea traced back to the original thirteen states before they formed a union), and that the Union had been created for mutual benefit. When the interests of the Union should be prejudicial to the interests of one state, that state was believed to have the right to withdraw from an unfavorable confederacy. Various northern states had threatened to secede previously, but had been restrained through diplomacy.

Texas had entered the Union but a short while before. Her entry was of her own volition, and she believed it was her right to withdraw, particularly should the federal government become involved in internal war.

Texas was essentially frontier, and there always had been but little slavery on the frontier. Only about ten per cent of the slaveholders and less than five per cent of all planters held slaves on a scale large enough to render an overseer expedient.

Nearly one-third of the votes cast were against secession. There was not the avalanche-like movement for disrupting the Union which was manifested in the Carolinas and elsewhere.

Next to the issue of state's rights in Texas, was the unassailable truth that the Union had failed to protect Texas from Indian and Mexican depredations, and refused to reimburse her for expenses incurred in defending herself. Texas disbanded its Ranger force, according to agreement, when it entered the Union and received assurances of federal protection. But the federal protection was inadequate and unsatisfactory.

Raids began increasing many-fold and Texas hurriedly reorganized her own frontier battalions. These Rangers could out-Indian the Indians, when it came to living off of the land, travelling light and fast, and staying in the saddle day and night, without rest, for long intervals. After the frontier was again under control, the United States refused any help in defraying expenses incurred.

Texas lawmakers and newspapers, before the slavery question became an issue, likened Texas to a maiden who, being courted by an ardent suitor, received many promises which were soon forgotten after the courtship was successful. Ill-feeling engendered by this circumstance swung many votes to the side of secession. Although most voters in Texas were from Alabama, Mississippi, Georgia or Tennessee, or were sons of fathers from those states, these human sympathies may not have influenced them completely had not the saber rattling occurred. But against the advice of the more seriously thinking minority, the mass populace, bombastic individualists, ranted of attempted Northern coercion, and opened their arms to war and disaster.

The Texas Convention adopted the ordinance of secession February 1, 1861. News of the attack on Fort Sumter was received in Austin on April 17, 1861. The American Civil War was on!

Within a week, the Confederate government called on Texas for 8,000 infantry. These were furnished. In less than six months there was a requisition for twenty companies for the defense of Virginia. Texas sent thirty-two companies immediately. Colonels Baylor and Young, commanding volunteer cavalry regiments, took over the federal army posts along the western frontier and in Oklahoma.

A county by county survey of arms was made. Forty thousand arms were reported. These included muskets, rifles of all calibers, shotguns of all bores, pistols and revolvers. This arms census probably was inaccurate, as it is doubtful if many citizens cared to register their weapons.

The male population of Texas in 1861, between the ages of sixteen and sixty, was approximately 95,500. The number of men entering the Confederate armed services was 68,500. From these figures it can be seen that the state had a considerable ordnance problem facing them. No arms were being manufactured in the state. No large federal arsenals were so located that arms could be confiscated for the arming of recruits.

The U.S. Army maintained a supply depot in the historic Alamo at San Antonio. These stores, valued at $1,500,000; were seized February 18, 1861, but they furnished few arms. Only parts of the many uniforms stored there could be used. The foods and medical supplies would have been a prize indeed, had not an accidental fire ignited the lard stored there, which destroyed everything except the nearly indestructible Alamo building.

Some men, on entering the army, carried their personal weapons. Others did not care to strip their homes of defense, for much of the state was yet subject to occasional Indian outrages, and the Mexican reaction was uncertain. The need for arms was urgent.

Let us examine the manner in which Texas attempted to provide arms and supplies for her soldiery. A Military Board was created consisting of Governor F. R. Lubbock, Comptroller C. R. Johns and Treasurer C. H. Randolph. This Board was empowered to take such steps as it considered necessary to furnish men, equipment, supplies, food and tax money to the Confederacy.

As the Confederacy's prime interest was the defense of Virginia, with the defense of the Mississippi Valley being of secondary importance, the defense of the Trans-Mississippi area received such small priority that the states west of the

Mississippi soon realized that they would have to defend themselves. Conditions in Texas were more acute due to unfriendly Mexico, the Indians in Oklahoma as well as on the western frontier, in addition to the threat of Union invasion.

The Board furnished the Texas quota to the Confederacy and increased their demands on the draft boards to organize state troops for home defense. The Board endeavored to receive credit from the Confederacy for men, arms and money so expended, but was unsuccessful. Thus with the draft boards carrying a double load, they became unreasonable in regard to granting exemption from military service. Manufacturers of arms and ammunition were fair game for the draft boards, and soon the stock of manpower in the army exceeded the equipment with which to arm them. But because the Confederate Armies were perpetually outnumbered in their campaigns and because the commanders constantly pleaded for reinforcements and replacements, this system of stripping the almost total manpower from the state prevailed until the end of the war.

In November of 1863 Governor Lubbock called for the drafting of boys of sixteen and recommended that there be *no* exemptions, except for total disability. There were already 64,000 men in the service.

As there are today many disputes regarding the war contracts of the Military Board, they are listed here as they appear in the official records of that Board. This record, which was recently found in the archives, should end all speculation in this matter. J. M. Moore and J. D. Wilson were appointed purchasing agents to act in Mexico. Their authority was vested in contracts.

John M. Swisher & Co. received a contract to purchase supplies for the Board in Europe. Short, Biscoe & Co., of Tyler, contracted to manufacture 5,000 rifles. Tucker, Sherrod & Co., of Lancaster, contracted to manufacture 3,000 revolvers. Billups & Hassell, of Plentitude, contracted to furnish seven hundred rifles. Whitescarver, Campbell & Co., of Rusk, contracted to furnish rifles in various quantities, and shortly before the end of the war, they contracted to furnish 1,000 revolvers. N. B. Tanner, of Bastrop, contracted to furnish five hundred rifles. Billups & Son received a contract for an unstated number of rifles.

The following firms received contracts to furnish gunpowder:

Gatewood & Co., George Pfeiffer & Co., Travis Powder Co., San Antonio Powder Co., and W. M. Bunt & Co. These were in addition to the State and Confederate armories at Marshall, Anderson and Austin. John D. Henderson contracted to furnish certain textiles. George Oetterlinger and Leavenburp & Bro. each received a contract for general supplies including ordnance items, but neither firm manufactured guns, pistols, revolvers or ammunition. Knives, pistol holsters, belts, cartridge pouches, etc. were included.

Johnson & Dewey received contracts involving the handling of cotton and the furnishing of certain machinery. Ball, Hutchins & Co., Groesbeck & Alexander, Wheat & Fletcher, and others not particularly interesting to the gun lover, were awarded contracts involving cotton—its purchase in Texas, its transportation and its sale in Mexico or elsewhere.

Late in the war, W. S. Reed & Co. received a contract to operate the State Foundry in Austin, which under state management, had been able to cast only one or two successful cannon up to late 1864.

The above was taken from a recapitulation of contracts and was signed by the Board. McKenzie Johnston of Hempstead corresponded with the Board concerning his manufacture of "long knives" and sabers. He is believed to be a subcontractor under either Oetterlinger or Leavenburp & Bro. Gunpowder was produced by Constantine Foster in Burnet, and one of the larger powder producers of the state was the firm of Rowin & Marchbanks in Waxahachie. Whether these firms were subcontractors, or whether the Board bought their output without benefit of a contract is not known. Correspondence on record authenticates such sale. Foster turned out only fifty pounds of powder per week. He received $1.25 per pound for it. The large plant at Waxahachie suffered an explosion April 29, 1863 which killed William Rowin and others. A batch of 2,000 pounds exploded. H. C. Marchbanks and Mr. Rowin's brother continued to operate.

In December of 1862 an ordnance mission attempted to recover Mexican cannon from rivers, where the remnants of the Mexican Army of 1836 had sunk them in their retreat. None were recovered. Six months earlier the Board had purchased the only cannon available in Texas. Briggs and Gard, of Houston, sold two Nichols rifled cannon to the State for $3,000. D. Bradbury's foundry at Port Lavaca offered to cast bronze cannon for the state, but when the Board requested them to do so, in April, 1862, they discovered the project was greater than they had anticipated. Bradbury was noted as a repairer of guns. This department of his business, prior to the war, was evidently quite large.

One of his gunsmiths was E. C. Singer, a nephew of I. M. Singer of sewing machine fame. E. C. Singer invented a "marvelous rifle gun." Singer never reported on his own invention, but Bradbury wrote the Board concerning it, as did others. John B. Burke of Indianola wrote the Board that the gun fired "four minnie balls extremely accurate." No replies from the Board are available.

A. I. Nave was another inventor of military arms which never materialized. His cannon would have cost six or eight hundred dollars each, he estimated, and would have been very similar to a rifle, only larger and "far simpler." The Board did not finance him.

On May 5, 1863 stock was sold and a company organized which was to manufacture a new type of submarine. This subsurface craft was rated a certainty to break the Union blockade. For some unexplained reason the blockade lasted longer than this new firm of naval constructors.

Cannon making in Texas, in 1863, required attention, stated the report of the Military Board. The report stated that only two cannon had been made in the state, those by Nichols, which were used in the Battle of Galveston. E. A. Blanch, of Marshall, had been sent by the Board to Hughes' Furnace in Cass County, and to the ironworks in what is now Marion County to negotiate cannon founding. But no cannon resulted. Eight months later Major Mason, from Rome, Georgia, visited these plants in the interest of Confederate ordnance.

The weights and size of cannon made them difficult to handle in the small foundries of Texas, even if the nature of the work had not been so specialized as to require experience and equipment totally lacking. An old ordnance file lists these standard barrel weights for the guns:

6 pounder — 884 lbs
12 pounder — 1750 lbs
12 pounder howitzer — 788 lbs
24 pounder howitzer — 1318 lbs

A letter, dated March 15, 1862, from Captain Lardner Gibbon, Inspector of Ordnance at Richmond, to Pryor Lea of Goliad, requests cannon for the army in Virginia. He wanted "3 inch 6 lb. guns, rifled, and 12 lb. howitzers of bronze or iron." He advised that better guns could be bought abroad than could be founded at home. Captain Gibbon further advised that infantry should be equipped with Harpers Ferry percussion rifles, or Enfield rifles from England. The cavalry, he said, required short Enfield rifles, holster pistols and good sabers. He opined that good rifles could be had from London Arms Mfg. Co. and from Liege, Belgium, for $19 per gun, though he advised allowing fifty per cent more in cost allowance to care for transportation.

Mr. Pryor Lea, the recipient of the above letter, had been appointed "Procurer" for the Military Board in a special dispensation signed by all members. He must have been a go-getter. Some of his purchases in Mexico were very important. He sent one wagon train out of Matamoros, Mexico, with 2,000 sabers, 20,000 pounds of gunpowder, 1,100 rifles (probably Enfields), 6,000 blankets and 2,000 pairs of French-made shoes.

Even so, he was often excelled by private traders. I. McAllen of Brownsville, made a business of importing lead for resale. John C. Baker, of Columbus, went to Monterrey and Zacatecas, Mexico, and freighted out by ox wagons an immense store of goods. He returned with 20,000 pounds of gunpowder, 40,000 pounds of sulphur, 16,000 pounds of saltpeter, 60,000 pounds of lead, 8,000 pounds of refined copper, 70,000 pounds of rope (he spelled it "roap," but regardless of spelling it's still a dozen wagon loads), 1,000 pair of shoes, and numerous other goods. Mr. Baker resold to Texas "at a nominal profit for my time and trouble."

On April 28, 1862, Inspector General Dashiell called the attention of the Military Board to a quantity of old flintlock guns that were stored in Austin. These weapons had been a gift of the federal government, following the Mexican War, to the local militia. The Texans had scorned the flintlocks, having been caplock men for fifteen years. But Dashiell knew how difficult new arms would be to procure. He insisted the guns be removed from storage and altered from flintlock to caplock. The Austin Armory attended the alteration.

Mr. P. De Cordova was secretary to the Military Board. If he bothered to answer most of the letters which he received, he missed a bet unless he employed form answers. His mail was chiefly: 1. Contractors wanting money; 2. Men wanting out of service; 3. Employers wanting men out of service; 4. People wanting materials; or 5. Screwballs with patents which could revolutionize warfare. At least one letter, April 25, 1863, must have given him pleasure in writing. The State Chemical Laboratory suggested that San Antonio Mills (San Antonio Powder Co.), makers of both rifle and pistol powder be complimented on the high quality of their product. Cordova's letter was an early day "E" award.

Before we begin a more detailed examination of some of the munition makers of the state, let us review the manner in which the Indian frontier was being guarded under the banner of the Confederacy. When Texas joined the Union, she dismissed her Rangers and expected the promised Federal protection. The protection offered was costly but inefficient. Indian raids began increasing. As the outrages mounted in number, the Rangers were reorganized. Now most of the old Rangers were with Terry, across the Mississippi.

Mr. John Henry Brown, in writing of the times, relates, "... many of the families of Gainesville gathered at the residence of James Elmore when warned of the Indian raid. Many of these families were simply women and children, the men being in the Confederate Army, and the few men in the county were armed with the poorest class of firearms, all the best guns having been given to those who joined the army."

This apt appraisal of Gainesville is equally descriptive of the whole frontier. A study of the reports of the Indian raids of this time reveals a pathetic poverty. Men pursued by Indians raced for their lives on old mules, or frequently blind horses. Of course, the riders were slain by the Indians. In account after account, one reads of faulty ammunition or guns causing loss of life. "James McKinney traded his pistol for provisions and while on the way home was attacked by Indians. He was killed when his gun missed fire"; or, "only two chambers of his six-shooter were workable and he was killed." The quotations are from J. C. McConnell, who gives a graphic description of conditions simply by relating numerous incidents.

The Indians stepped up their attack when the American flag moved in; it was increased even more under the Confederate flag. A Frontier Regiment was organized, at a cost of $800,000 per year. For three years Texas stood this expense of money and manpower without receiving credit for either from the Confederacy. In the last year of the war, Texas was allowed to count the manpower so expended as part of her quota to the Confederacy. Also there came a promise from the Confederate government to pay the cost of troops actively engaged on frontier service. As the Confederate government collapsed within the year, this failed to help.

The Frontier Regiment consisted of ten companies, designated "A" through "K." Each company with a strength of fifty to one hundred-fifty men, was given a sector to protect. Sometimes a company was divided in two camps in order to effect more complete coverage of the border. The camps were located one day's march apart along the entire frontier. They were not effective.

In the first place, the men were numerically deficient. So many miles were patrolled by so few men that in event of a collision with a war party of Indians, the whites were invariably outnumbered, often as badly as ten to one. Secondly, the arms and ammunition were decidedly second-rate. The percussion caps often had their linings fall out. The gunbarrels were of poor grade and often burst. The arms were of rough finish, the actions were often so uneven in operation that accurate sighting and squeezing off was impossible. Indeed, many of the arms were inherently inaccurate, so that polishing the action was useless.

Lack of discipline was at an all-time high. Being outnumbered in battle, their only chance of success was in coordination and spirit. Both qualities were lacking. When the officer ordered "Dismount," on the verge of one recorded action, one man answered, "Don't be a damn fool!" and a good many of the troopers rode away. Many losses in battle were explained by troops retreating while some of their comrades charged as ordered. Probably there was less bravery in this Ranger force than at any other time in history.

This is not an effort to depreciate many fine and brave men who were courageously attempting to perform a near impossible task under the most trying and discouraging conditions. There were many such men. But the first team was in another game, and the substitutes were of such varying quality and experience that victory could not be theirs.

Between the beginning of the war and late 1864 there were ninety-four Indian raids, possibly many more that were not recorded. In each raid there was loss of frontiersman life; sometimes as many as twenty-four or twenty-six whites were killed or carried into captivity in a single raid. Of course attendant outrages occurred, homes and barns were burned, livestock was stolen and a few maimed orphans were left with the dead.

The Indian defense was reorganized in late 1864, quadrupling the number of men assigned to protect the border. The First District, on the northern sector had 1,436 men under General J. W. Throckmorton. The central sector, under Major George B. Erath, numbered 1,529 men. The Third District, on the southern sector was commanded by General D. McAdoo who had 1,211 officers and men.

These groups were in addition to the Frontier Regiment which was placed under the command of Colonel James E. McCord. This placed the defense on a man for man equality with the Comanches, who could field about this number of warriors. However, the Apaches, Wacos, Cherokees, and others, as well as Mexican bandit raiders, kept the Texan defense numerically inferior.

This new organization claimed to have reduced the number of Indian raids by forty per cent. Actually, if recorded incidents are accurate enough to receive consideration, the raids continued in the same ratio of about three per month on an average. The Indians were simply trying harder, taking advantage of the temporary weaknesses of their white foes.

— Arsenals —

The State Foundry at Austin was more successful in the manufacture of percussion caps than in any other branch of manufacture. As there has been small praise of their caps, we may be troubled to laud this enterprise. Its chief disadvantage may have been its proximity to the seat of government. Too many ill-informed politicians had access to the plant, and from a consideration of their positions, their advice could not be wholly ignored.

Constant interference caused a long line of superintendents to display their questionable talents at this plant. Constantly changing the supervision, policies and plans of an organization has rarely induced distinguished accomplishment. The plant began manufacturing copper caps on a large scale. Speed, rather than quality, was evidently the criterion. Refined copper was obtained and shipped to Austin in sufficient quantities. The chemical laboratory, maintained by the state, apparently kept the explosive ingredients of the caps under proper control. The assembly setup was at fault. The cap-cutting men were paid $2.75 and $3.00 per day. The fillers, who added the explosive and inserted the liners to hold it in place, were paid one dollar per thousand caps. By rushing through their work, these laborers, if sufficiently negligent, often earned as much as twenty-five dollars per day.

These inferior caps lost their liners, both in transporting and in battle. The soldiers on the western frontier threatened to break off their Indian campaigns and open an offensive on the cap factory. This trouble was solved by reducing the salaries of the fillers from their favorable piecework rate to a salary of $2.50 per day. Some political favorites quit their jobs in indignation, but the caps improved in quality if they decreased considerably in quantity. Even so, large orders of caps regularly left the plant, one order being for $5,500 worth.

Mr. A. R. Roessler was clerk on March 14, 1863, when the position of superintendent became vacant with its usual suddenness. Mr. Roessler was given the supervision of the plant with no change of title. Possibly this rendered him slightly rebellious and impatient. His letter to the Military Board set off a small volcano, somewhat similar to the modern congressional investigations in Washington concerning governmental malpractice. Mr. Roessler called the Governor's attention to the difficulty of carrying forward the work at hand with his badly undermanned organization. His task, he continued, was not eased by the necessity of repairing plows and doing general machine shop work for everyone who had political influence, as everyone had, it appeared. As Mr. Roessler was indignant, some of the heat crept into his pen. Mr. Roessler resigned his position May 18, 1863 after sixty-five days of heroic effort among the plows. Hurrah for Mr. Roessler! May his progeny be numerous in Texas!

Ralph Hooker was the next superintendent of the State Foundry. His troubles were even more complicated. Over at Bastrop was a large supply of iron. This was made available to the foundry by reason of the departure of N. B. Tanner, the gunmaker, for greener pastures. Someone conceived the idea that the foundry should cast cannon, so Hooker was sent after the iron, one week after he assumed his new duties. Cannon casting was begun with great enthusiasm in Austin. After many faulty pours, it was agreed that the furnace must be rebuilt, as it was entirely unsuited to the purpose. This was done, and other unsuccessful efforts followed. On October 16, 1863, the Board was advised that statewide efforts were being made to locate a man who could cast cannon in a cupelo furnace such as existed in Austin. We presume they referred to a cupola furnace. Maybe it was a "cupelo"; maybe that was what was wrong with it.

This hopeful report was repeated on November 16, 1863. Next month's report indicated progress. Tools were being made with which to bore cannon. The report of February 8, 1864 reverted from progress to hopefulness. Casting a cannon in Austin was in prospect. But the report of July 21, 1864 was less cheerful—no cannon.

Late in 1864 the Board gave W. S. Reed & Co. a contract to manufacture cannon in the foundry. This organization speedily accomplished what state mismanagement had failed to do. They cast five batteries of six guns each that could pass inspection and proving. The guns were furnished complete, with carriages and caissons, for $800 each in specie. It has been said that the state finally cast one or two successful pieces before W. S. Reed & Co. took over the plant. The point is controversial and proof is lacking. It seems doubtful that W. S. Reed & Co. would have received their chance if success seemed at hand, at last, under the old regime.

ANDERSON ARMORY

Except for the manufacture of powder, it is believed that nothing was produced in Anderson until J. H. Dance & Bros. moved their plant there in 1864.

The Dances, who are discussed later, fled from Columbia to save their fellow townsmen from a bombardment by Federal gunboats, which desired the destruction of the valuable Dance equipment.

The Dance tools may have been utilized to manufacture a few revolvers here, but only a few. The foundry and forge was utilized to make bayonets, sabers and cannon balls. Other products may have been made also, but the claim that cannon and guns were manufactured in Anderson is discredited.

Records of this plant are obscure and slightly contradictory. As so much has been recorded concerning efforts to manufacture cannon, it is almost certain that successful attempts in Anderson would have been mentioned. Any records containing such mention have been lost.

The manufacture of guns in Anderson is discredited due to the lack of survival of the guns in quantities greater than would be probable for experimental models, and to the lack of knowledge of a possible source of gun manufacturing tools. Barrel making and rifling machines and other necessary special machine tools were scarce in the South in those days. All of them were known and indeed, the various states in the Confederacy quarreled over the possession of them in a number of cases.

There is no record of the source of such tools in Anderson, nor is there a record of the disposition of these tools at war's end. Defective guns, returned from active service, were repaired there for reissue.

MARSHALL ARMORY

Marshall, Texas, the wartime capital of Missouri, was actually a supply depot rather than an armory. It was under the administration of the Confederate States and not under the jurisdiction of the Military Board.

There was some manufacturing in Marshall. Gunpowder was manufactured, and late in the war, a cap factory got into production, using machinery transferred to Marshall from Arkansas. Saddles, artillery harnesses and miscellaneous other supplies were fabricated there.

Its great importance to the Confederacy, however, was due to its depot. Marshall was the gateway from Texas to Louisiana and Arkansas, hence to the Confederacy. New Orleans had fallen and the coast was blockaded. Materiel was freighted overland. The large supplies which came from Mexico, destined for the war east of the Mississippi, were massed here. The beef, textiles, raw and fabricated leather, foodstuffs, ammunition, guns and hundreds of items which Texas contributed to the Confederacy were checked in here, receipted for and consigned to their destination.

Marshall was important, but not particularly interesting from the specialized viewpoint of the gun student.

N. B. TANNER

A progressive gunsmith in Bastrop, N. B. Tanner, secured a state contract for five hundred Mississippi-type rifles. Heretofore he had repaired but had not manufactured fire-arms. Tanner had no stock of fabricated barrels to fortify his courage as he embarked on the venture, as many firearm contractors did have. He had a smart and analytical mind, however, and immediately secured the items he believed would insure his success. He acquired an early and adequate stock of iron before this commodity got scarce and dear. He secured the best tools obtainable, although they were not all that could be desired. And he obtained Mr. I. R. Nichols, reputed to be the best barrel man in the state, to attend this feature of his manufacturing. Nichols was to subcontract the barrels, delivery to be in the rough, at nine dollars each.

It is regrettable that a man of Mr. Tanner's energy, fore-sight and administrative ability should have no more success than he had. He knew whom to employ and he acquired skilled personnel. He was in production while most contractors were yet in the planning stage.

Whether due to inferior metal stock, inferior tools or some other reason, Nichols failed in his end of the production. Rifles were rolling off the line with cheerful regularity, but the inspector was rejecting an excessive percentage of them. Some of Tanner's rifles, after being accepted by ordnance inspectors, burst in the field. Bitter complaints began to accumulate against the Tanner rifles. The inspectors tightened up and rejects became more numerous.

Tanner must have been a forbearing character. According to Nichols' letters, Tanner remained cheerful and attempted to bolster the spirits of the discouraged barrel-maker. Nichols wrote the Board and stated that his barrels were not what they should have been. However, he believed he could rectify the trouble.

Tanner's forbearance in the matter was rendered less difficult by the excellent contract he had secured. He received $32.50 per gun. As money had not begun to depreciate at that time, since neither labor nor materials had begun their upward spiral, Mr. Tanner had a safety factor in his delivery price that would care for a high ratio of gun rejections in his new organization. A similar ratio would have been wholly unacceptable to established fabricators, who sold their guns for around twenty dollars.

The exaggerated account of faulty Texas-made guns was largely due to an unusual condition, or decision, in which no gunmaker was involved. The Confederate general commanding the Territory of Oklahoma had difficulty in obtaining guns for Indian troops. These troops were organized more for the purpose of enlisting their sympathies for the Confederacy than for the usual purpose. This action was based on the old premise that "if you can't whip them, you should join them!" As it was not considered essential that these Indian troops maintain more than token efficiency, the Commanding General made an unusual request.

He begged the Board for all the rejected arms from the various gun plants. This request is of record. Although the reason is not explained in official correspondence, the reasons are obvious and well understood in the Southwest. Various ordnance inspectors, usually junior officers of keen perception and unbounded ambition, did not suspect the true circumstances of these faulty arms. They observed them and reported them adversely. A study of their reports from the Confederate ordnance files has given arms students an entirely erroneous impression of Texas rifles. The present belief that Texas-made rifles were inferior, and were used only in arming Indians in Oklahoma, requires revision. It is a conclusion based on inference drawn from an incomplete knowledge of facts.

That the Confederate procurement officers illegally dipped into the state arms programs, and sent quantities of Texas rifles to the eastern sector is not generally known, although official records of it are available to all. Existing specimens of these rifles will compare favorably with rifles made elsewhere. But remember, the rejected rifles were also issued and some of them also survived. Probably in no other case have gunmakers' reputations been appraised by the quality of their guns that were rejected.

A sample of the adverse reports originating in Oklahoma follows in a portion of a letter written by J. J. DuBose, Captain and Chief Ordnance Officer of the District of Indian Territory, to General Maxey commanding the Territory: "...A few Enfield rifles were seen, with a few Mississippi rifles; the remainder were composed of double-barrel guns, Texas rifles, sporting rifles, etc....I would call your attention to the Texas rifles. A regiment armed complete with these guns is armed, but badly. These guns are nothing more than a cheat, badly put together, and very unreliable, being liable, a great number, to burst..." Other batches of these rejected rifles were sold into Mexico, their value being higher as rejects than as scrap iron, dear as iron became.

Tanner's first delivery of acceptable guns occurred early in 1862. His plant produced at the rate of about a gun per day, delivery being effected upon the completion of each unit of twenty-five guns. As his personnel left for active duty on the front, and replacement was impossible, the production rate declined. The plant averaged only fourteen rifles per month during the last seven months of operation.

Due to early imperfections in Tanner's guns, and consequent questionable reputation, nearly all the defective Mississippi rifles which turned up were attributed to Tanner. Faulty guns in use on the northern frontier have been attributed to him, whereas his guns were never sent to that front. "Give a dog a bad name..."

Nichols' tarnished reputation as a maker of gun barrels could no longer save him from the draft, although he placed a number of appeals. The other help was disappearing under the determined onslaughts of the draft boards. Tanner was closed up.

The last delivery of guns was May 20, 1863 when thirty-one rifles were accepted. Tanner did not mourn. Increased costs were ruining him. He had delivered two hundred and sixty-four rifles to Texas, but the profit he had made on early deliveries had been lost on later deliveries.

Tanner's rifles, as contracted, were the Mississippi type. This type of rifle is described elsewhere. The markings consisted solely of serial numbers, and identification of existing specimens is improbable except by tracing an individual gun through family ownership back to Tanner's shop.

— THE DANCES —

"The Dances? Ah yes, they are a magnificent race of men!" said a lady who remembers three generations of them. And who, suh, cares to dispute old southern ladies' opinions of their men? Lest you are misled by the title and expect a treatise on the terpsichorean art, permit us to explain that the Dances are an old pioneer family of Texas, and in helping to mold the destinies of that State, the women, as well as the men, have been magnificent.

Their home is called West Columbia, a prosperous community that grew along the railroad, on higher ground than the bluffs of the mighty Brazos River, where lies Columbia, the gem of early Texas. Indeed, when Texas won her independence from Mexico, set up an independent government over an empire reaching from the Rio Grande up into Wyoming, the capital was located provisionally in Columbia. The country is typically Old South, rather than western, with its large dwellings set well back from the roads, amid gigantic live oaks dangling their drooping moss and mistletoe over expanses of bright green grass.

The Dances are best known for their arms manufacturing activities during the Civil War. Their revolvers with percussion ignition, or cap and ball, are eagerly sought by museums and private collectors of rare arms. As greatly as Texans of 1863 desired these revolvers, the demand for them now is far, far greater. The hearts of twenty thousand collectors of rare American arms leap within them at the mere thought of acquiring one of these great rarities.

A daughter of the Dances, Mrs. Zula Winstead Loggins, conceived the idea of Father's Day, and strove with might and main until it became a national institution. When the once Capitol building of the Republic of Texas was to be torn down, only she thought to make a replica of it, carefully scaled and of the original materials.

David Etheldred Dance came from England before the American Revolution and settled in North Carolina. When war swept the colonies, and the Continental Army was organized, Etheldred took the field as George Washington's color-bearer. During the dreadful winter spent at Valley Forge, he became permanently crippled, due to frozen feet.

Prior to this, while on a furlough, he met his future wife. He and two companions were trudging the dusty roads of North Carolina, homeward bound, when the heat and dust reminded them of their empty canteens. Reaching a roadside plantation, they were granted permission to drink and rest in the shade on the broad piazza. Having drunk their fill and sprawled in the cool shade, the tired youths soon fell asleep, happy over their proximity to home and lulled by the breeze through the honeysuckle.

Several young girls of the house, the planter's daughter and her house guests, upon learning of the presence of the soldiers on the piazza, began peeping at them and giggling, as young girls will. Having selected the nicest boy, each to her own preference, and argued it thoroughly, they soon needed other amusement. The planter's daughter secured some snuff, a common household commodity when our country was young and virile, and tip-toeing softly she blew some in the face of Etheldred, whom she had selected as hers, and raced out of sight around a corner of the house before the young soldier awakened, coughing and gasping. But a man of arms awakens and goes into action at almost the same instant, and he quickly pursued the now frightened and rapidly disappearing young lady, vowing vengeance as he ran. He soon caught her and kissed her and they looked at one another, the laughter leaving their expressions, a deep and intense understanding filling their eyes. She was Miss Delilah Watkins.

They were married after the war and had three children—John Henry, Rhoda, and James. Rhoda became the wife of a nephew of Stonewall Jackson. James settled in Grimes County in Texas.

Most of the men of that day were craftsmen. They could do things with their hands, and do them expertly. John Henry became better than most, possibly because of greater incentive. His father could no longer walk more than a step or two, and John Henry determined to build him a wheelchair. Never having seen one, John Henry actually was an inventor, and a number of chairs were constructed before John Henry and Etheldred were satisfied. But his failures added practice to his skill as a mechanic, and he became more and more skillful, whether working with wood or metal. He followed the building trade the remainder of his life, being a carpenter, cabinetmaker and ornamental metal worker.

After the death of Etheldred, John Henry, who had married and fathered five sons and three daughters, moved to the community of Utah in Alabama, where he reared his children, lived his life and was buried.

Joe John Dance, the eldest son, left home early and went west. In 1849, when gold was discovered in California, he shared the adventures of crossing a raw and savage continent. He never returned. Joe John Dance was reported dead in California in 1852.

James Henry Dance went to Texas in 1851 at the age of twenty-eight, after the death of his father, John Henry. He liked what he saw and sent for his brothers and sisters. His brothers, George Perry Dance, born March 27, 1829, David Etheldred born May 24, 1833, and Claudius born in 1835, and their sisters, Della Elouise and Melvina followed their older brother to Texas in 1852. Little Sally Ann died before the Texas trek.

Although George was a skilled metal worker, and David was an equally skilled worker in wood, both trades learned from their father, the entire clan determined to become plantation owners in Texas. So they purchased nine hundred fertile acres at Cedar Brake, which was to become West Columbia.

As the Dance brothers and sisters were unmarried, they decided to build one large home as the family seat, and all of them occupy it. A large southern colonial mansion was built, of fine workmanship, and fine material—for the house was built of selected grain cedar throughout! Much of the furniture was made by David and fine furniture it was, and is yet!

The county they selected was Brazoria, then one of the richest counties in Texas. As early as 1848 Brazoria County produced over five million pounds of sugar and over ten million pounds of cotton. Famous plantations sprawled in the fertile valley of the Brazos River.

The Josiah H. Bell plantation joined the town of Columbia. On this land the first Congress of Texas assembled under a giant oak tree which is still standing, and later, the first capitol of Texas was built nearby on land granted by Bell. Bell soon realized that the capitol was attracting the growth of a town, so he banished the capitol to Houston, explaining that a new town would ruin his hog pasture.

Other famous plantations were General Coffee's Halcyon; Peach Point, where Stephen F. Austin, the Father of Texas, died; the Mills brother's Low Wood with its bells cast from Mexican silver dollars; China Grove, the home of General Albert Sidney Johnston, who fell at Shiloh, famous for its profusion of wild Cherokee roses; and Orizimbo, owned by Dr. Phelps, where the Mexican dictator, Santa Anna, was held prisoner after the Battle of San Jacinto.

One of the most impressive homes was that of the McNeels. This house was a two-story brick home containing twenty-one rooms. Galleries supported by immense columns ran the west and south lengths of the house. The marble hearths and mantels, the carved ceilings, the luxurious carpets and handsome mahogany and walnut furniture

were credited with making for the McNeels the most pala-
tial home in Texas. Marriage united the McNeels and the
Dances nearly a century later.

The early history of the county was chiefly the history of
the Brazos River. Lafitte, the pirate, erected a fort on the
river in 1818. The first permanent white settlers on the river
came with William Andrus, who built a fort in 1819 for protection against both Indians and pirates.

The river, over nine hundred miles long, was first called
Los Brazos de Dios, the Arms of God. This name was be-
stowed by a Spanish priest prior to the advent of French or
Americans. It was given this name because the good man
and a band of converted Indians saved their scalps from a
war-whooping party by crossing the river and hiding in a
canebrake.

It was at Velasco, near the mouth of the river, that the Tex-
an-Mexican violence began, and it was there that it ended
with the Treaty of Velasco, which expelled the Mexicans
from the north side of the Rio Grande.

Because there were many plows running on the Dance
plantation, a blacksmith shop was deemed expedient. This
fell within the jurisdiction of George, the metalsmith. From
forge and anvil, his farm smithy gradually expanded in size,
equipment and personnel until he had a full-fledged metal
working machine shop.

Because the need for a machine shop catering to public
trade was acute, and good profits were forthcoming from
this new industry, the machine shop was moved from the
plantation to the town of Columbus, where it occupied a
spacious building within a hundred yards of the river front.
Operators of cane mills, sugar refineries, cotton gins, saw-
mills and steamboats had long felt the need of a good machine shop. A large boiler and steam engine were procured
and installed with the forges, trip-hammers, presses, drills,
lathes and other equipment which made George's eyes spar-
kle and brought a stream of hopeful customers bearing their
iron-working problems.

The term machine shop was not applied to this type of business in those days. It was designated a "steam factory." The firm name honored the eldest brother—J. H. Dance and Bros. Actually George controlled it. James Henry was content to be a senior, silent partner.

But while the Dances prospered, and the plantation in the rich Brazos valley yielded its cotton, corn, cane, cattle and horses, and as the machine shop grew and secured more and more business from up and down the broad and darkly muddy river, storm clouds gathered.

The War of Secession was looming on the horizon. Despite the dissenting voice of Sam Houston and their other leaders, despite the advice of Robert E. Lee, who commanded the Army Department of Texas, public opinion veered to secession. With the beginning of hostilities, James Henry Dance, the eldest brother, entered the army and was stationed at Galveston and Matagorda. The Confederate garrison in Galveston withdrew without a fight when the island was subjected to a large scale Union invasion. Reinforced and reorganized, the Texans under General Magruder recaptured the island after a bitter land and sea battle, and thereafter James Henry was sent to Matagorda and remained there until the end of the war.

George was sworn into the Confederate Army but never was required to report for active service because his mechanical and executive ability was sorely needed on the home front.

About the time the war broke out, there appeared in Columbia, Jesse Parks and his nineteen-year-old brother, Anderson. Anderson was to cause some controversy among arms students in later years. The Parks brothers found employment in the Dance machine shop.

The files of the Military Board contain over one thousand letters of complaint from firms contracting with the Board. All of them deplore the draft boards constantly stripping them of nearly their entire personnel, of having to pay one dollar per pound for steel, for receiving only forty dollars for a firearm when it would bring two hundred on the black market. Most firms had to have sizeable advances in cash before they were able to tool up and begin production. After these advances were awarded, the Military Board received complaints and delays rather than arms. Their patience was worn thin, no doubt, by the time they received a petition from A. Underwood, attorney for the Dances, signed by numerous friends. This letter is reproduced because it reflects the type of business letter and business procedure of that era, and because it contains many names which are a source of Texas pride today.

Columbia, April 22, 1862

To His Excellency
F. R. Lubbock
Governor of Texas

The undersigned friends and acquaintances of your Excellency beg leave respectfully to represent that our fellow citizen, George P. Dance, is by nature and experience a mechanic of great ingenuity, reliability and energy whose services our State and Country may be made of great utility and importance in the manufacture of army revolvers, now so much needed to increase the efficiency and add to the invincibility of our brave Texas soldiers.

With the aid of five thousand dollars machinery can be added to the large steam factory of J. H. Dance and brothers in this place which will enable him to employ fifty hands and turn out fifty army revolvers weekly.

Our object therefore in this is to ask your Excellency with the least possible delay, to place at the disposal of said Dance the sum named, and also to intervene with the proper military authorities to detail not only said Dance but all mechanics and others whom he may select to the manner named labor, to aid him in his manufactory. He will appropriate the factory and his own time to the entire use of the State, or with the aid asked will furnish the pistols at prices greatly reduced from the present market value to those in the service of our State and Country.

The undersigned will guarantee that money granted as above will not be misapplied. The utmost promptitude should be used; details may be arranged hereafter. Let the work commence immediately.

With respect, your friends,

A. Underwood	R. R. Brown	A. M. McMaster
W. F. Swain	W. Baker	Thos. E. Heill
C. T. Patton	W. B. Gaines	I. M. McCormick
D. Walcoh	Alex McCloy	A. L. Weems
I. A. Corkex	S. W. Perkins	John Sweeny
H. T. Tinsley	Fred K. Vogel	Wm. Tewneck
Rhos. I. Givcemy	S. W. Dannon	Milton Aubrey
T. W. Benson	Thos. Brooks	O. T. Howard
Anthony Winston	R. H. Boxley	

The answer was not overly promising but advised attorney Underwood to have his client contact the Military Board. That the Dances were motivated by a sense of loyalty to the state and earnestly desired a contract with the state, which could not be advantageous from a monetary point of view, is shown by George Dance's letter of May 2, 1862.

Columbia, May 2, 1862

To His Excellency
F. R. Lubbock
Governor of Texas

The undersigned, a member of the firm of J. H. Dance & Brothers of this place, hereby places the steam factory belonging to said firm at the disposal of your Excellency to be used for the manufacture of army revolvers and other arms and further offers his own services to conduct said business.

An advance of from $2,000 to $5,000 in proportion to the amount of business proposed to be carried on will be necessary to furnish additional machinery and stock, which advance will be repaid by arms furnished. The undersigned further proposes that the rent of the factory and the value of his own services may be determined by Your Excellency, or by disinterested persons appointed by you, to assess the value thereof; or should Your Excellency choose to receive the arms at a fixed value, the value of said arms may be determined in like manner, Your Excellency contracting for arms sufficient to justify me in entering into the enterprise.

As I have already been sworn into the Service, this whole proposition depends on the exemption not only of myself, but of other mechanics employed by me from military service.

Very respectfully your obt. svt.

G. P. Dance

The answer to this letter is missing, but subsequent events reveal its nature very well. George Dance received an exemption, but no money or contract. The lack of contract is almost certain, not because there is no copy of its extant, but because the Board made a long report on their contracts in 1864, and Dance is not included therein. His employees or associates received no exemptions. He was urged to make revolvers as rapidly as possible, and was advised that a ready sale of them could be had by contacting a procuring agent of the Board whenever the number of his completed weapons would justify an inspection. The Dances determined to manufacture revolvers without a state contract.

In 1862 George went to work on a design, patterns, templates and tooling up. A Colt revolver, long a familiar article of apparel in Texas, was chosen as a model and from this arm the patterns and templates were made, subject to some minor revisions in design.

Occasionally, when firing a revolver of that era, not only the load which was indexed, but all the other unfired charges in the cylinder would shoot at the same time. This was so dismaying to the shooter that he usually, if physically able, discarded the revolver for a single shot horse pistol.

George Dance, like other revolver manufacturers all over the world, had his ideas on this problem. All models of revolvers were equipped with shields just behind the caps which were supposed to protect the shooter. George decided this shield should be eliminated, on the theory that sometimes a cap, exploding under the hammer, ricocheted along the shield in fragments, and burst one or more other caps which in turn, would ignite all charges.

He determined to his satisfaction, that these fragments always traveled laterally and could not be a menace to the shooter if the customary shield be eliminated. This theory was incorporated into the design, with the result that the Dance revolvers are the only percussion revolvers made without recoil shields.

The number of workmen employed by the revolver factory is not known. The number probably varied from time to time, certainly labor must have been the bottleneck. The firm which had secured the state contract for revolvers at one time during production had their payroll shrink to three men, when they threatened to quit.

The Dances must have been a little more fortunate. George and his department completed the iron and brass parts. David, the furniture maker, made the grips and assembled. Claudius, the youngest brother, could not help due to sickness, and soon after the pistol project got underway, he died and was buried in West Columbia. The two Dance girls had married and left the family seat, and their husbands were not available. David had also married, Miss Elizabeth Grey, of Pine Bluff, Arkansas. The other Dance brothers were bachelors.

The Parks were available, as were several other older or physically handicapped employees. New hands were hired whenever available, but more help was needed. It has been shown that a large per cent of Texas men entered the service. In fact, the army roster of Texans was larger by 4,700 men than the state roster of voters. Consequently, help of any kind was very difficult to procure.

There was a Dance family in Grimes County, four brothers and an unmarried sister, who were cousins of the Columbia Dances. An appeal was sent them which brought help promptly. Their names were Harrison, James, Spencer and Nancy Dance. These cousins proved to be excellent workmen in the shop. Nancy served coffee several times a day to the workmen, was a morale builder and helper to everyone and soon became known as the "Mother of the Factory."

Another of Nancy's brothers from Grimes County was John T. Dance. He enlisted in the military company which was raised at Anderson. This was Company G, Texas Fourth Regiment in Hood's Brigade. Company G was commanded by Captain Buffington, father of Judge T. P. Buffington, present resident of Anderson. John T. Dance served with distinction throughout the long and difficult campaigns before Richmond. His only relief from active duty came while he was hospitalized by a grievous wound suffered in the battle of Gaines Mill.

The revolvers manufactured were well-made. The quantity turned out in Columbia is unknown, but production certainly must have been larger than is indicated by the number known to be in existence today. Stocks of materials were assembled for several months before production began, and good equipment and some trained machinists were on hand. It is reasonable to suppose that this plant would outproduce some factory which was established after the war began. A little theorizing is perhaps in order.

As noted above, there was no contract between the Dances and the state or the Confederacy, while the factory existed in Columbia. A regular freight and passenger service existed by sea between Columbia and New Orleans, via Galveston, before the war. Some of these sailing masters continued an irregular service until New Orleans fell to the Federals. After that, their ships were available for contraband transport whenever the chance of evading the blockade was good. Revolvers on the Mississippi in 1863 brought prices far in excess of government contract prices.

The few existing Dance revolvers have not been found predominantly in Texas, in fact they were extraordinarily rare in Texas as far back as 1868. From these related facts it is possible to believe, although this is admittedly an assumption, that the Dances ran a portion of their output along the coast to brighter markets. If that is true, there must have been a day, or a night, when a stealthy blockade runner fell under the stern muzzles of a federal man o' war. The contraband was discovered and destroyed, many cases of precious revolvers, several months' work at the Dance factory, consigned to Davy Jones. And the bill of lading revealed to the Federals not only the name "Dance," but the *location of the factory!*

Near the end of 1863, the Dances received word by river grapevine that the Federal gunboats, stationed at Velasco near the mouth of the Brazos, soon would come up the river to shell Columbia and burn the pistol factory. Great excitement prevailed among the townsmen. Work at the factory was suspended, a conference held and a decision reached. They determined to move to Grimes County, out of reach of the gunboats. The airline distance was one hundred miles but the rail distance was one hundred and sixty miles. The stock and equipment was ferried across the river and loaded on the cars of the Houston Tap & Brazoria Railway, which had built into Columbia in 1859, thence by the Houston and Texas Central Railway to Grimes County. Fortunately the H. & T. C. had reached Millican, in Grimes County, with their rail laying when the war forced suspension of construction.

It may be appropriate to note here, regarding railroads, that Houston, a little town fifty-five miles from Columbia, was quite a rail center, even in those days. Four railroads radiated from this little city on the Bayou. One of them, the Buffalo Bayou, Brazos & Colorado, was constructed in 1852 and was the first railroad in Texas. An interesting feature of this first Texas railroad is that John A. Williams of Boston, who was chief engineer of location, design and construction, chose a gauge width of four feet, eight and one-half inches. This was the same gauge employed by the Romans on their racing chariots in Biblical times. It was not until 1878 that this gauge was adopted as standard in the United States, so Texas' first railroad had the distinction of adopting the standard gauge twenty-six years before it became general in this country.

Moving the heavy engine, forges, furnace, machinery and metal stock under such short notice, and under such trying conditions, reflects a huge capability and an indomitable spirit. Once the town had wanted a pistol factory; now they definitely wanted to be rid of it. Nor could the Dances rest until they had removed the threat of destruction from the homes of their friends.

As the plant had to be moved, it was moved. Other Southern war plants moved as far as the exigencies of war dictated and, regardless of the splendid courage and vigor displayed by the arms makers, the loss of production must have been calamitous. That the hurried move served its purpose is reflected by the fact that Columbia was never shelled by the Federals and the old factory stood unmolested until destroyed by accidental fire years later. Mr. T. L. Smith is the present owner of the land on which the steam factory once stood.

In Grimes County, the pistol factory was established on land owned by John and Mary Graves. The Grimes County Dances were not land owners, and were unable to offer a site. Their friends, the Graves, had a fine spring of water near the road, which was not in use. They offered this factory site for the duration of the war. Mr. Fritz Pistler now owns this tract, which is located about three miles north of Anderson.

While the millwright work of setting up the machinery was proceeding, or shortly thereafter, the Military Board took over the plant in the name of the Confederacy. Other items were more urgently needed than revolvers. A powder plant was already in production there. It was decided that this plant should furnish artillery ammunition for the coast defense guns, which were almost helpless due to the scarcity of ammunition. In spite of the continued practice of calling the plant a pistol factory, it is believed few, if any, revolvers were turned out by the Dances at their new site.

A monument erected at the site of the Grimes County plant by the Texas Planning Commission, under the guidance of the Texas Historical Society, is inscribed:

SITE OF
A MUNITION FACTORY
of the Southern Confederacy, established in 1861, in operation until 1865. Cannon, cannon balls, guns, pistols, swords, sabers, bayonets and gunpowder were manufactured.

Cannon balls, a few bayonets, a few sabers and various ordnance items, as well as powder were assuredly manufactured here. Pistols, meaning revolvers, may have been. Cannon and guns, meaning muskets or rifles, are doubtful products of this factory. We discredit the claim that guns were made here, as neither the rifles have been found, nor any authenticated record of them. Neither is there a record of the source of disposition of the tools necessary to manufacture rifles. Possibly a few were made by increasing the handwork and utilizing the revolver tools.

Before the Dances left Columbia, they had made at least three rifles and probably a few more. As none were made to pattern, they obviously were not made commercially. It is believed that some of the workmen made these rifles on their own time for their own use, or they could have been experimental models. The existence of a few of these so-called Dance rifles may be the basis for the inscription on the monument.

The most probable source of this misconception is due to the repair shop which was opened at the pistol factory. It is referred to as a pistol factory because that is the name by which it was then known, and is known locally today. Disabled guns were sent to this plant for repair preparatory to reissue. Christian Mann was superintendent of the repair shop. When the war was over, he had a number of these guns on hand. When he moved his residence to another county, he gave them to his nephew, Henry Lange, who operated a blacksmith shop in Anderson. These guns—stacks of them—remained in the blacksmith shop for years. Eventually they were put up in the Lange residential attic. Mrs. Lange, knowing that the guns frequently were returned for repairs while still loaded, feared for the safety of her children. She had the guns hauled off in a wagon and dumped into a deep creek. Many later day citizens of Anderson, who had seen the old guns in the blacksmith shop, assumed they had been manufactured in the pistol factory.

Any cannon founded there must have been experimental and unsuccessful. The Military Board had spent large sums at various plants in Austin, Jefferson, Rusk, Port Lavaca and Houston trying to manufacture cannon. The cannon procurement file of the Board is a continuous recording of hope and of failure.

Until July of 1864, only two small cannon which would withstand ordnance tests had been founded in Texas. These were made by Briggs & Gard of Houston, and were used in the Battle of Galveston. Shortly before the end of the war, as we have seen in a previous chapter, a few successful batteries were founded in Austin.

Many records are missing from the State Archives. Miss Harriet Smither and her capable staff have labored for years under a deluge of material which cannot be ideally cared for, due to an inadequate manpower and ridiculously cramped quarters. Activities of the Civil War era have become quite obscure in many instances. Mr. L. W. Kemp, president of the Texas Historical Society, advised that the inscription on the monument was written in Anderson, and reflects the opinion of the older residents of that county. It may be correct in all details, although seventy years elapsed before the inscription was written, and present records do not support it in its entirety. The persons who dictated the inscription acknowledge uncertainty as to its accuracy, although the inscription was believed to be true when it was written.

Cannon balls must have been produced in large quantities at the plant. These balls were for the six-pound field pieces, the twelve-pound howitzers, the forty-eight pound coast defense guns and the eighty-pound, hollow, Columbia bombs. Many of these balls existed until World War I, when a scrap iron drive induced the citizens to gather them and render them as scrap metal. World War II scrap metal drives took their toll, and now there are very few left.

During the Civil War, these iron cannon balls were taken from the Dance forges to a loading depot in Anderson. The hollow bombs were charged with gunpowder and stored until they could be barged down the river. One day some boys, who worked in the depot, were rolling loaded balls on the floor. An explosion of the chain reaction type occurred. The workmen miraculously escaped death, but the depot was demolished. As this accident occurred near the close of the war, the depot was not reconstructed.

Generally, morale was poor in the latter part of 1864. This is indicated by the number of desertions, the price of slaves, the sale and price of government bonds and in other ways. All three attempts to invade Texas had been repulsed, but across the Mississippi, affairs were not favorable for the Confederacy. Texans could see the handwriting on the wall. George and David Dance began planning their future when they would return to Columbia.

Iron and more iron was the need of the Grimes County plant. The limited scrap supply had been consumed. Up in the red hills of northeast Texas were large iron ore beds. A charcoal blast furnace was located at Rusk, and Reece Hughes owned and operated a similar furnace and mine near Hughes Springs. Mr. Hughes' iron had been going into plows, wagons and farming implements. The Military Board took over his furnace and established ox wagon transport to Grimes County, and possibly other ordnance plants.

The writer's great-grandfather has told him of the long wagon trains, the many camps, the river fords and the long journeys. From Hughes Springs to the Grimes County pistol factory, there stretched two hundred and fifty miles of mud, or dust, segmented by five major rivers. One makes the round-trip in a day now, but it required two months then. A yoke of oxen was worth a hundred dollars, and a wagon was worth a hundred and fifty dollars. Strong, cumbersome wagons of bois d'arc, bound with iron and with iron axles were used. Their wheels were five and one-half feet high, with tires six inches wide. Their load approximated 7,000 pounds, which required ten to twenty mules or twenty to thirty oxen to draw it, depending on the season and weather conditions. In spite of the work involved, the quantity of iron delivered probably was very small.

After the Civil War, the federal government took over Mr. Hughes' furnace and operated it as long as it would function. When finally it was returned to him all the equipment had so depreciated under the management of two governments that he was unable to resume private operations. His personal wealth was depleted, as were nearly all Southerners, and failing to secure favorable action on his claim for damage, he died an impoverished, frustrated old man.

Because of inadequate communications, the last battle of the war was fought in Texas. About a month after the war had ended elsewhere, a column of Federal troops was sent to occupy Brownsville. They expected no resistance, and apparently were prepared for none. The Texas commander, Rip Ford, ignorant of the trend of national events, assumed this to be another invasion attempt, and attacked vigorously. Only after he had routed a force which failed to fight with the customary Yankee courage, did he learn of Lee's surrender. His three hundred prisoners convinced this puzzled officer that his country was again at peace, upon which he then surrendered his command to the occupying force.

With the coming of peace, George and David Dance and Anderson Parks returned to Columbia. The Dance plans were made and after an interval of preparation, they began the manufacture of cotton gins. These gins were of ten to twenty mule power and could gin from five to ten bales of cotton per day. A few are said to have been built to derive their power from overshot water wheels, an installation designed for use in conjunction with a mill dam. Of course, a steam engine was used to power all gins where the owners possessed the mechanical equipment, but the equipment hardly was available to new entrants into the ginning business in the eighteen-sixties.

James Henry returned from the army, and the brothers and their widowed sister, Mrs. Winstead, and her little girl Zula, occupied the old family home for years. Miss Zula grew up and went away to school where she met her husband, Mr. R. B. Loggins. Years later, Mrs. Zula Loggins lay in a hospital bed in San Antonio on Mother's Day. Being a cheerful soul, she pondered how fortunate she was that she had had such a fine mother and three fine fathers. The three fine fathers were James, George and David Dance, her uncles, whom she had regarded as fathers since early childhood. Her affection for them was so great she was prone to wonder why fathers had never received the same honor as accorded mothers on Mother's Day.

Immediately she began writing letters. Her confinement afforded her plenty of time and once the idea obsessed her, she worked tirelessly at it. Newspapers, clubs, magazines, public officials and others received her urgent pleas for a Father's Day. Sooner than she had dared to hope, newspapers began to play up the idea and gradually it was presented to the public. It began in 1913, and even as late as World War II, she received thanks for her efforts from servicemen overseas. These letters were carefully filed with the official thanks she had received from governors' offices.

John Grey Dance, the son of David, is the last member of the Columbia branch of Dances to bear the name. His two daughters bear other Texas pioneer names. His grandson bears the given name of David Ethelred in honor of the old color-bearer, six generations removed, but he is a Dance in tradition rather than name.

The Dance cemetery is at West Columbia, once Cedar Brake. There rest the Dances. There is still some of David's furniture and a few, too few, of the colorful Dance revolvers.

There has been a slight controversy over whether the Parks were part owners, with the Dances, of the revolver factory. They have been referred to in these pages as employees.

Mr. Richard Dennis Steuart in collaboration with Mr. Claud E. Fuller, has written most interestingly on the Dances. Mr. Steuart possesses some old notes, or memos, jotted down by firearms enthusiasts of an older generation. These notes indicate that Anderson Parks was co-owner in the revolver enterprise. Mr. Steuart accordingly and properly gave Parks recognition in his book. When Anderson Parks returned to Columbia following the Civil War, he engaged in gunsmithing. He followed this trade there until after the turn of the century, when he closed his shop and moved to New Orleans. Columbia heard he was dead in 1912.

For many years he was the sole survivor of the factory personnel, having entered the armory as a lad of nineteen. He told many stories, some quite humorous, of the activities of the Civil War era. The pronouns employed in his conversation concerning the plant were "we" and "our." It is believed that this may be the basis of a misconception. Several old acquaintances of Mr. Parks have stated that he never claimed partnership in the revolver factory. The present generation of the Dance family deny such co-ownership. There is no record of the Dances transferring part ownership in either the real estate or the equipment to Mr. Parks, but of course, Parks could have received such a deed and failed to record it. Uncertainty remained until June of 1948, when some old letters were found which had been written by the Columbia firm in 1863. The firm name had not been changed from J. H. Dance & Bros.

Bill Longley is reputed to have carried Dance revolvers from his youth until 1873, when Colt introduced the Peacemaker model. If Longley's name doesn't register in your memory, you aren't an authority on Western gunfighters, for Bill was the father of them all. Mr. Eugene Cunningham, writing of a notorious gallery of gunfighters, calls Longley "Number One of the modern gunslingers."

During the Reconstruction period, following the war, many good men were outlawed. White people were denied a vote and were ruled by blacks, who were backed up with Northern bayonets. It was this shortsighted, unjust, carpetbagger rule which engendered the racial question in the South and nourished hatred for the Yankees for so long. Do not attribute it to the war, which created a vast respect in each side for the opposition. It was the cruel Reconstruction period which scalded such a crippling sore, that the cure has been not even yet.

The negroes of 1865 were hardly the same race as our modern negroes. Some of them, not too far removed from the African bush, were as primitive as our American Indians. Through no fault of their own, they were ill-equipped to administer their own affairs, much less the affairs of State. Failure of the whites to resent this imposition would have demanded qualities far beyond the frailties of a mere human being. Where abusing a negro before the war stamped a man as an uncouth boor, negro-hating during the carpetbag era was apt to make a popular figure of him. But whatever the qualities of the law, opposition to authority breeds outlaws.

It was during this period that Bill Longley became an outlaw and rode from bad to worse. He lived near the Grimes County plant and secured a pair of Dance revolvers while but a youth. Becoming proficient in their use, he killed his first man before he was sixteen. From then on, he was a "longrider" and a "hard case," staying alive by his dexterity with his weapons, riding from the Rio Grande to Wyoming, always hunted, always attracting trouble, as steel draws the compass needle, always spreading the gospel of rapid leather-slapping—the quick draw. Dozens of men were to achieve fame, or notoriety, for their indifference to the results of a blazing gun fight. Bill Longley was the first.

Mr. Cunningham describes Longley as riding into an assembly of drinking, roistering negroes and engaging in a gun battle with the lot, killing two and wounding six. Maybe this is the same incident related by Mr. Ruffin Farmer, who was a friend of the participants and possessed full knowledge of the event, and who tells of a negro preacher, a leader with dangerous ambitions and an inflammatory tongue. So much trouble was being stirred up by this carpetbag leader that it became recognized by the disenfranchised whites that something must be done. Bill Longley was the something.

He was masked as he strode up the aisle at the next public meeting of the negroes, and consequently could not be recognized, on oath, by spectators. But as he shot the carpetbagger off of the speaker's platform, several recognized the Dance revolver. This was in 1868, and indicates the Dance pistols were even then rare in Texas. This same revolver later became the property of Mr. Farmer. Its serial number is 4 and indicates it was made in Columbia, rather than in Grimes County.

In 1873, Longley longed for the Colt six-shooter using brass cartridges, instead of the old style cap and ball revolvers. He obtained a pair of Peacemakers and soon staged a leather-slapping contest in which he shot a man twice through the head. "These certainly are fine guns! They shoot right where you hold them!" he said.

Admiral Nelson once said, "When in doubt whether to fight, I always fight." Bill Longley had the same philosophy, but never had any doubts. Bill was no hero. He was brave, but he was also brutal, merciless and domineering. He was a creature of his times, a product of his environment. He reputedly killed thirty-two men before being hanged at Giddings, Texas, October 11, 1878.

The antique arms trade in America is well established. Several dozen dealers throughout the nation buy collections of arms whenever they are offered for sale, and dispense them to collectors and to museums. These dealers also import antique arms from all over the world to satisfy the demand of their clients. They are professional procurers of rare firearms, and their activity is limited, not by the number of persons who desire rare arms and who will pay well for them, but by the dealer's inability to secure the rare arms.

Of course, old firearms do not have to be rare to be salable. Mimeographed and printed lists are exchanged by the hundreds among collectors, offering to buy, sell or exchange various weapons. A small proportion of the arms thus offered are rare or very expensive. Occasionally a fortunate purchaser will obtain an antique firearm for a few dollars and discover it to be worth hundreds. An acquaintance of the writer paid two dollars and fifty cents for an old revolver and sold it for twelve hundred dollars. He could have had fifteen hundred for it by waiting a while longer before he sold. This adds an exciting treasure hunt air to the collecting game, whether firearms, paintings or other items are being collected.

The market price on antique pistols is subject to periodic fluctuations, but thousands of active collectors can tell at a glance the value of nearly any firearm that is shown them. I say nearly, for some weapons are so rare that they are never offered for sale, hence no quotations on them pass among the gun collecting fraternity.

Major W. G. C. Kimball, of the Kimball Arms Co., is a professional dealer in antique firearms with nearly fifty years of collecting lore to his credit. He states that he has never known of a Dance revolver being sold, and has no idea what one would be worth. Not more than two dozen are known to exist in museums and private collections. Some of these probably cannot pass a rigid test for authenticity.

In order that you may identify the Dance revolvers among the other cap and ball revolvers you may examine, the specifications are presented here. The revolvers were made in two sizes, one patterned after the Colt second model Dragoon, and the other patterned after the Colt Navy model. The large, or Dragoon model, was of .44 caliber and the smaller, Navy model was .36 caliber. When the State awarded a revolver contract to Tucker, Sherrod & Co., these two calibers were specified. It is believed this contract influenced the Dances to attempt two models.

Specifications of the large size are as follows: caliber .44, six chambers, single action. Eight and one-sixteenth inch round barrel, rifled with seven grooves. Total length is fourteen inches. Weight, unloaded, is three pounds, six ounces. The cylinder is one and seven-eighth inches long. A brass knife blade front sight is dovetailed into the barrel. The rear sight is a notch cut into the hammer, which aligns properly at full cock. The frame is of iron, with an oval trigger guard and backstrap of brass. A loading aperture is ground into the right side. A conventional loading lever operates the rammer. The grips are shellacked walnut.

Assembly is effected by driving a wedge from left to right into the cylinder pin. But the outstanding and remarkable trait is the absence of the recoil shield. The arm does not bear the company name or address. The only mark is the serial number which appears on the trigger guard, below the barrel, on the hammer, frame, rammer and cylinder.

On some of the later models, the hammer does not stand quite as erect as on most similar weapons of that day, and the hammer spur is unknurled. This slant is reputed to be designed for the maximum rapidity of fire when "fanning the hammer," a mode of shooting popular with Westerners at very close range, before the advent of double-action revolvers. On earlier models the hammer stands erect, and is knurled to prevent thumb slippage.

The .36 caliber, or small size, Dance revolver measures twelve inches overall, and has a six and one-eighth inch barrel. The barrel is round with a brass bead front sight. It has the same flat frame, without recoil shield, of the larger type. In regard to trigger guard, grips, backstrap, wedge, rifling, loading aperture, etc., it is the counterpart of the larger size.

One of the peculiar quirks of the arms collecting game is that the Dragoon, or large size, is considered more desirable by the professional collectors. This is odd because fewer revolvers of the Navy size were made, and a smaller number are extant. By the yardstick of rarity, the Navy size should command more respect than its big brother. When the facts become generally known, the selectivity in preference may be reversed.

Lest you be tempted to throw the switch on your lathe and make a genuine Dance revolver in your home workshop, you are warned that you must first successfully imitate the original metal. First, you will require iron blasted in a charcoal furnace, quite different from the modern article. Then it must be wrought and tempered in the Dance method. The markings must be made with dies exactly after the Dance dies. There are a number of ways to detect a fraudulent Dance revolver, some of which are easily checked, yet they have not been discussed in printed matter which bears on this subject.

This partly explains why valuable antique arms are not often faked by skillful frauds. Experts can identify fake firearms with less trouble than must be exerted to authenticate rare paintings.

— Whitescarver, Campbell & Co. —

One of the most interesting gun-making plants in Texas during the Civil War was located at Rusk, in Cherokee County. There was an established iron mine and blast furnace here before the war, but no gun industry. John L. Whitescarver, William H. Campbell and Benjamin F. Campbell organized a company, styled Whitescarver, Campbell & Co., for the purpose of fabricating guns for the duration of the Civil War. Other men who had prominent roles in this gun manufactory were M.H. Tanner, R.H. Guinn and M.H. Bonner. Mr. Bonner was the ordnance officer selected to represent the state at this plant. As all of the six men resided in Rusk and were personal friends, so the spirit of teamwork and cooperation which prevailed is not surprising.

The Campbells settled in Rusk prior to 1850, and were prominent from the first. Thomas D. Campbell was head of the clan, and father of Tom, a future governor of Texas. William, one of the partners in the armory, was a doctor by profession.

John L. Whitescarver moved to Rusk in 1856. His estate adjoined that of Dr. William Campbell, and the two became fast friends. After the war, Whitescarver formed a partnership with W. N. Hughes, and Whitescarver, Hughes & Co. became the foremost gunsmiths and cabinetmakers of that section. Before the war, John L. Whitescarver served as the second elected mayor of Rusk.

R.H. Guinn opened a law office in Rusk in 1847. He was among the first six to be admitted to the Cherokee County bar at law. The Guinns have practiced law in that location ever since, there being no lapse in the hundred and three years when a Guinn was not a member of the bar.

M. H. Tanner is believed to be the son of John L. Tanner, who bought lands near Rusk in 1843. M. H. Tanner became a combination banker and investment broker after the war. Before the war, he was conducting an iron business, a small charcoal furnace south of Rusk, which founded iron utensils of various types.

Thus the men who entered into the gun manufacturing enterprise were all substantial citizens and prominent in affairs of the county.

Following the formation of Whitescarver, Campbell & Co., attorney Guinn was retained to obtain a contract with the Military Board. Mr. Guinn was both influential and efficient. A series of letters to the Military Board and a trip to Austin by Mr. Guinn, and the trick was turned. He may be credited with performing his job with neatness and dispatch. The contract was even better business for the Board. They got their best contractor, and at a very favorable price.

The contract was dated April 18, 1862, and called for three hundred and fifty Texas rifles, to be delivered in lots of fifty, at a price of twenty-five dollars each. The contract specifications were: barrel thirty-two inches long, iron ramrod, sights similar to the Mississippi rifle, back action percussion lock, walnut stock, single trigger, iron mounts, two barrel bands with a bore thirty-two to the pound. This meant that thirty-two bullets should weigh a pound, or expressed in more modern phraseology, .54 caliber.

Whitescarver, Campbell & Co. made a deal with Tanner for iron. Slaves were busied constructing a railroad from the furnace to the gun factory which was located in the western outskirts of Rusk. This railroad was narrow gauge, and the rails were wooden. Molten iron was delivered to the gun works from the blast furnace in small cars with kettle shaped beds lined with fire clay. Mules pulled the cars along the track.

Tanner sold iron to two other Texas gunworks. The Tyler arsenal and Billups & Son, both within fifty miles, are on record as having used Tanner iron. In 1864 a large stock company was organized which acquired control of the iron industry of this locality. It is probable that Tanner was inducted into the army, and sold out to the new iron firm.

T. L. Philleo was prominent in the stock company, called the Cherokee Furnace Company, and the furnace was named for him. The Cherokee Furnace Co. continued to furnish iron to Whitescarver, Campbell & Co. After the war, the Cherokee Furnace Co. was reorganized and renamed the Cherokee Iron Works. The latter operated until the mid-seventies.

M. H. Bonner, the ordnance officer representing the State, may have been one of the few civilian officers in this type of service. Although ordnance files mention a Major Bonner on a few occasions, there is no definite link to M. H. Bonner. The reports directed from Bonner to the Board are signed simply M. H. Bonner. Whether this action indicates a lack of military rank is not known. There were no printed forms in that day; the reports were more informal than would be entailed by the same nature of business now. Evidently Mr. Bonner, or Major Bonner, should they be the same person, was efficient, industrious and diplomatic. Apparently, the firm had no intention of taking advantage of personal friendship in dealing with him. He was never embarrassed by being harsh with his intimate friends, nor by accepting inferior workmanship or materials. There is no record of friction between him and the contractors. The team of Bonner, Whitescarver, the two Campbells and Tanner was a group of personalities which blended well to display considerable talent and driving force.

It is reasonable to suppose that Bonner was quick to perceive the good qualities and efficiency of the new company. Happy to have been so fortunate in the raffle of post assignments, he must have aided in securing the second contract. It is also reasonable to assume that Guinn had assurance of

additional contracts while the first contract was being negotiated. These men hardly would have been content with a
three hundred and fifty gun contract otherwise.

The State Military Board advanced Whitesrarver, Campbell & Co. $2,500 to aid them in their initial tooling up.
General Magruder, on a tour of inspection, visited the Rusk
rifle works and heaped praise on the operators for their determined and practical approach to a difficult problem.

If the efforts of these early Texan manufacturers seem
insignificant, visualize the conditions under which their
attempt was made. These men lived on the fringe of civilization. They were without technical training, without
previous experience in any sort of manufacturing. Their
tools were crude, their transportation facilities negligible,
their help was scarce and unskilled. Gunmaking had always
been considered a monopoly of the effulgent East, where
mechanical engineers, highly skilled artisans and the best
of power tools had combined with years of experience to
produce guns. When the accepted sources of guns were no
longer available, and Texas must have guns, these pioneers
were no less than heroic in their efforts to produce them.

For some unexplained reason the Military Board requested that it be advised the ages of all citizens connected with
the Rusk plant. Fortunately, the letter dated July 4, 1862,
which furnishes this information, has been preserved:

The firm: John L. Whitescarver, 34; William H. Campbell, 38; and Benjamin F. Campbell, 34.

Hands: W. H. Hughes, 38, who later became Whitecarver's
partner, and who presently has descendants in Rusk; William Totley, 28; John C. Campbell, 40; John H. Benson, 30,
whose family long was prominent in Rusk; Allen W. Campbell, 36; Richard G. Hardy, 33; Robert Harrison, 48; John
R. Newton, 28, whose son resides in the old Newton home
on Fifth Street, near the gun factory; John H. Derrough, 27,
who also has descendants residing locally; Freeling Ham-
mons, 17; Charles Mankins, 46; William J. Gregory, 36;
J.W. Vining, 29; Robert Pryor, 35, who has three daughters

and a stepdaughter in Rusk; Jefferson Whitescarver, 31. M. H. Bonner is listed as 34 years of age. The negroes employed are not listed.

The second contract, let before the completion of the first contract, called for another three hundred and fifty guns. This was dated June 30, 1862. The specifications remained the same with two exceptions. The Mississippi type gunsights were abandoned and the Sharps sight substituted. A sword bayonet was specified to be attached by the Enfield method. The new contract price was $35 per rifle.

State Ordnance Officer M. H. Bonner reported to the Board on October 13, 1862, that Confederate Army officers had appropriated eighty guns from the Rusk plant which had been manufactured to apply on the state contract. Bonner had protested. This procedure was calculated to disrupt the accounting between Texas and the Confederacy, and certainly slow down the contractor's deliveries unless guns appropriated by the Confederacy applied on the state contract.

The Confederate officers probably needed the guns to equip an Arkansas company for immediate action in Tennessee. The urgency of their requirement prevented their following the proper procedure which then, as now, was entwined in red tape. They needed the guns, they took them; they did issue a receipt. The Confederacy was not scorning Texas rifles. The inventory at Marshall on August 23, 1863, listed four hundred and fifty Texas rifles crated for transportation across the Mississippi.

The reader observed, no doubt, that the ages of men employed by Whitescarver, Campbell & Co. made them subject to military duty. As this list was compiled early in the war, it probably was not effective long. Some of the men enlisted. From month to month the draft boards got others. Very shortly, manpower in Rusk, as elsewhere, became a problem. This problem became so acute that the authorities relented in January of 1863, and nine skilled gunsmiths and munitions workers were detailed from active service to the points of their former employment. Whitescarver, Campbell & Co. received two men among these returnees.

The rate of manufacture in Rusk was about four finished rifles per day. The first contract was completed on March 25, 1863. Letters from the contractors to the Board were mailed in March, April and May endeavoring to collect for the last fifty guns of the first contract. Payment, $1,250, was made on May 11, 1863. As time passed, the rate of production declined in this plant, as in all others in Texas. This was due, of course, to the shortage of labor. As the draft boards "scraped the barrel clean," the contractors saw their personnel, which they had trained at considerable expense and trouble, taken from them, gradually but surely.

It is hard to understand the reasoning of the governor who headed the Board that placed these plants in operation. He, of all people, was in a position to realize their importance. He knew of the work and money poured into their creation. With plants established, valuable machinery installed, metal stocks assembled, a small force of men, possibly thirty or forty at each plant, could have rendered tremendous aid in furnishing arms to the pitifully armed recruits. If these gunsmiths were more valuable at the front than five or ten thousand stand of arms would have been, why was money and time wasted on the construction of the plants in the first place? This was the question asked by the contractors. The Board governor's answer was his stentorian, "Let there be *no* exemptions..."

From March 1863 to June, Whitescarver, Campbell & Co. delivered four hundred and forty rifles and were paid $4,500 on June 30, and $6,500 on July 4, 1863. They, among others, refunded two and one-half per cent on gross sales. As this rate of production would have been around five guns per day, it is probable that a portion of these guns were made in the previous period and had not been accepted.

In the next three months, Whitescarver, Campbell & Co. delivered sixty rifles, for a production rate of two-thirds rifle per day. These delivery figures furnish ample testimony as to when the draft board's axe fell at Rusk. By the last of the year, 1863, this firm had made and delivered eight hundred and seven rifles, three hundred approximately having been passed on to the Confederate forces at Marshall for service east of the Mississippi.

With production dragging at a little over one-half gun per day, it is not difficult to guess why Whitescarver proposed to the Military Board, January 1, 1864, that they award him a revolver contract. By this time, most of the other contractors were threatening to throw up their hands and quit. It was a novelty for one of their number to solicit more work.

Whitescarver, Campbell & Co. were making guns for $34.12 each, after sales tax. Considering the inflated cost of labor and materials in 1864, either they were losing heavily or they were miracle men. Rather than attempt to renegotiate their rifle contract, they preferred an entirely new contract, with a new product. Revolver manufacture required less material but more skill than gun manufacture. They had less material available, but had acquired more skill and experience during their latest rifle contract. They intended that any new contract should provide more financial security against unstable money. That is the reasoning which motivated their offer to the Board. The price proposed was $100 per revolver.

The Lancaster revolver plant was a fiasco. The Dances were fearing federal raids at any moment and all revolver production in the state was about to grind to a halt. The Board awarded Whitescarver, Campbell & Co. a contract for 1,000 revolvers at $100 each. This firm never manufactured any revolvers.

Rifle-making was continued while plans were drawn for retooling and reorganizing for the revolver project. On March 29, 1864, fifty more rifles were accepted by Bonner on the state account. On July 1st another fifty were accepted, which completed the third contract, which had been for two hundred rifles. The firm had now delivered six hundred rifles to the state and three hundred and seven rifles to the

Confederate authorities. Had it been their intention to dis-
continue rifle-making, it would seem that this was the logi-
cal time to suspend operations.

The Board reported in November of 1864 that Billups
had made seven hundred rifles and Whitescarver, Campbell & Co. had completed nine hundred rifles. This indicates that the Rusk firm either had suspended gunmaking
after July 1864, or their output was going to the Confederacy in its entirety. As a record exists which records that
Confederate ordnance drew five hundred and forty-seven
rifles from this plant, they must have fabricated the difference between five hundred and forty-seven and three
hundred and seven, or two hundred and forty more rifles
before the end of the war.

Final production figures are not available on the firm. So
little is known of the rate of survival of their rifles that no
estimate of production can be made, at this time, from that
angle. It is safe to state, however, that the total production of
rifles at Rusk was at least 1,147. Possibly it exceeded 1,500.
But for the policy of the draft boards, the production might
well have been 4,000. It is fair to point out, however, that
this shortsighted policy of the draft boards was not peculiar
to Texas. Apparently, it was an evil which had been adopted
as Confederate policy.

On October 13, 1864, J. Gorgas, chief of Confederate
ordnance, wrote J. A. Seddon, Secretary of War, "…at least
50,000 arms will be necessary for the coming year and unless the armories can be placed on a permanent footing by
declaring all skilled mechanics engaged on them absolutely
exempt from military duty…I cannot lay too much stress on
the necessity for legislative action on this point."

The above excerpt, taken from Fuller & Steuart's *Firearms of the Confederacy*, is only one which portrays so vividly
the damage done the Southern cause by the no-exemption
policy.

General Robert E. Lee previously had written General
T.H. Holmes:

The demand for arms from all sides is so great and their scarcity so keenly felt, that I deem it proper to call your attention to the importance of making a judicious distribution of the rifles recently sent you. I am advised of the inability of the state of North Carolina to arm the regiments now in camp at Raleigh. I suggest you place the rifles in the hands of the flanking companies of the regiments, and give the balance muskets or such private arms as can be procured. The rifles will thus be made to do much toward enhancing the efficiency of each regiment. If you can use them and desire it, I can order a number of pikes to be sent you. Owing to the lack of firearms some of these have been sent to nearly every army in the field.

There you have General Lee, uncomplainingly shouldering the responsibility of winning battles with inferior numbers of men armed with spears, while their numerous opponents were armed with the latest breech-loading rifles!

On the other hand, President Jefferson Davis closed the armory at Columbus, Mississippi, with the remark, "If they can whip Grant, they will have all the arms they want, if they can't whip him, they will not require arms."

— BILLUPS & SON —

Probably the first machine shop in Texas was established in conjunction with a cotton gin, by James S. Hanks in Anderson County at Mound Prairie, prior to 1850.

Mound Prairie was a community of about four hundred population, excluding slaves. It was located about six miles north of Palestine on Mound Prairie Creek, a large stream now known as Hurricane Creek. One of the attractions of the village of Mound Prairie was the institute of the same name which was conducted by Reverend J. R. Malone for young men and women of the better families of this section of the state. Although a thriving town, Mound Prairie did not afford a post office. Plentitude, a smaller village one-half mile to the north, furnished this utility. Neither Mound Prairie nor Plentitude exist today. A forest now grows where Mound Prairie once stood; the land is now owned by Mr. Tom Davis. The post office at Plentitude was discontinued about 1880.

A firm titled Lawrence and Billups, in 1851, bought the gin and "mill factory," which was located on one hundred acres. John D. Billups acquired full control of the plant before the Civil War.

John Billups was born in Georgia in 1816, a descendant of George Billups, who came to Virginia from Wales in 1650. John was trained in metal working and manufacturing, being an employee of various cotton gin manufacturers. Billups moved to Alabama as a young man and his first son, Joseph, later to become his partner in the gun business, was born there in 1840. John Billups brought his family to Texas in 1850. After acquiring ownership of the Hanks machine shop from his former partner, Lawrence, Billups engaged in the manufacture of cotton gins. This was the leading industry of Mound Prairie before the war. With the advent of the war, Billups determined to secure a contract to manufacture guns.

D. D. "Dan" Hassell was an intimate friend of Billups and the latter succeeded in arousing Hassell's interest in the enterprise. They formed a partnership known as Billups and Hassell, and secured a contract from the Military Board. The contract, dated July 1, 1862, called for seven hundred Mississippi-type rifles at thirty dollars each.

A copy of the specifications is not available, but the description "Mississippi" is adequate for our purpose. Billups and Hassell's specifications were doubtless similar to those of Whitescarver, Campbell & Co., of Rusk.

Colonel Alexander M. Watts was appointed ordnance officer to the Mound Prairie rifle works. Colonel Watts wrote a number of letters in which he deplored his sweetness being wasted on the desert air. There is doubt whether the same fine spirit of teamwork existed here as was displayed in Rusk.

Hardly had the gun contract been secured and the arrangements made for tools and buildings before Mr. Hassell died. John Billups was considerably grieved by this occurrence, as he and Hassell had been close friends of long standing. Although the plant was developing well, Mr. Billups attempted to cancel his contract with the Board. He pointed out that he had lost a fine partner in the business, and that he was incapable of supervising both the iron business and the rifle factory. Billups' health was poor, and he feared that overwork and worry would bring him to an early grave. He may be excused from feeling so depressed. Hassell was a dear friend. Although Mr. Billups did not hesitate on occasion to tell the Military Board how to conduct their business, the Board seemed genuinely fond of John Billups. In this instance they praised him highly and reminded him of his duty to his country. They had no intention of terminating his contract.

The production of iron was the joker in the deck. Several months had been frittered away while Billups & Hassell negotiated with various persons to furnish them iron. Although several had promised to operate the small charcoal furnace and smelt iron, none had moved to do so. In December of 1862, Billups advised the Board that he would operate his own iron production business.

As the ore for the small furnace had to be transported twenty-four miles by ox wagon from Cherokee County, Billups' task was rendered more difficult. A solution was found. The iron business was sold to Mr. J. B. Bussey, a man of considerable means in the locality, who was able to maintain this end of production by supplemental purchases of iron from Tanner, at Rusk.

Mr. Billups changed the name of his firm to Billups & Son, honoring his eldest son, Joseph, twenty-two years of age. In subsequent records, the firm is alluded to by both names: Billups & Hassell, and Billups & Son. As the latter seems to be the proper one, we shall refer to the plant by that name, although the letter or record referred to, might possibly bear the other name.

Mr. Nat Hassell, brother of the dead partner, had moved to the plant site to help on the project. He continued in Billups' employ. Billups & Son received an advance of $5,000 to aid them in establishing the rifle factory. This amount was repaid the state in acceptable rifles at the contract price.

John Billups had a well-equipped machine shop and ironworks prior to the war. Most of his many slaves were skilled workmen in an industrial sense. He was running a forty-horsepower engine and another fifteen-horsepower engine from his steam boilers. Yet there were special gun tools he had to acquire. Where this machinery was obtained is not known. The State Board must have obtained it for this contractor, or paid for it. The Military Board required an inventory of all tools, machinery, etc. to be filed with them. So far as can be determined, this was required of no other contractor.

Colonel Watts notified the Board that Billups & Son had finished their tooling up and organizing, and had gone into production on November 20, 1862. As the iron situation had not been satisfactorily worked out at that time, it is probable that iron from Rusk was used in this first production. On December 29th, Watts reported that the contractor had crated fifty Mississippi rifles, and that another fifty would be ready for crating in two weeks.

Hardly had production begun before the firm received help with their labor problem. It was January 28, 1863 that the army transferred six skilled gunsmiths from active duty to Mound Prairie. The rate of production noticeably increased at once. Colonel Watts reported on May 21, 1863, that he had just accepted four hundred rifles. These were produced at a rate of about three rifles a day.

On June 6, 1863, Major A. S. Cabell receipted for nine boxes containing two hundred and seventeen guns, complete with bayonets and wipers, from Colonel Alexander M. Watts. As the transfer was effected in Bonham, it is probable that these rifles were intended for use in the Indian Territory. It is also probable that the shipment contained all the rejected guns which had accumulated in Mound Prairie until that time, plus only enough good rifles to complete the order.

It would be interesting to know how the state paid the contractors for rejected rifles, which were accepted under peculiar circumstances for use by Indian allies of the Confederacy in the Indian Territory. No mention of this can be found in the records. It is plainly revealed in the records that these rejects did not apply on the manufacturer's contract. How, then, did the Military Board acquire title to these defective guns? Possibly the ordnance officer was instructed to accept two rejects as one acceptable rifle. This thought is pure conjecture, but the records do not reveal any payments at a reduced rate.

On Colonel Watts' return to Anderson County from Bonham, he made a discovery which dismayed him. In a very indignant letter he advised the Board that Mr. Billups was "going into the whiskey making business within thirty feet of his own armory." Anxiously Watts queried what could be done to prevent this catastrophe. The Board's answer is unavailable and the fate of the distillery is uncertain. It is better than an even bet that Billups built his distillery. It may have turned out the finest bourbon ever distilled by gunsmiths.

On June 29, 1863, two hundred and thirty-three Billups rifles were sent to the northern district for use by the frontier regiment troops who were fighting Comanches. Shortly thereafter, Billups & Son was about to fulfill the Billups & Hassell contract of seven hundred rifles, and it was deemed proper to negotiate a new contract. This contract was drawn in the name of Billups & Son. The product being manufactured was to remain unchanged. There was a price adjustment, however. Billups & Son received $60 per rifle on their second contract of September, 1863. The number of rifles specified in the new contract was five hundred.

The first contract for seven hundred rifles was finished in August of 1863, before the formality of the second contract had been completed. However, there was no lapse of work. The second contract was assured and production continued. By January 1, 1864, Billups & Son had delivered three hundred rifles on the second contract.

The labor situation in 1864 hurt Billups as it did the other contractors. After losing money on the seven hundred rifles he manufactured for $30 each, he had high hopes of recouping on his contract which paid him $60 for each rifle. Due to the labor shortage and money depreciation in 1864, Billups probably did not make a profit on his second contract either.

The number of guns made at Mound Prairie in 1864 and 1865 is not recorded. The Confederate world, falling apart in 1865, was not conducive to uniformly kept records and neat recapitulations. The total production of Billups & Son can be fixed at a certain 1,100 rifles, and possibly 1,600 guns, counting the rejects which were issued. To be sure, five hundred rifles is a wide gap of uncertainty, but so many of the reports are obscure. Some records of manufactured guns seem to duplicate the same arms with a slightly different report, the date varying two days to a week. There is no chronological record available which is apt to contain entries of all deliveries.

At least four hundred rifles from this plant were issued to Confederate Ordnance for use outside Texas and Oklahoma. Whether these rifles were a direct sale from Billups & Son to the Confederacy, or whether they were transferred from the State of Texas to the Confederacy is not plain.

Billups & Son made between 1,100 and 1,200 rifles for the state of Texas, plus "accepted rejects." If they made an additional four hundred for the Confederacy, their production was easily 1,600 rifles.

A total production of 1,600 guns would have entailed an average monthly rate of forty guns per month over the last phase of the contract. The average monthly production for the prior fourteen months was seventy-two guns. It is doubtful if the production could have been maintained through the last phase on fifty-six per cent of normal rate. As there are no rate-of-survival figures at hand to aid us, we shall form no opinion on total production. Until more information is at hand, the figures 1,100 to 1,600 must suffice.

Mr. Walter Billups of Dallas is the only surviving child of John Billups' five children. Mr. Walter Billups is convinced that his father dealt directly with the Confederacy on at least one contract. If so, the production figure of 1,600 is more authentic than the lesser figure of 1,100.

After the war, John Billups moved to Neches, a new town on a new railroad, about four miles from Mound Prairie. There he resumed the manufacture of cotton gins. He died in 1877 and is buried in the Mound Prairie cemetery. Joseph, his son and partner, died in 1870. He had married Miss Katherine Venoy and two children had been born to them, both of whom had died in childhood.

— TYLER —

James C. Short moved to Tyler from Nacogdoches in 1858. His family originally was from Alabama. Short was an excellent gunmaker with a statewide reputation. He made hunting rifles and beautifully balanced double-barrel shotguns. He also had some musket manufacturing experience, having made some cheap muskets for Indian trade.

Mr. Short was not a maker of barrels. He bought his barrels from other fabricators. Known specimens are marked with names which are unlisted in compilations of American gunmakers. As none of these lists pretend to be complete, it does not necessarily follow that his barrels were imported. It may be, however, that his barrels were bought abroad, shipped to New Orleans and thence to Shreveport via Red River steamboats. The last stage, one hundred miles, would have been by wagon freight.

When the Civil War began, the Military Board offered Mr. Short a rifle contract. On April 28, 1862, he declined their proposition, explaining that his stock of barrels was very limited, and he had despaired of obtaining more. This statement indicates his barrels were being purchased in the northern states. If not, Mr. Short showed remarkable ability, for a backwoods gunsmith, to forecast events. How could he know of the fall of New Orleans and the tight Union blockade which was to stifle the South?

William S. N. Biscoe and George Yarbrough were two men of means in Tyler. Mr. Biscoe went to Tyler in 1855 and bought land and negro slaves. The county deed records contain many accounts of his slave purchases; he once bought thirty-seven in one day.

The Yarbroughs were an old family in Tyler at the time of earliest record. They subscribed to the first steamboat line on the upper Sabine River in 1848. George Yarbrough, with Alfred W. Furguson, ran a substantial mercantile business in Tyler prior to the Civil War. George also dealt in land. The records reveal a dozen land sales by him, prior to the war, amounting to over 1,500 acres. During the same period, he purchased over 4,000 acres of land.

William Biscoe and George Yarbrough, when they learned of Short's opportunity to secure a gun contract, prevailed on him to enter upon the project. They proposed to furnish adequate capital. Accordingly, a firm was organized under the name of Short, Biscoe & Co. The Military Board was advised of their readiness to negotiate a contract. The new firm bought a tract of land, two hundred and forty-eight acres, upon which was situated a large brick building. This was acquired from F. F. Foscue on September 9, 1862, and cost $3,954.76.

Gunbarrel making tools were acquired and installed. These tools are reputedly within thirty-five miles of Tyler at present. Short's other tools were removed from his shop in Tyler to the large brick building, that was then a mile south of Tyler. A letter to the Board on December 5, 1862, described the acquisition of the property, and advised that steam power was being installed.

Short, Biscoe & Co.'s contract was signed November 5, 1862. It called for 5,000 Mississippi-type rifles at $35 each. The specifications were similar to those of Whitescarver, Campbell & Co., of Rusk, except for the bayonet and barrel length. The length of the barrels to be made in Tyler was specified as thirty-three inches.

James Short had previously designed a bayonet, presumably for use on his Indian muskets. The Indians were never bayonet fighters, but may have been more greedy for guns so equipped. Short asked the Board to consider the use of his bayonet, as he was experienced in its manufacture. The Board viewed it "as a very effective weapon," and the firm was authorized to furnish these "improved Short bayonets" with the rifles.

George Yarbrough had been a man of many activities before the war, and had many men in his employ in various capacities. When the rifle contract was obtained, he selected a number of his better employees who had entered the service, and began a campaign to have them restored to him. He was partly successful, both then and later. This firm probably secured as many exemptions for their men as the other combined plants in Texas. These exemptions and the size of the contract reflected the confidence James Short enjoyed with the Board. Even these relatively large exemptions from military service did not insure Short, Biscoe & Co. an adequate labor supply.

Obtaining metal stock, walnut lumber for gunstocks, and other materials and tools occupied the early part of 1863. No iron was smelted in Tyler and all of it had to be freighted overland. The haul from Rusk was short, and the Cass County furnaces were not too distant. Of course, scrap iron was utilized when it was available.

In June the firm had expended most of their capital, and faced with the rising costs of labor, freighting and materials, they applied to the Board for an advance of money. The Board advanced them $25,000. In July, Short, Biscoe & Co. applied for military exemption for R. Carleton, explaining that he was vital to their plans as he supervised the labor of one hundred negroes. The records contain frequent references to slave labor in other gun plants, also. The negroes were employed to cut and haul wood to the boilers and other non-skilled work. It was ironic that they were thus forced to help forge their own bondage chains. Whether Mr. Carleton was excused from military service is not known. Certainly the firm must have kept numerous men out of the armed service. On October 8, 1863, the Army formally requested a review of the Short, Biscoe & Co. operations due to what was considered an excessive number of military exemptions demanded by them. In nearly a year, it was pointed out, the firm had not delivered a gun.

In their anxiety to fulfill the large contract which had been awarded them, the firm tried to fabricate too many arms at once. This had been guarded against in some of the other plants by specifying delivery should be made in lots of twenty-five or fifty rifles. Short, Biscoe & Co. attempted to complete 1,000 arms in each increment. They repented this decision on September 17, 1863:

> We can deliver 100 guns in two weeks from this date. We have been much troubled about stock timber, and a large number of our hands have been sick. We have been delayed on account of inexperienced hands, having to take such as we could get, and as we have invariably been refused gunsmiths from the Army, and we are much annoyed by hands wanting advanced wages, as everything has so much advanced above the usual price of living. We are already losing money at the price of the gun.

> We have 500 barrels bored and turned ready for stocks, and 250 bored, and fifty welded, making in all, 800 barrels. We have made about 500 bayonets, and have nearly ready all the pieces for the locks for 800 guns. We have a lot of timber seasoning which we will push as we are steaming it, and will put them together as rapidly as possible.

Mr. Claude E. Fuller, in his capable *Firearms of the Confederacy*, relates that the armory was turned over to the Confederacy about October 12, 1863, and the State of Texas paid for, and had delivered only one gun from this plant. He further relates that the bore was changed from .54 caliber to .577 caliber in compliance with the wishes of the Confederate War Department. Mr. Fuller assumes that the Short bayonet manufactured was some kind of saber bayonet, since one specimen of the rifle which he had examined, had a lug for this type of bayonet. We will add to this meager store of knowledge that the old muskets manufactured by Short prior to the war also had lugs for this type of bayonet.

This furnishes a measure of substantiation that Mr. Fuller's assumption is correct.

On October 22, 1863, Major Thomas G. Rhett advised Major J. P. Johnson, assistant adjutant and inspector general, that he was negotiating for the purchase of a manufactory of small arms located in Tyler, which was in the process of furnishing arms to Texas. The Confederate States' purchase of the Short, Biscoe & Co. armory rendered necessary the cancellation of that firm's contract with the state. This contract was one of only two contracts cancelled by the state until near the end of the war.

On December 30, 1863, "Lieutenant Colonel Gabriel H. Hill, acting as agent of the Confederate States of America," purchased one hundred and twenty acres of land out of the original two hundred and forty-eight acres of the Short, Biscoe & Co. armory. The one hundred and twenty acres were specified as that "upon which is situated a brick building now used and occupied by the Confederate States as an armory." The consideration was $30,000.

The above wording indicates that the Confederacy had not waited on the formal conclusion of legal matters to occupy and use the property. Thus Mr. Fuller's approximate date of Confederate occupation is not contradicted.

The State of Arkansas had two rifle manufactories at Little Rock, a percussion cap factory and a powder mill at Arkadelphia, a repair shop at Fort Smith and a depot at Camden. The Confederate authorities spirited one rifle works away from Little Rock before the Union forces gained control of the Mississippi River. This plant was relocated in Alabama. Arkansas received the apologies of President Jefferson Davis in payment. When Union armies began advancing inside Arkansas a few months later, the Confederate authorities seized the remaining plants and moved them out of the state. The other Little Rock rifle plant was moved to Tyler. The Camden plant was moved to Shreveport and the other plants were moved to Marshall, where the percussion cap factory was placed in operation.

The Confederacy combined the Little Rock plant with the Short, Biscoe & Co. factory in Tyler. Captain George S. Polleys was superintendent with Lieutenant Colonel Gabriel H. Hill in overall command. This plant was now quite well-equipped, boasting sixteen forges. As the workmen were moved from Little Rock with the machinery, the manpower problem was not increased.

A variety of calibers, lock markings and design types from the Tyler armory has puzzled gun students for many years. Before Short, Biscoe & Co. sold out to the Confederacy, they assembled two hundred rifles. These were not delivered to the state, and when the contractors released their armory to the Confederate Ordnance Department, the two hundred rifles, as well as eight hundred incomplete rifles became the property of the Confederacy. Thus we have two fabricators—Short, Biscoe & Co., and the Confederate States Ordnance, and two plants—Short, Biscoe & Co., and the Little Rock rifle works, to contribute to the confusion of Tyler products.

The disparity in calibers in the Tyler rifles is explained by the above situation. The 1,000 complete and partially complete rifles on hand when Colonel Hill took over the plant were .54 caliber. They obviously were not rebored to .58 caliber. This explanation also answers questions on design. Short, Biscoe & Co.'s rifles, two hundred complete and eight hundred partially complete, were Mississippi-type rifles. They were completed as such. Subsequent production turned to the Enfield type, and began a new series of serial numbers. Thus, no Tyler rifle of the Mississippi type should bear a serial number greater than 1,000. No definite limit can be placed on the serial numbers of the Enfield type, as the final production figures are not known.

A few facts may be established from a study of existing guns or their parts. All the lockplates were attached to the guns in a peculiar manner. In each case, a single screw, located just forward of the hammer, served this purpose. No other known military guns are so constructed.

None of the guns were dated except those manufactured in 1865 (with one exception, which is not standard in other respects). The serial numbers were stamped on the fore end of the lockplates, "CS" for Confederate States, was stamped behind the hammer on the lockplate.

From the markings in the center of the existing lockplates, inferences may be drawn. The Short machinery continued to turn out Texas rifles, that is, they were marked "Texas Rifle Tyler Texas," and some also carried the caliber designation. The other plant, which had been brought in from Little Rock (these plants could not be completely integrated as that would have involved shutting down and rebuilding the first plant when the second arrived), marked its lockplates "Enfield Rifle Tyler Texas" and also in some cases, the caliber designation. The highest "Texas Rifle" serial number known is 802; the "Enfield" serial numbers exist up to 500. The two hundred rifles completed by Short, Biscoe & Co. had plain lockplates except for the serial numbers and "CS" in the rear.

Now the complications set in. There are both guns and lockplates which are marked "Austrian Rifle Tyler Texas" and others which are marked "Hill Rifle Tyler Texas." The serial numbers on the first have been found no higher than 49, on the latter the highest serial number known is 337.

Mr. L. D. Satterlee has described a short rifle with a barrel length of only twenty-seven inches and with all means of attaching a bayonet omitted. This gun obviously was made for saddle use. The lockplate was marked "Hill Rifle Tyler Texas." Until more information is at hand, we can assume that carbines for cavalry use, made in Tyler, were marked Hill Rifle in honor of Colonel G. H. Hill, chief of the plant. They had a separate sequence of serial numbers.

The guns marked "Austrian Rifle Tyler Texas" are copies of a popular European gun of that period. Why the plant changed to this design in the dying days of the war is not known. Serial numbers 11, 26, 42, and 49 are known. There couldn't have been many made.

Production in Tyler could not have been less than 2,750 rifles, nor is it likely to have been more than 3,300. The armory operated until the end of the war and was destroyed by occupation forces several months after the end of the war.

Mr. Short left Tyler in 1866. He sold his home at a loss, and probably departed in a near bankrupt condition. It is not known where he sought his next opportunity.

Mr. Biscoe, who lost the thousands of dollars he had invested in slaves, continued to prosper in Tyler. He bought land and paid in gold.

The Yarbroughs also continued to live and do business in Tyler. They were too secure to be completely wrecked by the financial upheaval of a defunct government.

— Sherrard, Taylor & Co. —

Texas' most publicized makers of arms during the Civil War were the least effective. There is an inclination to dismiss them with a few curt paragraphs, but as their products are among the most sought after pieces among firearm collectors, and as considerable controversy exists among arms historians concerning them, we will discuss the gentlemen who accepted the responsibility for arming the Texas cavalry.

A firm composed of Labon E. Tucker, A. W. Tucker, Pleasant Taylor, W. L. Killen and J. H. Sherrard was formed to obtain an arms manufacturing contract with the state. These men were residents of Lancaster and Dallas, two small adjoining towns in Dallas County.

The Tuckers were of a military family and knew guns, although they were not manufacturers. They had a relation in the Confederate Army who ranked as a general. J. H. Sherrard was the local blacksmith; little is known of W. L. Killen. Other members of the story have connections with the Rawlins and Myers families.

The Rawlins family, headed by Elder Roderick Rawlins, went to Texas from Illinois in 1844, and settled in Lancaster. The Myers family, also from Illinois, followed the Rawlins family to Lancaster the following year, 1845. These two families had intermarried and remained very close to one another. The Myers' daughter, Nancy, married Pleasant Taylor, a tall Texan, who was to become a partner in the pistol factory. Pleasant and Nancy had three children, Alfred,

Alonzo and Addie Paris, all of whom were killed by a pet bear.

A. S. Clark, who figures prominently in this story, also came from Illinois to Lancaster in 1845. Probably he followed Sarah Myers, for they were soon married. He and Pleasant Taylor thus became brothers-in-law.

Mr. A. B. Rawlins, of a later generation, in his story of the pistol factory, as recorded in *Firearms of the Confederacy*, refers to Mr. Clark as a "Northerner" who married into his family. The expression, Northerner, is not clearly understood. Clark and Myers were in Lancaster within a year after the Rawlins located there. Possibly Clark's sympathy remained with the North, while the rest of the clan had turned "Texan" without reservation. This is a purely conjectural explanation for Rawlins' phraseology. Northern gun students, on the strength of that remark, have gibed at Texas for the necessity of importing northern know-how.

The newly organized company, composed of the above listed members, was styled Tucker, Sherrard & Co. Before proceeding further, let us explain the irrelevance in the firm's name, which has puzzled so many for so long. The above name, "Sherrard," is undoubtedly correct. It appears on dozens of letters written by the firm from their Lancaster plant. It never appears in any other manner on papers which originated in Lancaster. It also assumes this spelling on engraved revolvers, the parts of which were manufactured at this plant. On their contract, in the Military Board's reports, in the accounting files, in all state papers, without exception, the firm is referred to as Tucker, Sherrod & Co. This consistent misspelling of Sherrard's name by all governmental agencies is puzzling but true.

Having organized for the purpose of manufacturing armament, the selection of the article of manufacture was made. Their choice of revolvers was intelligent. Texas was a pistol state. Nearly everyone was a horseman. Successfully fighting from horseback and using a pair of revolvers had come to mean one and the same thing in Texas. Cavalry elsewhere in the South preferred the .36 caliber Navy size revolvers. Possibly remembering the partial failure of light Colt revolvers in Texas, and the later success of the Colt Dragoon models, Texas preferred the heavy guns. The North was using .44 caliber revolvers on a lighter frame. Texas decided to use the heavy dragoon frame for both their .44 and .36 caliber revolvers.

No doubt a successful revolver manufacturer in central Texas could have enjoyed a good many years of commercial success after the war was over. There is little doubt that Texas would have bought more revolvers than rifles, during the war, if a successful arm had been available.

Having made their choice of products the firm required a contract. Being Lancaster and Dallas men, their first thoughts were of John M. Crockett. Mr. Crockett, a resident of Dallas, was a past mayor of that promising little city, and a first class politician. At that time he was Lieutenant Governor of the state, having been elected on the same ticket with Governor Lubbock. He and Governor Lubbock were close personal friends, and Lubbock headed the Military Board. Then, as now, public officials in high places may be retained as legal counselors. Mr. Crockett was retained. Tucker, Sherrard & Co. got their contract.

On March 20, 1862, Crockett wrote William M. Walton, secretary to the Board, urging haste in preparing the contract. The Board prepared the contract, calling for 3,000 revolvers at $40 each, 1,500 of .44 caliber and 1,500 of .36 caliber. The revolvers were to be modeled on Colt's. The contract was dated April 11, 1862, and was signed July 21, 1862. On July 3, 1862 (note the date and the firm's name) Tucker, Sherrard & Co. wrote a letter to the Board asking questions concerning revolver design and possible materials to be employed in their coming production. No definite plans had been made and nothing accomplished. On August 18, 1862 (note the date and the firm's name), Sherrard, Taylor & Co. advised the Board that they were about to begin work on the first one hundred revolvers at Lancaster.

The men who organized the company seemed to have had no particular knowledge, talent or skill to aid them in their new enterprise. Mr. Sherrard, being a blacksmith, may have been valuable in the forging room. The contributions the others were in a position to make are not known. During the uncertainty of those first few days, vast differences of opinion, or a struggle for control, forced the Tuckers, and possibly Killen, from the partnership. This happened during the latter part of July, or the early part of August, 1862. The firm was to operate under the name of Sherrard, Taylor & Co. until their contract was cancelled. A letter to the Board, formally confirming this, was dated September 2, 1862.

George Todd, of Austin, a skilled gunsmith who had made a few revolvers in imitation of Colt's weapons, after the Colt patents had expired, was brought to the Lancaster plant. He could have rendered considerable aid, but he did not care for the setup, and moved on to another armory in Alabama.

In April of 1862 the Military Board gave the struggling firm an advance of $5,000. A second advance of $5,000 was made in September. On October 7, 1862, Sherrard, Taylor & Co. notified the Board that their men must be given more protection from the clutches of the draft boards. The firm could not keep over a dozen men in employ, and could make very little progress toward production.

Only four days later the firm again wrote the Board that men on their payroll for whom military exemptions had been secured were causing trouble with the townsmen. It seems the people in Lancaster resented their men going to war while the revolver firm's employees were being exempted. This second letter no doubt halted any move which had been instigated at the behest of the first letter. On November 20, 1862, Sherrard, Taylor & Co. reported all of their employees were gone except three. All operations were in a state of suspension. At about this time the Board received a series of letters from the Lancaster firm requesting an increased price for revolvers to be delivered on their contract.

Finally, on January 28, 1863, Sherrard, Taylor & Co. advised the Board that the firm would not be able to finish their contract unless the state furnished them ample manpower, and metal must be cheaper than the dollar per pound they were paying. They explained that the factory was tooled to produce two hundred revolvers a month, but that they had never had enough men to realize the potential. Their materials had been contracted for in New Orleans, which had fallen to the Federals. There were no local sources of wood or metal around Dallas except such scrap as could be collected.

The contractors told of having four hundred revolvers nearly finished, lacking only a few parts. A short while before they had reported one hundred revolvers nearly finished, lacking only a few parts. Some item was a bottleneck—they were increasing their stock of nearly finished revolvers without being able to deliver a single one.

A year passed without a pistol delivery. The firm was under fire. The state had advanced money and granted military exemptions. The firm purportedly had made some consumer goods which may have brought very good prices. Could it be that revolver manufacture served as a front for military exemption, while the firm's equipment, labor and metal stock went into consumer goods? Mr. Crockett was again retained.

Crockett wrote the Board in May of 1863 explaining the lack of revolver production in the "north Lancaster" plant with great facility. A new governor and lieutenant governor had taken the executive chairs in Austin. Lubbock had not run for office in 1863. Governor Murrah replaced him. Crockett's best friend was no longer the head of the Military Board. Crockett became a press agent. His expansive interview with an Austin newspaper, the *Texas Almanac*, led the reporter to declare that Colonel Crockett was the head of a large armory which was in successful operation, and that the Colonel was offering the government four hundred completed revolvers at one-third the market price. Indeed!

This typical misquotation of a public figure by the press has misled writers and compilers since it appeared in print. The firm never delivered any revolvers. They probably never finished more than half a dozen which were used for display in Austin. If more revolvers were made, they were sold where they would bring the best return. Crockett displayed a pair of Sherrard, Taylor & Co. revolvers to the Military Board, and to an awed press. Were these revolvers completed in Lancaster in their entirety?

It is probable that they were not. If they were, they were pilot models. These guns were finished so far ahead of completion date of anything on plant schedule, that a suspicion of their entire authenticity is in order. This firm may have been the first in history to alter a Colt revolver in order to produce a Confederate-made firearm.

An examination of the revolver bearing serial number 2, which well may have been one of those displayed by Colonel Crockett in Austin, reveals a frankly Colt cylinder. Of course, this may have been a replacement by an owner at a much later date. Other noticeable discrepancies are the crude parts which stand out from the well finished parts. While a few of the parts are obviously handmade, other parts are well-turned and display a finish Colt could not improve upon. Possibly the more crudely made parts were the parts uncompleted when Crockett was prepared to start to Austin, and enough of them were hastily made so that he might have complete weapons to display at the Capitol.

In these days of cost-plus contractors, it is hard to censure a firm of amateurs, injudiciously located for their type of project, who were faced with so difficult a task under the most trying conditions. We may discount insinuations regarding the absence of a proper sense of duty. The fact that those men created four hundred nearly complete revolvers in a little frontier town, all within a year—a chaotic year— is ample evidence of sincere effort. Inventory the factors which were unfavorable for them, and then hunt for some advantageous factor of greater import.

In the summer of 1863, the state cancelled the Sherrard, Taylor & Co. contract. As $10,000 had been advanced them, the firm had to repay that sum with interest. The interest amounted to $814.44. That ended Sherrard, Taylor and Company. Military exemptions were withdrawn, the salable equipment was sold.

There were four hundred unfinished revolvers left behind. Two completed specimens have been found with "Clark, Sherrard & Co." engraved on them. The Clark was A. S. Clark, brother-in-law of Pleasant Taylor, a foreman in the plant during its operation.

When Sherrard, Taylor & Co.'s contract was cancelled, the transportable portion of the factory was removed from the building that had housed it. This building was owned by the Rawlins family. No doubt, Clark had salary due him which he perforce took in unassembled revolvers. Or possibly the firm merely cashed in their assets to repay the state, moved away, and left the partially finished and unassembled revolvers. However the transaction, Clark acquired the pistols.

After the war and before cartridges rendered these percussion revolvers obsolete, Clark, evidently with Sherrard's help, undertook to finish as many of these revolvers as he could. In order to complete them, Clark may have introduced some Colt parts, with the numbers appropriately changed. Several of the existing guns are mongrels. The Clark & Sherrard revolvers are actually, of course, Sherrard, Taylor & Co. guns.

The fanciful engraving on the "Clark" revolvers shows a star, the words "Texas Arms," a shield showing thirteen stars, crossed cannons, scrollwork and two halberdiers. The engraving is signed L. S. Perkins. The arms world is waiting for an identification of L. S. Perkins.

It is doubtful if Clark, and Sherrard, the blacksmith, made any attempt to finish or assemble pistols during the war. It is believed that Sherrard entered the army immediately after the contract cancellation. The problems which had prevented the revolvers being finished until then still existed. Clark hardly could have solved them single-handedly. Whether it was a lack of spring steel, abrasives or other shortage, only the end of the war could bring relief.

Clark was attempting sale of these Sherrard, Taylor & Co. revolvers in 1867, over two years after the end of the war. The following letter is addressed to S. W. Stone, who was a hardware merchant in Jefferson.

Dallas, Texas
June 1, 1867

S. W. Stone, Esq.
Jefferson, Texas

We have about 400 cal. 44 old style army revolvers that we plan to finish and embellish into high class merchandise. We are prepared to furnish you a dozen at twenty dollars, gold, each.

Your servt.
A. S. Clark

Sherrard's name is not included, but it is highly probable that he and Clark are the "we" referred to. The wording indicates that the plan to finish the revolvers is strictly in the future. It does not preclude the possibility that a portion of them had been finished and sold at a prior date and intentions were held to complete the entire four hundred.

Colt revolvers of newer design were retailing for $30 in Texas at that time. The wholesale price, delivered, was probably between twenty and twenty-five dollars.

Existing specimens are numbered 23, 103, 160, 126, 241, and 402. Most of the revolvers with intervening numbers never were finished. The entire production, during and after the war, could not exceed an approximate four hundred. As Mr. A. B. Rawlins has testified to the large number of unassembled parts scattered around the factory site years later, we may be certain that very few revolvers came from this plant.

It is painfully evident that some of the numbered specimens listed above are of doubtful origin. Proof that those cylinders bearing the long, narrow rectangular stops were made in Texas would be interesting to all arms students. We believe Jonathon Browning of Utah should receive credit for this type of cylinder.

One thing noted by arms students on revolvers attributed to the Lancaster plant, was the tendency to decorate the wooden grips with inlaid silver stars. Others have decorated cylinders, not done by stamping on the design, but by laboriously hand etching the design in the metal with the use of acids. Various writers have explained that this was done at the factory to enhance the sale of the revolvers. As the factory existed only during the Civil War, we deny this procedure. As Texans were literally crying for revolvers during the war, it is inconceivable that hours of extra work could have been expended on the weapons, when man hours were very, very dear. The following letter may emphasize how scarce were revolvers at that time, and the length to which Texans were prepared to go to obtain them.

Bastrop, Texas
April 10, 1862

P. De Cordova, Esq.
Secretary to the Military Board
Austin, Texas

Dear Sir,

There is a sixshooter in the hands of Captain J. H. Gillespie here belonging to the State that I wish to get if possible. I will pay for it, receipt for it or put other arms in the place of it. I want it to use in the service myself having lost two in the fall of Arkansas Post and find it impossible to buy. It seems to me that it had as well be in the service doing some good as lying here benefitting neither State nor Confederacy. If there is any way by which I can get it, please write me or Captain Gillespie about it by return mail...

Yours respectfully,
H. S. Morgan
Capt. 18 Texas Cav.

It is evident that the adornments are postwar. That cylinders should be hand-etched, and grips silver inlaid under the conditions of labor shortage and pressing demand, is ridiculous. Our explanation for the stars in the grips is that they were put in by their owners. Before "white plowhandles," ivory and bone grips became popular in the West, this sort of adornment was used to relieve the plainness of the wooden grips. One Texas collection of percussion revolvers shows a number of such star-spangled grips. They are on Colts, Manhattans, Coopers and other makes of revolvers.

May this discussion of pistol grips give pause to those collectors who throw away the original wooden grips on a fine old dragoon model, and install handsomely carved ivory grips of an obviously later date. Pistols equipped with ivory grips are, and should be, more valuable than their plain counterparts, but only while they remain in character.

The most important trait attributed to revolvers made in Lancaster is the absence of a loading aperture on the side of the barrel lug. One theory is that the cylinders were supposed to be removed from the revolver for loading, hence no aperture was necessary. It would be equally true that no attached rammer would be necessary. Why did they not save some of the work and materials which went into the rammer? Could it be that some of the barrels left the plant before they were finished? We think so.

Mr. A. B. Rawlins, whose family owned the land on which the Lancaster factory stood, remembers that long after the war the factory building served as a warehouse. Scattered around were numerous and various revolver parts. Let us remember that, when we are tempted to classify all the various shaped trigger guards, cylinders, etc. which reputedly were made in this plant. Anyone with some spare dragoon parts, and these were not uncommon in 1870, might have obtained a complete revolver of questionable merit, by sorting through the old warehouse, doing a little hand-fitting, and possibly buying a spring or two. Maybe there wasn't an aperture in the lug. If the gun was for use, the aperture was ground in; if the gun was for sale, maybe no grinding was done. We do not pretend to know the answer, but neither can we overlook these possibilities.

Another point to remember is that imitation dragoon models were made in at least two locations outside of Texas. Each variance in design doesn't have to be explained in Lancaster.

Considering the above, we can dismiss this arms factory as unimportant from the standpoint of production. It is important from a standpoint of interest and color. Probably more collectors are interested in this product than in any other Confederate firearm. It would be difficult to prove authenticity of any revolver made in Lancaster, except for those marked Sherrard, Taylor & Co., or Clark, Sherrard & Co., unless the history of that specific revolver could be traced directly back to the factory through family ownership. Even that can be tricky.

A .36 caliber percussion revolver bearing the name, Tucker & Son, has come to light. The "son" purports to be Elihu Tucker, son of Labon. As this revolver was obtained from the Tucker family it was reasonable to believe it might have been a product of the Lancaster plant. But the State Archives contain undeniable proof that the Tuckers were separated from the Lancaster plant before any pistols were made. Instead of proving that the Lancaster plant actually manufactured some .36 caliber revolvers, which has been claimed for this specific revolver, it proves nothing.

Prior to 1900, many dealers in commodities, from guns to pianos, had their names stamped on the products they sold. Two or three revolver manufacturers were willing to implant their customer's name, rather than their own, on the product. Labon Tucker and his son had been gun dealers in Marshall before the War.

This is not written to minimize the importance of the "Tucker" revolver. It is a fine piece and very historical. It must be placed in its proper historical niche, however. When records exist which are public property and available to all, it is amazing how many misconceptions and distorted facts can cloud issues which need not be obscure. To you Texans who have a Lancaster-made revolver—guard it well. The collectors will stack up the greenbacks to tempt you, and we do not mean Confederate money!

Part V -
Rimfire, Centerfire

— Cattle —

Long ago, some aphorist rhymed: Other states were carved or born, Texas grew from hide and horn.

Few subjects have been as widely discussed in literature as the winning of the West. Hundreds of able books analyze the growth of the cattle industry, the big push westward by the railroads, the recession of the Indians and the rapid settlement of grange lands by swelling tides of pioneer farmers. We shall not expand on this well-reported subject, but rather examine it from the gun lover's point of view. We cannot refrain from one observation: the winning of the West occurred as soon as the development of firearms permitted—it could not occur before!

Detailed study of firearms during the Civil War doomed the muzzle-loading gun. Breech-loading weapons were well known, of course, before the war. None of them, however, had made themselves indispensable, and the Civil War was fought almost exclusively with the muzzle-loaders.

After one large battle between the North and South, the abandoned guns were recovered from the field and sent to an armory for examination and a report. It was found that many of the guns had the powder loaded on top of the bullet, thereby insuring a misfire. An unbelievably high percentage of the guns were loaded from two to eight times, one load on top of the other. The excited soldiers could not be depended upon to properly handle the muzzle-loader. Notable improvements in firearms rarely have occurred during wartime. The need and incentive for such improvements invariably appear in war.

It has been seen that Colt made a tremendous contribution toward repeating fire with his revolver. Before the end of the war, Remington, Whitney, Starr, Manhattan, Joslyn, Freeman, Cooper and others were making good percussion revolvers. All were used in the cattle country after the Civil War.

The Remington revolver particularly deserves discussion. Most of the returning veterans carried one or more revolvers home from the war. If the veterans interviewed by the writer were a typical cross section of the entire state, many hundreds of Remington revolvers went to Texas because their new owners became enamored with them at the front. This small personal survey indicated that of the revolvers obtained by the returnees about thirty-five per cent were Remingtons, about forty-five per cent were Colts with the remaining twenty per cent composed of all other makes. In 1872 government sales of used revolvers to veterans reveals the sale of 9,875 Remingtons as compared to 9,047 Colts.

Eliphalet Remington made his first gun in Ilion, New York, in 1816. It was a flintlock rifle. His gunmaking prospered, and in 1845 he began obtaining contracts for government arms. In 1856 Remington admitted his three sons into the business. The following year the firm began manufacturing percussion revolvers. Eliphalet Remington, Sr. died in 1861, and the firm passed from the control of his family in 1888, when the name was changed from E. Remington & Sons to the Remington Arms Co.

While this firm ever has been noted for excellent shotguns and rifles, its revolver manufacture reached its peak during the Civil War era and held until the end of the percussion period. Over 200,000 good cap and ball revolvers in .44 and .36 caliber were made by Remington.

Since the advent of metal cartridges, Remington's power as a maker of handguns has declined. Their double-barrelled .41 caliber derringer has been their most popular pistol until about fifteen years ago, when they discontinued all handgun manufacture.

As the star of Remington's revolver production declined, that of Smith & Wesson ascended. Before the Civil War, Smith and Wesson, two young and progressive gunsmiths, made a lever action repeating pistol. Its action is familiar to all gun lovers, even though they may never have seen one of these early pistols. Reverse the actual evolution and imagine the well known Winchester 94 carbine as a pistol, the manipulated lever, underneath the frame, ejecting the empty shell, cocking the hammer and removing a fresh cartridge from the magazine beneath the barrel. Then, when the lever is closed against the stock, the cartridge is seated in the firing chamber and the action is locked.

That was the first Smith & Wesson, with one exception. Their pistol had no ejector—none was needed. Their cartridge was a hollow bullet, the cavity containing the explosive. The paper back burned with the charge it retained, so there was no ejection problem. This special cartridge was not popular, the detonator was too corrosive. Smith & Wesson sold out to a firm controlled by Oliver Winchester, who was a shirt manufacturer. Winchester agreed to make rifles or long arms with the patents he was purchasing from Smith & Wesson, they in turn agreed to confine their future interest to handguns.

Accordingly, Winchester had the repeating pistol redesigned as a rifle, equipped with an ejector, as it was proposed to fire the new metallic cartridge. Winchester's gun expert, designer and superintendent was B. T. Henry. The new and successful repeating rifle was known as the Henry rifle. The metallic cartridge was rimfire.

The Henry Repeating Arms Co., controlled by Oliver F. Winchester, was formed July 7, 1865, and became the Winchester Repeating Arms Co. on May 30, 1866. The first model Winchester gun appeared in 1866. It was not greatly different from the Henry rifle. Indeed, the later models of 1873 and 1894 are the same basic guns as the original Henry rifle, except that centerfire replaced the rimfire ammunition.

Smith & Wesson deserve great credit for the development of the rimfire metallic cartridge. They manufactured the first successful rimfire weapon in 1856. This was a .22 caliber revolver. The small caliber was necessary, for cartridge-making had not progressed beyond that point. The heads of the cases were blown off of larger caliber shells due to the lack of annealing.

By 1861 Smith & Wesson were making a .32 caliber rimfire revolver. These were fine little guns, although the Civil War passed without them earning much credit for their makers. The South bought hundreds of them just prior to the war, and all the available .32 caliber rimfire ammunition. Within a year after the war began, the South had expended their supply of ammunition, and as no more was forthcoming, the Smith & Wesson revolvers were withdrawn from service. The North did not use them, though a few officers were self-equipped with the fine, but small-bored weapons.

In 1869 copper annealing processes had insured dependable centerfire ammunition in any desired caliber. Smith & Wesson came out with their "American" model, .44 caliber revolver, beating Colt by four years in the manufacture of a large caliber revolver chambered for metal cartridges. Colt used centerfire on its .45 caliber "Peacemaker" which appeared in 1873.

Colt had manufactured rifles from 1847 (a few were made prior to this) until the Civil War. These would have been popular in the West but for their high cost. These guns really were but long-barreled revolvers with a shoulder stock, and were, of course, percussion. Many times, in accounts of Indian raids or other violence, mention is made of the "six-shooting rifle." Remington, Wyler and others also manufactured these revolving guns.

The Sharps carbine and the Spencer carbine emerged from the Civil War as fine saddle guns for frontier use. Both were breech-loaders. The Spencer was rated as the finest carbine of the war by the Ordnance Department. The Sharps was more popular in Texas.

Now that we have examined the cattleman's fighting tools, and have found him equipped with a pair of six-shooters and a long range .50 caliber Sharps or fast shooting Henry rifle or Colt revolving rifle, we note that he has the firepower of several Indians, plus an advantage in range. The Comanches had withstood the whites successfully until the advent of repeating firearms. As Indian attacks never occurred unless the red man had numerical superiority, slow firing, tediously loaded guns could not cope with them. The post-Civil War Texans were equipped to handle a problem hitherto impossible. Not only were the Texans able to traverse hundreds of miles of Indian territory, they were able to carry along and protect large herds of cattle.

When the hungry, ragged, heartsick Confederate soldiers straggled home to Texas in 1865, there was a silver lining in the black cloud of their despair. They were not long in recognizing it. Unfenced Texas was a natural cattle ranch. In its mild climate and rich pasturage, cattle had multiplied and re-multiplied, running wild and untended during the war years.

Enabled by the new arms we have discussed, the railroads were moving westward. Large numbers of the nation's people, their lives disrupted by war, were moving westward. The supply of free meat and cheap hides could not long withstand the western surge. The American buffalo disappeared. Thousands were destroyed in gigantic slaughters because their hides were worth fifty cents each. Soon the meat hunters for the railroad and mining camps, for the Army posts, and for the established Indian reservations, could not supply meat. The East had been making swords rather than plows, and now they were hungry. In the West, pioneers located on potentially rich ranches, but they needed cattle with which to stock their luxuriant acres. Never before was there such a market for cattle. Texas had the cattle. Thus the stage was set for the cattle business in the southwest.

Men pooled their money and labor. Herds were rounded up and branded. Trail drivers were selected for their knowledge of cattle no more than for their proficiency with guns. Indeed, many trail drivers were wholly inexperienced in handling cattle; none were signed who could not shoot fast and straight. "Sure as shootin" became a byword with the trail hands.

Cattle were bought in Texas for two, three or four dollars per head. Driven out of Texas, up the frontier to Dodge, Abilene, Newton or some other market, they were sold for eighteen, twenty, or even thirty dollars per head. Some cattle were lost along the way, the drives were long and costly, and the trail drivers were sent back to Texas. But the margin of profit was high if the herd came through. If it was lost by storm, stampede, Indian attack or disastrous river crossing, the operators were bankrupt.

The routes of the various cattle trails, the Western, the Chisholm, the Loving and many others are well known. The excitement, the hardships, the brutal rawness of the drives has been described over and over. The drives established the cattle business throughout the West. Texas reaped full benefit. As competition by the trail drivers for the acquisition of herds increased, the Texas price increased. As cattle money poured into Texas, and as the inventory value increased, more thought and money were devoted to the production of cattle.

Cattle barons sprang up. These men, or often corporations, controlled large spreads of land. They owned in fee, leased, held public land by force of arms, or by a combination of these methods. Each holding might embrace several hundred square miles. George Littlefield, Shanghai Pierce, Richard King, Samuel Maverick, Mifflin Kenedy, John Chisum, Oliver Loving, Charles Goodnight, C. C. Slaughter, Thomas Bugbee, Dan and Tom Waggoner, Ike Pryor and Burk Burnett are among the individuals who "grew a state from hide and horn." There were many others.

Many of the large corporations, such as the XIT and the Matador, carved their separate empires. These outfits would think little of leasing 500,000 acres of land, of moving 10,000 head of cattle, or building a fence seventy-five miles long. They maintained large payrolls, and among the employees there probably were one or more "protection" men or "stock inspectors." These men were the strong-arm boys of the ranch.

The employees of the ranch, their families, and those many little cattle towns which were supported by cattlemen's patronage, were protected by the trigger men of the big cow outfits. True, these fighting men served primarily to check cattle rustling and to prevent encroachment on their range. As the frontier was yet wild and lawless, family residences, freighting services and the small outfits could not have existed without this left-handed protection.

The wildness of the cowboys cannot be denied. Yet their wildness is understandable when the conditions under which they lived are known. In fiction and motion pictures the cowboy may rarely leave town, and when he does he may ride back in again in thirty minutes. Actually the cattle towns were far between, to use an authentic expression. A man might work two hundred miles from a town. His work, as well as the distance, prevented much urban activity on his part.

After a few months in the wilds, he naturally wanted to kick up his heels when he got to town. He had worked hard, long hours in good weather and in bad. He had stood night watch in the rain or sleet. He had slept short hours in cold wet clothes, on a cold wet blanket. The more rugged his life, the more human and comprehensible was his desire to live high and have fun when the rare opportunity presented itself. But what sort of towns were available to him, and what did they offer in the way of recreation?

The towns ran chiefly to a pattern. The one wide, dusty street was lined with irregularly spaced wooden or adobe buildings. Each building was one story, false-fronted, and most of them were unpainted. Each had a hitching rack in front. A water well was in the center of the street, and it supplied the entire commercial portion of the town and many residences. There were general stores which sold desirable hardware and undesirable patent medicines, cheap clothing and high-priced saddles, good tobacco and poor matches. There were feed stores, livery stables and blacksmith shops. There was apt to be no courthouse or jail, no school or church. There was no theater or library. There was an abundance of saloons and pool halls. There were the little one- and two-room homes of the dance hall girls out back of the saloons, or maybe a large "fancy house."

Much of the cowboy's sport involved either his gun or his horse. They were about all he owned. As his amusement was self-created, he liked to race horses for bets larger than he could afford. He enjoyed poker and monte, mostly for very low stakes. The big games occurred when the professional gamblers locked horns. The cowboys played pool, but due to lack of practice, he was usually a dub with the cue. He was no tyro with his revolver and after a few drinks, he liked to shoot up something, all in fun. The more damage he had to pay for, the drunker he must have been. The bigger his drunk, the more worthwhile his eight day ride for two days of celebrating. Thus he reasoned. He was a simple soul, generally honest, friendly and kindhearted.

Mrs. Temple Houston, a refined and cultured lady who lived in Mobeetie, a rough cattle town, has written sympathetically of the wild ones. She describes the boys riding up the street with a bottle of whiskey in one hand, shooting high, wide and handsome with the other hand. The boys often rode their horses into the barroom and drank without dismounting. But, she protested, they were just a bunch of fine boys celebrating the end of a long solitude. Mobeetie has been described as a "bald-headed whiskey town." It was no worse than Tascosa or Toyah or many others of the same pattern.

Mr. C. L. Douglas has written of an interview with Billie Blevins, former Texas Ranger turned bartender in Toyah. Mr. Blevins described the boys riding in, tired and grimy from the range. They had a few drinks and then left to clean up. Soon they returned for the night's entertainment, and the town suddenly became very lively.

Quoting Blevins: "I knew how to get along with the boys. When they'd start shooting the balls off of the pool tables, I'd grab my .45 and shoot the fifteen ball. And I always managed, too, to get one of the lights before the boys put 'em all out. I had to use a lot of putty on those pool tables."

Toyah, Lampasas, Mobeetie, Clarendon, Colorado City, Fort Stockton, Fort Worth, El Paso, Big Spring, Cuero, Giddings, Denton, Denison, Uvalde, Cotulla, Laredo and Tascosa were among the woolly and wild towns. Let us hasten to add that these were not the only ones. In those days, practically every town in Texas could qualify for the above list to some extent.

Tascosa was probably the worst. Twenty-seven graves were dug in Boothill cemetery there within nine years. Each grave contained a corpse which was buried just as he fell in a gunfight, many without a burial ceremony and without cleansing the body of gore. Raw and brutal, it happened beyond civilization.

The cattle industry has passed a number of serious travails. Sheep challenged. Homesteaders and water-grabbers posed a problem. In the eighties, barbed wire brought trouble measured by the mile. Other problems kept the ranchers fighting for survival, rustlers and Indians furnishing their share of the woe. But the industry has grown. The longhorn passed as did the buffalo. The stockmen began upbreeding their cattle in the early seventies. Modern methods are not as romantic as the old ones, but the pioneers snorted at the idea of romance in any stage of the industry.

Rodeos capture the color of the old West on fiesta days. On other days, the cowman is strictly a businessman. A helicopter is used on the Waggoner ranch to herd the cattle from the brush into the open where the cowboys are waiting!

Shades of old "brush-breakers!"

The gun did its work well. Now it's left hanging over the mantel.

— Outlaws —

Lawlessness prior to the Civil War has been noted. Poverty and despair, carpetbag rule and the natural psychological state of the beaten war veteran were not conducive to a reduction in crime. Law enforcement in Texas became more lax than usual during the period of Reconstruction, and crime gained such a foothold that twenty years were required to stamp out gun rule.

Nearly all cowboys had the gun skill essential to a true gunfighter. Most, fortunately, did not have the disposition. This required disposition involved indifference to loss of life, the ability to think clearly in moments of great excitement, the art of coolly squeezing off a shot when utmost haste was a matter of life and death, and above all, the temperament to remain constantly prepared and alert.

There were several classes of gunfighters. The protection man, or stock detective, was not an officer, because he operated where there was no law. Actually he was more than a peace officer, for he apprehended, judged and administered punishment. His court was presided over by Judge Colt. The U. S. marshals, the county sheriffs and their deputies, the city marshals and the Texas Rangers were the gunmen on the side of the law, and many were as proficient in arms as the best. Being under restraint, they killed less frequently than some of the outlaws. There were the guards for railroads and stagecoaches. This class was little different than the protection man, except the guards were not horsemen. Both groups owed allegiance only to their employers.

There was a class of gunfighters who were outlaws by reason of a murder charge. They were not bandits, indeed they were not dishonest. Hot words, whiskey or even self-defense resulted in many men becoming long riders, looking back with regret, looking ahead with defiant surliness.

Then there were the bandits, trigger men, robbers, murderers, rustlers, horse thieves and cutthroats. Their ranks were filled with jackals and with lions. They can't be classified—they were all types. Where some were jovial and carefree, others were surly and brutish. Where some were reckless and indifferent, others were coldly calculating. A cross section of the criminal element of 1870 probably would reveal the same varied strata of motives and mental processes shown by the criminal element of today. There would be one exception.

That courage existed in copious quantities in the old style outlaw cannot be questioned. When he entered a town to rob a bank, he knew there would be stiff opposition. Nearly all citizens had handy firearms and could use them. Modern bandits need not fear the unarmed and incapable public. Only the police will be marksmen, and only the police will have arms quickly available.

A member of the Dalton gang, riding out of Longview, Texas, after robbing a bank and engaging in a full scale battle with the citizenry, was shot in the face with a light load of bird shot. Whirling quickly to fire at his assailant, the bandit saw the young boy. The lad, mouth agape, was partly hidden by the huge front gate post before his home. Smoke curled from the right barrel of his father's shotgun. The bandit wiped the blood from the side of his face and ear and dismounted to recover his big black Stetson. Grinning at the frightened boy, he spoke, "Look out thar, Bub, you're liable to hurt somebody with that thar gun!" Men were dead back there in Longview, and he was not yet out of town, but he was both calm and good humored.

Texas long had been a refuge for wanted men. During Reconstruction, many Johnny Rebs throughout the South ran afoul of the law, and overlooking the fact that Texas, also, was ruled by carpetbaggers, they went to Texas. The GTT (gone to Texas) mark appeared after names on the rosters of churches, clubs and police records alike.

Many of these men went west to begin a broken life anew in fresh surroundings. A few had nothing but skill with arms and a love for adventure. The latter type was prone to become gunfighters, some with the Rangers, others with the outlaws. Texas outlaws were in no particular need of reinforcements. The State Treasury in Austin was robbed in 1865 by local talent. With the out-of-state help, the robbers' roosts filled and became a major problem.

Many of the robber gangs maintained headquarters in Indian Territory (Oklahoma) or New Mexico. Both territories were even more sparsely settled than Texas. Billy the Kid's gang shuttled back and forth across the western border of Texas. Horses stolen in New Mexico were sold in Texas. Cattle rustled in Texas were sold in New Mexico. His business was so prolific that the ranchers put gunmen on his trail. These men were James H. East, Lon Chambers, Leigh Hall, Cal Polk, Charles A. Siringo, Bob Robinson, Tom Emory, George Williams and Louis Bousman. The Kid's gang consisted of Tom Pickett, Charley Bowdre, Tom O'Folliard, Bill Wilson and Dave Rudabaugh.

The pressure on the Kid and his gang was considerable, and Billy's death at the hands of Sheriff Pat Garrett followed. Garrett then, with the influence of the pleased Texas ranchers, obtained a captain's commission in the Texas Rangers.

Belle Reed's husband, Jim, was a member of Jesse James' gang. After Jim was killed in a Texas gunfight, Belle married Sam Starr. They made their home in Younger's Bend, in Indian Territory. Sam was an outlaw also, which did not displease the unattractive Belle. In fact Belle, by her forceful personality, shrewdness and unscrupulous character became the leader of the gang, and a thorn in the side of north Texans. Belle Starr was killed by Edgar Watson, another outlaw, who used a sawed-off shotgun loaded with "blue

whistlers." She was forty-three. Her gang suffered a somewhat similar fate. Sam Starr, Dan Evans and Felix Griffin
were killed in gun battles. Jim French was killed resisting
arrest. Jack Spaniard and Blue Duck, both half-breed lovers
of Belle, were slated to hang. However, Blue Duck escaped
the noose in favor of the cell by the narrowest of margins.

The Cook-Skeeter gang, the Dalton gang, the Younger
boys, Jesse James' gang, the Doolin gang and the Hole-in-
the-Wall gang dipped in and out of Texas in a flurry of violence. Cherokee Bill, with thirteen notches on his plowhandles, was an unwelcome visitor from the Territory until he
danced himself to death on the end of a rope. The Rangers
broke up Bill Cook's gang of bank and train robbers which
ranged in the Panhandle.

Bob Dalton was the leader of the Dalton gang. He and his
brother, Grattan, after a career of crime, were killed during
a bank robbery at Coffeyville, Kansas. Emmett Dalton went
to the penitentiary. Bill, a brother too young for the gang,
grew up and joined the Doolin gang, but soon died with his
boots on. Frank Dalton stayed on the side of the law. He became a deputy U.S. Marshal, but he, too, died in a gunfight.

The Youngers and James used Texas as a place of refuge
for a long while, refraining from robberies within the state.
In financial embarrassment, the James gang finally robbed
a Texas stagecoach, which applied the heat to them all.
The Youngers were headed by Thomas Coleman Younger,
known as Cole. His brothers were James, Robert, John and
Bruce. Other members of the gang were Clem Miller, J. F.
Edmundson, Bill Chiles, Bud and Tomlinson McDaniels,
and George and Olle Shepherd. Practically all died of gun-
shot wounds, or in prison.

The James gang was headed by Jesse and Frank. Other
members were Jim Reed, the first husband of Belle Starr,
Charles and Robert Ford, Charley Pitts, Bill Chadwell,
Hobbs Kerry, Clell Miller, Arthur McCoy and Bill Greenwood. Their fate was similar to the Younger's except more
of them were shot down, and fewer went to prison.

Frequently modern bank robbers are picked up within a few hours following a robbery, and one hears the remark, "They haven't a chance now." The voice inflection on "now" indicates escape was formerly a sure thing. Consider the Hole-in-the-Wall gang, one of the most famous in the West. They ranged over Montana, Wyoming, Nevada, Utah, Idaho, Colorado, Oklahoma, New Mexico and Texas. The two leaders, George Parker, known as Butch Cassidy, and Harvey Logan, called Kid Curry, along with Harry Longabaugh, "The Sundance Kid," all committed suicide at various times to avoid arrest. George "Flat Nose" Curry, Will Carver, O.C. Hanks and Lonny Logan—a brother of Harvey—all were killed resisting arrest. John Logan, another brother, was killed in a gunfight. Ben Kilpatrick, "the handsome Texan," was killed during a train robbery. Robert Lee, the only member who did not die by the gun, served a long prison sentence for train robbery. Retribution was not as speedy in the old days, but about as certain.

Bill Doolin led a gang closely allied to the Daltons. Doolin was killed by Marshal Hack Thomas. When Doolin drew his revolver, the Marshal hit him with twenty-one buckshot. Charles Pierce, Charles Bryant and George Newcomb, members of the gang, were also killed resisting arrest. Newcomb was known as "Bitter Creek," and he was the lover of that lovely young lady of romance, the "Rose of Cimmarron." Bill Powers and Dick Broadwell, other members of the gang, were killed in the same bank raid. Ol Yountis, part-time member of the Daltons and part-time member of the Doolin gang, was killed by a posse headed by Chris Madsen and Heck Thomas. Retribution was pretty certain.

Why did they turn to outlawry? Some were naturals, some became outlaws as a result of carpetbag rule, some started small, but once outside the law, they robbed to live. Sometimes whiskey was their downfall. With Joel Collins it was gambling.

Joel led a group of trail drivers from Texas to Kansas where he sold a herd. The herd had not been his and the money from the sale had to be returned to Texas. Joel lost this money at poker, and dared not return without it. He decided to rob a train to recoup his loss. His fellow cowboys agreed to help him. Their haul was rich enough to spoil them, $60,000 in gold coin. Instead of going home and paying off the debt, these young men decided on a career of crime. But Joel Collins, Jim Berry and Bill Heffridge were killed resisting arrest. Jack Davis disappeared in New Orleans and may have gotten away. Sam Bass and John Underwood, "Old Dad," returned safely to Texas.

Sam Bass proceeded to organize a band of Texas train robbers. Arkansas Johnson was Bass' lieutenant. James Murphy, Frank Jackson, Bill Collins, a cousin of Joel's, Henry Underwood, brother of "Old Dad," Sam Pipes, Albert Herndon, Jack Davis, Tom Spotswood, Billy Scott, and Seaborn "Sebe" Barnes were members who spread terror among Texas railroads. The hauls were small, so the robberies had to be frequent. Probably Sam was too jovial and fun-loving to be leader of such a desperate enterprise.

As the gang struck furiously, and train after train was robbed, large rewards soon were offered, and intensive manhunts kept the boys on the jump. The Texas Rangers killed Arkansas Johnson at Salt Creek. James Murphy betrayed the gang for personal immunity, and then regretting the scorn of fellow Texans, killed himself. A bank was to be robbed in Round Rock, the old stage station near Austin. The Rangers were tipped off by Murphy, who managed to avoid the company of his three companions while in that town. These three men, the residue of the gang, were Sam Bass, Sebe Barnes and Blocky Jackson.

A local officer tried to beat the Rangers to the quarry, and touched off the battle prematurely. This officer tried to disarm Bass and company and was instantly killed. The outlaws took to their horses, the bank forgotten. The Rangers, who were scattered around town, went into action. Ranger Dick Ware shot Sebe Barnes to death. Ranger George Harrell shot Bass from his saddle.

Then Jackson did a heroic thing. He was in the lead and had almost ridden from range of the guns into safety. He turned back, saw that Barnes was dead and that Bass was wounded. He dismounted, and as the rifles and six-guns pumped at him, he lifted Bass on a horse, remounted and led Bass' horse out of town on a run, while some of the best shots in Texas were reaching for him!

Jackson, having won the admiration of the Rangers, and a million to one gamble for his life, was never seen again. Who knows but what somewhere, sometime, a Ranger looked straight up to avoid recognizing Frank Jackson.

Sam Bass was found not far away, dying.

Bass has captured the imagination of Texas, and remains its favorite outlaw. Bass loved a horse as well as any man. He loved his joke and was quite humorous. Bass was not a killer by instinct. He was generous and loyal. He was brave even in death, that is, "he died nice." Texans admire all these traits. But a sticky loop deserves a killin' and Sam had to go.

Frank Stevenson's gang, the Sand Creek gang, the Daniel and Robert Campbell gang, the Joe Beckham gang, the Sid Woodring, the Bill Brookens, the Kimble County gangs all made their splash, created their excitement, shed their blood and died.

Burt Alvord, the Baker gang, the Marlow brothers, Ham White, Joe Horner, Jim Moon were six other desperate gangs of outlaws. The McCampbell gang and John Kinney gang add to the list which could stretch to monotony. They all add up to murder and violence. They were all burrs under the saddle of a fine Ranger force and a brave assortment of county peace officers. Each of those names is a story, an exciting chapter in outlaw history. Before we dismiss organized bands, let us consider one of the most unusual.

Meet King Fisher!

Fisher, in 1876, was a young, handsome man of gaudy dress and few scruples. He affected the silver adorned clothes of the Spanish Dons. The excessive cost of his clothes, horses, hacienda and ranch in Dimmit County did not concern him greatly. He had parlayed personality, gun skill, diplomacy and aggressiveness into a fabulous southwest Texas empire. Both the criminals and the courts in half a dozen counties in this section paid him homage and followed his orders. Never less than fifty, often over a hundred gunmen rode at his beck and call from Castroville, near San Antonio, to Eagle Pass, on the Rio Grande. King Fisher did not hide behind his wall of gunmen. He led them. They respected him as a leader and as a dangerous man personally, for he boasted twenty-six notches on his own guns.

Following the wave of injustice and crime which accrues from the absolute rule of any one man, the Texas Rangers were assigned the task of reducing Fisher's organization. The Rangers, unaware of Fisher's control of various courts, undertook to capture him after obtaining enough evidence for conviction. This feudal lord was bearded in his den. Ranger McNelly captured him after a dangerous campaign, but seemingly Fisher was immune from justice. He was freed by the court, recaptured and again freed by a different court. At last the Rangers managed to jail him in San Antonio, where he had less influence. He was confined there only eight or nine months before his influence or money had him back in the saddle with his guns tied down.

At last a lady accomplished what the Rangers had not. Cupid laid King Fisher low. His love for a good woman, and her proper guidance reformed King. Willingly, he destroyed his empire of crime and violence. He became an officer of the law in Uvalde, under a court he no longer controlled. A night away from home, a short fling with former friends, and he was killed. With Ben Thompson, Texas' most famous gunman, King attended a variety show in a San Antonio saloon. His companion for the evening was ill-chosen, for Thompson had been marked for death at his next appearance there. No doubt the San Antonians believed King Fisher was there to side Thompson through trouble. When the gun slugs cut down Thompson, the domesticated King Fisher was slain also.

Not as famous as the mountain feuds of Kentucky and Tennessee, the Texas feuds were more impetuous and deadly. In Texas, they called their feuds "wars."

The Salt War of El Paso derived from a dispute over the use of a salt lick which supplied the local salt requirements. It was precipitated by a shotgunning, and so much violence followed that a company of Rangers was dispatched to the spot. No one distinguished himself in the fighting; both sides proved adept at murdering their disarmed prisoners. Ten men lost their lives, eight of them unarmed, in this "war." Lieutenant Tays, a temporary appointee, conducted Ranger activities in a manner which brought shame and mortification to the regular force. This war was important because it aligned Mexicans against Americans and contributed to later racial hatred.

The Horrell-Higgins Feud existed in Lampasas from 1873 until 1877, when both sides signed a formal treaty of peace witnessed by Major John B. Jones of the Texas Rangers. The Horrell faction was led by brothers of that name, Tom, Mart, John, Bill, Ben and Merritt, with Bill Bowen and Ben Turner. The boys were reputed to have had a method with cattle unappreciated by the other side. J. Pinckney Higgins led the other faction. Higgins, called a "good badman," was a relentless killer. In spite of being a family man who usually stood for moral living, he killed twenty men. Among his victims was Merritt Horrell. After much violence and bloodshed, the Horrells migrated to New Mexico, but did not stay long. While there, Tom and Mart Horrell, Bill Bowen and Ben Turner shot up Lincoln and killed three men. Later they shot up a Mexican village and killed four more. Ben Turner and Ben Horrell were killed by gunfire, Tom and Mart Horrell were mobbed. The others moved back to Lampasas after their New Mexico trouble which is reputed to have taken the lives of fifty men.

In Clinton, former county seat of DeWitt County, there occurred the Taylor-Sutton War. About one hundred and fifty armed men were aligned on each side, but there were no general battles involving the total resources of either side. Paid gunmen were imported by both sides, and these mercenaries succeeded in prolonging the desire for blood.

In 1874, the sporadic fighting was fanned to white heat when Will Taylor and a companion killed Will Sutton and Gabriel Slaughter. Taylor was killed also. Captain McNelly and a company of Rangers were dispatched to Clinton. They could do little, as the court was corrupt. As practically the entire county was involved, the governor withheld permission for the Rangers to settle the issue in the manner of their inclination—by force of arms. The Taylor brothers, Buck and Scrap, ramrodded one faction after Bill's death. Joe Tumlinson directed the other side. Both sides were described in Ranger reports as being mean and treacherous.

Of Tumlinson, Captain McNelly wrote, "He is a man who always rights his own wrongs. He has never felt that civil law could and should be the supreme arbiter between man and man. I am satisfied he will refuse to go to court without his arms and men as he has done heretofore. I feel entirely able to whip Tumlinson..."

Bill Taylor has been described as a young man who loved horses, women and guns. The more angry he became, the colder and more calm he became, which perhaps explains his reputation as a fighting man. Buck Taylor was ambushed and killed at a dance. Scrap Taylor was hanged by a mob on a rustling charge. The Rangers ran John Wesley Hardin, the gunman with the longest certified list of killings in the entire West, out of the county and the war. Manning Clements, nephew of Hardin, was killed in a saloon brawl. Brown Bowen, Hardin's brother-in-law, was hanged in Cuero. Hardin's brother Joe, and his cousins, Tom and Bud Dixon, were hanged by a mob. Jack Helms, DeWitt County sheriff, was killed by John Hardin. The Rangers killed Alexander Barrickman and Hamilton Anderson.

These events are not listed here in chronological order, but each death is significant since it brought peace in DeWitt County a little nearer.

As the Salt War aligned Americans against Mexicans, the famed Mason County War aligned Americans against Germans. The Germans had not been Confederate sympathizers during the Civil War. One act of violence had occurred then between these German settlers and the rebel Texans. Trouble smoldered thereafter.

When the Reconstruction period ended, the sparks were blown by the winds of hate, and in 1875, the conflagration roared. The Texan faction had a stigma of cattle rustling and general outlawry. It was led by George Gladden, Maze and John Beard and Scott Cooley. The German faction, exonerated by law, was led by the sheriff of the county, Clark. The local processes of law failed, of course, due to Clark's alignment with one faction.

After a period of terror, dry-gulching and night-riding, the advent of the Rangers ended the trouble. Moze Beard was killed by Rangers. His brother, John, departed for Arizona. George Gladden went to the penitentiary for twenty-five years, and John Ringgold, a noted gunfighter, was sent to prison for life.

Major Jones, of the Rangers, handled this situation well. Most of the Rangers sympathized with the outlaws, as they resented the war record of the Germans. Scott Cooley, who had precipitated the war by killing two men, was an old trail driver and an ex-Ranger. He was a close friend of many of the active Rangers on that detail. Major Jones wisely transferred many of his men and replaced them with unbiased forces.

There were other "wars," but those mentioned, reflect the temper of the people prior to 1880. The courts of law were not then fully relied on. Colonel Colt and Judge Winchester yet formed the board of arbitration.

The death toll of the individual gunfighters of Texas, and of all the West, was greatly exaggerated. A man's reputation among his fellowmen was based on their sincere judgment of him. If a man possessed the qualities of a gunfighter, the physical talent of rapid drawing, fast and accurate holding and squeezing, along with the psychological qualities, indifference to killing, natural aggressiveness and the absence of any inclination to panic, he was known to be dangerous. Such a man need not have a record of past performance, among those who knew him. He could perform and this was recognized and respected. The mention of a past record was the shortest way, the most convenient way, to acquaint strangers with the man's dangerous qualities. To exaggerate is a human trait. Reports circulated orally, on any subject, are apt to be distorted. This distortion rarely tends toward depreciation. Almost invariably, it is exaggerated.

The fame of the gunmen outgrew accuracy. Wild Bill Hickok's gunfighting career was largely a lie. He never killed one-third the men attributed to him. But he was physically and temperamentally fitted to have killed them, hence the ease with which his legend grew.

Texas' Ben Thompson was as dangerous a man as ever lived. He was an ex-convict, gambler, Confederate soldier (during the war he killed three Confederates and no Yankees), railroad guard and peace officer. Reputedly dozens of men were killed by him. Actually, he is known to have killed six white men, none of them his equal in reputation, and none of them killed in the publicized fashion of quick draw. If, however, the occasion had offered, he doubtless would have done everything, and more, that legend attributes to him. Surely he was more gunman than brainy. He emptied a theater by yelling and firing his revolver among the audience. He broke up a large banquet of cattlemen in the state's largest hotel by shooting out the lights and shooting up the dishes on the tables. He shot up his own gambling hall while in a rage. He shot up Leadville, Colorado, when that rough camp was at its toughest. He stood off Ellsworth, Kansas, and all its fighting men. He was feared in Abilene, the town dominated by Wild Bill Hickok. No, Ben Thompson had no private cemetery, but it was the other fellow's caution and not Ben's reticence which was responsible.

Bill Longley is credited with being the earliest gunman to achieve notoriety in the West. He probably killed eighteen men, though he is credited with twenty-six. Of his victims, one-third were Mexicans and negroes, not Longley's equal in skill with arms. Two men died at his hands in quickdrawing contests, yet Longley is called the "Father of the quickdraw."

John Wesley Hardin, credited with forty notches, possibly killed fifteen white men, and as many more negroes, Mexicans and Indians. These latter groups are segregated, not because they are not as human as the whites, but because they were usually not as well armed, had not the time and money for constant practice with arms, and hence were not acceptable opponents for the building of a gunman's notoriety. Of Hardin's victims, at least a dozen were murders, pure and simple. His quickdraw killings are more numerous than any other Texan's—seven.

Both Hardin and Longley rate with Thompson. All were conscienceless killers, and were prepared to kill more often than the occasion offered. It may be noted that their victims never were gunmen of reputation. Hardin didn't fight Longley, although they were enemies. Hickok and Thompson did not meet, although each desired the death of the other. Their collective reputations were accumulated on small fry.

Wyatt Earp, for ten years, enjoyed the reputation of being one of the five best gunmen in the West before he killed his first man. His mechanical skill had been displayed in shooting matches. His courage, aggressiveness and toughness were constantly paraded. Hence, the Westerners catalogued him, not on his feats, but on his potential. Wyatt's record of "credits" eventually reached five. He killed two men with a shotgun, and three more with his twelve-inch barrelled Colt. One was a prisoner. None were killed in the tradition of the quickdraw.

Buffalo Bill, Earp and Hickok were victims of poor press agentry. They lived in railroad towns and were readily available to "western reporters," who would travel no farther into the West than a railroad coach could carry them. These writers featured lurid sensationalism more than factual reporting. Legends have become accepted as truths as a result of their efforts.

Hickok adored it. Buffalo Bill used this notoriety professionally. Earp professed to detest it, but his interviews never gave a journalist an opportunity to describe him as a mere man. Many of the "factual incidents" relating to Wyatt Earp are not only physical impossibilities, they are superbly ridiculous.

Billy the Kid killed a lot of men; nearly all of them were murders rather than combats. He has been called "sure thing killer."

Luke Short and Clay Allison were exceptions. Allison, of Hemphill County, Texas, was prone to ride a hundred miles to challenge some big-name gunfighter merely to see if the fellow was as good as his reputation. The fact that these challenges were declined with some loss of face, bears out the contention that the notorious fraternity was not entirely reckless with their personal safety. It was a game to the bearish Allison. Like a small boy, he just loved to fight.

Luke Short did not have Allison's reputation for proficiency with the cutters. He could, therefore, get big-name competition. Luke left Texas driving a herd of longhorns to Kansas. He abandoned trail driving for the more lucrative business of selling whiskey to the Indians. Luke became a gambler and made the big boom towns—Leadville, Dodge, Tombstone and Abilene. Short was a descriptive name. Luke was only five feet, six inches in height. Possibly his physical lack contributed to the idea that he could be ridden over. Despite his supposed lack of prowess with the revolver, he killed some of the best in the West, Charley Storms in Tombstone and Jim Courtright in Fort Worth, for example. Luke became a peace officer, serving as Marshal of Dodge.

We are not depreciating Hickok, Thompson et al in the above paragraphs. We are merely depreciating their supposed accomplishments, those deeds of fantasy rather than fact. Their bravery cannot be doubted. It is no accident that they have been singled out from the masses, their exploits exaggerated, their deeds romanticized. But they were not fearless. They had their bump of caution, even as you or I. Their fame found foundation as much on oral embellishment as on their true accomplishments.

It is easy to say Hickok killed a hundred men. But who were they? Where were their homes? Where are they buried and who are their relatives? In answering these questions, the number of notches in each case necessarily must be scaled downward.

— Rangers —

If Texas is a state of braggarts, credit it to their esprit de corps. Since 1870 much has been accomplished in Texas. Texans spur one another to greater efforts with a pat on the back and shameful, but unashamed bragging. Texans will boast of anything in Texas, even abominable weather, for it, too, can be superlative in a negative way. Their favorite and unfailing brag is the Texas Ranger.

It is with difficulty that one thinks of a Ranger as a mere man, filled with ordinary human frailties, including fear. From a review of their accomplishments, from the attitude of the people they served, one views the Ranger as through a defective mirror, distorted into an infallible giant.

What enabled them, through trial and tribulation, year after year, to succeed where greater forces failed? How could their prestige, their invincibility, be maintained forever against the most cunning, brave and determined warriors produced by the Mexicans, Indians and American outlaws?

Two concise sentences voiced by two great Ranger captains tender some answer to our queries. Captain Bill McDonald: "No man in the wrong can stand up against a fellow that's in the right and keeps on a-comin'." Captain J. A. Brooks: "My men are crack shots and I am not afraid of them getting the worst of anything!"

There you have the Ranger. First, he was a hand-picked fighting man, endowed with both natural and acquired skill with weapons. Secondly, he believed in the infallibility of his organization. From his association he acquired an indomitable will. The mental conditioning of a Ranger was more important than his physical assets. As he acquired his indoctrination from his captain, and from his comrades in an unplanned, day-by-day process, the sincerity of it was doubly effective. His intestinal fortitude, his unmitigated gall, stemmed from absolute self confidence and unequaled determination. The by-word of the Rangers, used like a battle cry was, "The Hell I can't!"

The Rangers in the years B. C.—before Colt—were handicapped. In an earlier examination of their equipment, we have seen them armed with long-barreled, single shot rifles and single shot pistols. In 1840 they acquired a few Colt revolvers, but these were of insufficient stopping power, difficult to reload and too fragile to maintain. One thousand Walker model revolvers were delivered to the Texas Rangers at Vera Cruz. The B. C. period of the Rangers ends in 1848.

The Rangers were organized October 17, 1835, three companies of twenty-five—twenty-five and ten men being first authorized. Two weeks later, another company of twenty men was authorized. The four captains, called superintendents in 1835, were Garrison Greenwood, Silas M. Parker, D. B. Frayar and G. W. Davis. Within a month, a reorganization established three companies of fifty-six men each under Captains I. W. Burton, William H. Arrington and John J. Tumlinson, all under the command of Major R. M. Williamson.

This organization was planned as non-uniformed cavalry, detached from both the regular army and the militia. They had no ordnance department, no quartermasters, no medical auxiliaries. The men furnished their own rations, clothing, horses, saddles, arms and ammunition. They were to treat their wounds themselves with their own medical supplies. No wonder they used bullet molds as forceps to extract arrows from their bodies. The first Ranger pay was a dollar and a quarter per day. Officers received the same base pay as a U. S. Army cavalry officer of similar rank, plus a dollar and a quarter per day while on active duty.

At its inception, the sole duty of the Ranger force was to protect the frontier of Texas from Indian attack. They failed for evident reasons. Their numbers were insignificant, and in battle they were forced to dismount and fight on foot. The revolver solved the last problem to the complete satisfaction of the Ranger. With a pair of sixes, he was the equal of the Indian in mobility, and superior to the Indian in firepower.

Between 1835 and 1848 the Ranger force was the subject of many Congressional actions. The force was increased, it was reduced, it was abolished, it was reestablished with rapidity, sometimes one bill passing before the preceding act had time to take effect. This was a result of economic expediency, the dictates of politics and other reasons. We may assume this confusion was not beneficial to the Rangers, who were feeling their way, building a tradition and rapidly becoming indispensable. Great Rangers who made their names before the Mexican War were Big Foot Wallace, John Coffee Hays, Edward Burleson, Mathew Caldwell, Ben Mc-Culloch, Rip Ford and Samuel H. Walker.

After Texan annexation and the Mexican War, Texas looked to Federal defense against Indians. The Rangers were disbanded. The Indians were not. They raided with the same Apache and Comanche gusto as of yore. The Texas frontier could not be defended by the federal government exactly as was the other American frontier.

Texas was the only state in the Union at that time, which had hostile Indians within its borders. No reservations had been established for the Indians; they were in effect, citizens of the state. The Army was prohibited from attacking Indians unless the savages were caught in the actual act of depredating. This was beyond the comprehension of the Texans. With them, it always had been war on sight with Indians. The Army had little chance of catching the red men in the act of depredating. The forts were too far apart, troop movements were too slow. Indians, moving their women and children, tents, stock and all their worldly possessions could stay ahead of the troops who were in active pursuit.

Texas heartily disliked President Taylor, who returned their regard with interest. We have noted his adverse reports on Texas regiments during the Mexican War. Taylor was accused of degrading the Rangers, and as President, of deliberately withholding protection from Texas. It was pointed out that he sent thirty-two companies of troops to Florida to whip six hundred Indians, and four hundred troops to Texas to whip 20,000 Indians.

No doubt Taylor was blameless. The same hue and cry was raised in Texas during the Reconstruction era, when the Rangers were deactivated. Texas claimed then that she was disarmed and bound and laid on the sacrificial altar at the mercy of the savages. This claim, though exaggerated, was not altogether without basis, for in 1867, H. H. McConnell, a Union soldier wrote:

> The fact that this is a frontier does not seem to be known in Washington. When blazing dwellings of Texas pioneers light the skies from the Red River to the Rio Grande, when murdered women and captured children are everyday occurrences along the entire frontier, General Sheridan reports, "No Indian difficulties of any importance have occurred in my department!"

The fact is, Texas liked the way the Rangers fought the Indians, and were impatient with other methods. The Rangers were prone to kill men, women and children, and take scalps to mortify their enemies. By treaty, when the United States assumed the defense of Texas, other agencies were excluded. Officially, there could be no Rangers. However, the Rangers were called up intermittently for a few weeks at a time throughout the period extending from 1849 to 1858.

In 1858 Texas decided the Rangers must operate again on a full-time basis. John S. "Rip" Ford was made Senior Captain in charge of three or four companies of Rangers. Ford was told to cooperate with the U. S. Army and the Indian agents, but to let nothing interfere with his program of border defense. Governor Runnels advised Ford that only good judgment could steer the Ranger fortunes through a delicate situation. Ford's actions not only were condoned by the U. S. Army, aid was rendered Ford by General D. E. Twiggs. President James Buchanan was more friendly to Texas than Taylor had been. His Secretary of War, John B. Floyd, approved an army offensive against the Indians.

Between 1858 and 1860 reservations in the Indian Territory were delineated for Texas Indians, and an effort was made to induce the Indians to occupy them. As there were no more Indians legally in Texas, there could be no further uncertainty by the troopers concerning the propriety of attacking an Indian band.

There was no Ranger force from 1861 until 1874. The Civil War funneled the Rangers into regular military service. From 1865 to 1874 were nine years of carpetbag rule backed up by State Police. The less said of the State Police in Texas, the better. When the Rangers were reactivated, Major John B. Jones was given command of the Frontier Battalion, charged with protecting the border from Indians. Captain L. H. McNelly was given command of the Special Force, which was to suppress trouble along the Mexican border.

Since 1859 the Mexican bandit problem had been serious. Cortina's War on the Rio Grande had involved more than 1,000 men, had resulted in many deaths and the sacking and burning of a large portion of the lower Rio Grande Valley. As Mexico and Texas had never cooperated in suppressing crime, Indians, Mexican and American outlaws raided on either side of the border, crossing to the other side for refuge. Jefferson Davis, when Secretary of War, had pointed out that this international boundary rendered Texas the most difficult part of the frontier for the army to defend, since it served as a barrier beyond which the army could not pass, while obstructing the raiders not at all.

A third division of the Rangers should have been organized. Texas needed an internal section to combat outlaws. The feuds, train, stagecoach and bank robberies, large scale cattle rustling and other lawlessness were rampant. Local authorities, in many cases, were totally inadequate. Rangers were summoned so frequently that all requests for them could not be complied with. The reorganized Rangers remained irregular cavalry. Their salary was fifty dollars per month. They furnished their own clothing and horses, but the state furnished their guns. There were no quartermaster or medical attachments. The state replaced any Ranger horse which was killed on duty. The first issue of carbines to the Rangers was .50 caliber Sharps, which were known as brass bellies. A few of the men preferred to use their personally owned Henrys or Winchesters.

The second time new guns were issued, in 1876 or 1877, Winchesters were selected. The new Winchester carbines, model 73, delighted the Rangers and there was much rivalry to secure one of the new guns. The revolvers used were the Colt Peacemakers, .45 caliber single action centerfire with a seven and one half-inch barrel. Winchesters won instant approval in Texas, yet they seemed to have been singularly scarce for a long time.

Texas used new innovations in arms before they were accepted in other sections. An improved firearm probably could not have been offered to a more eager public than in Texas. Spencers, Sharps, the Mississippi rifle, Colt revolving rifles and Colt revolvers are known to have achieved very early acceptance in Texas. But all records of arms types in the state indicate that Winchesters, prior to 1873-1874 were quite scarce.

The state's use of the Rangers is illustrated by this one of many like incidents. Sheriff John McClure's telegram to Austin, "Is CAPT. MCNELLY COMING—WE ARE IN TROUBLE— FIVE RANCHES BURNED BY DISGUISED MEN."

McNelly's report to Austin a few weeks later reveals what happened when he arrived there.

> ...About seven o'clock next morning I came in sight of them (twelve cattle thieves), about eight miles distant. They discovered my command (eighteen men) about the same time and commenced running the cattle. They drove about three miles and, finding we were gaining on them, they drove the herd

onto a little island in a salt marsh, and took their stand on the opposite side, and waited our approach for a half-hour before we reached the marsh.

On arriving I found them drawn up in line on the south side of a marsh about six hundred yards wide, filled with mud and water, eighteen or twenty inches deep, and behind a bank four or five feet high. I formed my men as skirmishers and rode into the marsh, not allowing my men to unsling their carbines, or draw their pistols. As soon as we struck the water, the raiders commenced firing on us with Spencers and Winchester carbines. We advanced at a walk, not firing a shot or speaking a word, and keeping our line well dressed.

On our nearing the position they held, perhaps within seventy-five or one hundred yards, they wheeled their horses and galloped off at a slow gait. When we got out on hard ground, we pressed forward and soon brought ourselves within shooting distance. The Mexicans then started at a full run, and I found that our horses could not overtake them. So I ordered three of my best mounted men to pass to their right flank and press them so as to force a stand.

As I had anticipated, the Mexicans turned to drive my men off, but they held their ground, and I got up with four or five men, when the raiders broke. After that it was a succession of single hand fights for six miles before we got the last one. They were all killed. I lost one man, L. B. Smith, of Lee County...

The above was used by Walter Prescott Webb in his studious *Texas Rangers*. In that work the author has taken many pithy reports from the Ranger files and reproduced them to convey the atmosphere and spirit of the Rangers. The man of action shines through many of these labored reports. Through Indian troubles, border trouble, outlaws, feudist alarms, fence cutters, smugglers, bootleggers and boomtowns the Rangers have galloped. Unquestionably they were one of the most colorful and effective law enforcement organizations in the world.

The lone Ranger's work is not all fiction. Not all of their work was done in companies. Many one man details went out, and in nearly every case the mission was successful.

Rangers actually joined outlaw gangs as spies, in the best tradition of the movies. And in one case, for shame, an outlaw gained entrance to the Rangers for the same purpose.

The Texas Rangers killed over 5,000 outlaws—reflect on that figure for a moment—and captured many thousands of others. There are few marks against their record, extraordinary when one considers that fighting men were the chosen recruits. Rangers liked their men "on the proddish side." Men who were prone to go on the "prod" might be expected to precipitate a regrettable incident sooner or later. That the Rangers did not speaks volumes for both the men and their officers.

It is impossible to name all the great Rangers who have become a tradition in Texas, men whose names have been a byword to Texans. Captain J. A. Brooks, Will Scott, L. P. Sieker, Junius Peak, Frank Hamer and Tom R. Hickman are such men. But the Big Seven of the Rangers are Major John B. Jones, Lieutenant John B. Armstrong, and Captains L. H. McNelly, Leigh "Lee" Hall, G. W. Arrington, W. J. "Bill" McDonald and John R. Hughes.

On August 10, 1935, ninety-nine years and ten months after its inception, the force of Texas Rangers was merged into the Department of Public Safety, virtually ending this historical organization.

PART VI -
THE PRESENT

— NOW —

There is no reason for the modern Texan to know that a horse pistol can be loaded, without a ramrod, by banging the butt on a table top. He need not know that a small wad of paper placed in the holster, under his revolver, speeds the draw. The modern Texan doesn't know how to prop up a wagon tongue to make a gallows out on the treeless plain. He doesn't know that the man who wears only one glove, also wears a hide-out. If he knows that the quickest way to open a stopped vent is by exploding a cap on it, with the gun barrel empty, the knowledge is not particularly useful. Eighty years ago, such knowledge might have saved his life.

The gun in Texas today is not an essential if there is to be meat on the table. A Texan may wear his hair to his grave without having to defend it with firearms. However, the gun still can put meat in the larder. It still can save life, which is prolonging death, by furnishing adventure, zest of living, recreation and contentment which belong to a man, with a gun in his hand, roaming the great outdoors. Few other things impel so strong a sense of well being, such a panacea for the troubled mind.

Being in the outdoors, communing with nature, relegates the trivialities of day by day living to their proper place. Add a gun to the picture, change the phrase to "hunting in the outdoors," and you add the thrill of anticipation, the fascination of exploration, the exultance of achievement, the many medicines which are remedial to an ailing soul.

Fortunately, there is an abundance of hunting available to Texans. East Texans have quail, doves, ducks, geese, woodcock, brant, squirrels, deer and rabbits, as well as predators, the wolves, bobcat, armadillos, opossums, fox, an occasional panther, and other game. West Texas affords quail, doves, turkey, prairie chickens, ducks, geese, chachalaca, antelope, bear, deer, wolves, coyotes, cougars, prairie dogs and other local and migratory game. South Texas boasts all of the game found in the other parts of the state and whitewings, Mexican lions, ocelots, plover, javelinas, and other game also.

Game laws vary from county to county and all varieties of available game may not be taken concurrently. Indeed, there may be no open season on part of the above named game in a given year. The increase in population, resulting in fewer hunting areas and an increasing number of hunters, poses a problem for the Texas Game, Fish and Oyster Commission. The increasing tendency of land owners to post their land poses a problem for the hunters.

It is feared that urban life is robbing many Texas gunners of the true concept of fair play and the highest type of sportsmanship. Rural landowners complain of rich city men, with five-hundred-dollar dogs and an expectation of hunting elsewhere next season, cleaning the quail coveys too closely, of breaking down fences, leaving gates open, and of shooting too near livestock. It is a problem which can be solved only by courtesy and the proper regard for the other man's rights. Unless the farmer's past experience has been too bitter, he will enjoy being your host if properly approached.

Game hogs have always existed. They probably always will. David Crockett killed twenty-four bears on one hunt in northeast Texas. Once duck hunters killed sixty to a hundred ducks in one shoot. Quail hunters once carried wash tubs in the back of the buggy in which to bring home the quail. The white man never has limited his kill to his needs; that is why the Indian fought him so bitterly. The slaughter of the buffalo is an indictment against the American gunner.

Skeet and trap-shooting absorb a vast amount of the Texan's love for a gun, without diminishing the supply of game.

The generally mild climate of the state permits shooting for practically the entire year. The trap-shooters of Texas enjoy a high national ranking. Four of them earned places on the All-American team of 1949. No other state won so many places. Grant Ilseng of Houston, D. Lee Braun and Charley Mason of Dallas, Charley's wife, Janice, and Walter Wells of Houston, held national honors for the year.

This sport also furnishes satisfaction in achievement, and satisfies a demand for competitive action. That Texans also shoot a lot of skeet cannot be doubted if one studies the record of championships. Lest we be accused of boasting (Texans occasionally have been so accused), we will not dwell on the fact that Texans won twenty-two championships out of thirty-eight classes in the last National Championship meet. Glenn Van Buren, Herman Ehler, Grant Ilseng, Lee Braun, Mikey Michaelis, D. W. Conway and J. C. Adams are national names in the sport. Of course, there are many other men, and women, who are proficient enough to hold National Championships, thereby upholding the prestige of Texas arms. Obviously we cannot name the dozens of Texas skeet experts who have won, or are on the verge of winning, national acclaim.

What the skeet club is to the shotgun man, the various rifle clubs are to the sharpshooting riflemen and pistol men. No more ardent sportsmen are found anywhere than are those who shoot for X's on the target range. With their heavy barrels, their slick actions, their high power scopes and spotters, their contracted patterns furnish a thrill. As soon as a Texan shows you his photograph of Junior, he may show you Saturday's target with all holes in the ten ring at one hundred yards.

The national champion in this sport also is a Texan. Robert E. McMains shot a sizzling 3,189 out of a possible 3,200 in a gusty wind to top the 1949 competition. And what superb competition! Think of the sharpshooters those two hundred competing marksmen could train! All of those lads could hold and squeeze. And how they love the sport! For the good of the nation, upon what better sport could a man bestow his enthusiasm? He is learning at his own expense, on his own time, the things his government will want to teach him most in case of national emergency. When statesmanship fails, when the gun is called on as the inexorable answer, how wonderful to be a nation of gun lovers!

But the citizen's ownership of a gun is not agreeable in all corners. Insidious movements are constantly afoot with the objective of curtailing private gun possession. The attack is through legislation, and the method involves a gentle and gradual infringement on the individual's rights, so gradual that no resistance is incited. One law introduced in a few states requires that all guns be registered, presumably as a crime prevention measure. Despite any number of these laws, the criminals would no more register their guns than a moonshiner would register his distillery. A proposed law in other states would enact high taxes, prohibitive tax, on guns. Reasons for the proposals are always desirable, but the proposals themselves are wrong. Most states have had to defeat anti-gun laws. Let Texas remain in the forefront by defeating all anti-gun legislation, however small the concession entailed.

Such laws crippled Europe in the last war. There were few marksmen, fewer guns and those guns were registered. When the Nazis occupied a country, the records revealed the ownership of all guns. It was a simple matter to disarm completely such a people. The allies found it necessary to parachute arms to the Norwegian, Belgian and French underground. Who would parachute arms to us?

As this is being written, the morning's newspaper relates that the Communists have ordered police to confiscate all firearms in citizens' hands in Czechoslovakia. The firearms are registered and there will be no withholding them. A disarmed populace can give a police state small trouble. One well-armed man can safely control hundreds of unarmed men. It could happen here. There is no right more inherent to an American than the right to own a gun. Owning, and properly using guns made America possible. The nation, like Texas, grew and expanded only because guns made such growth attainable. Let us not give up our guns if we expect to retain our liberty, for our liberty was won with them. If anti-gun laws are a panacea for criminality (ridiculous!), then the cure is worse than the disease.

Both the rifle and revolver are of American origin. Had our ancestors not loved these weapons and been skilled in their use, our history would be vastly different. Our American Revolution, the War of 1812, the Texas Revolution, the Mexican War and the vast project of winning the West were not terminated successfully due to superior numbers or better organization. We won because we had superior small arms and could use them. We won because of the spirit of our men. They were unregimented individualists, resourceful and courageous pioneers, magnificent men who heroically, without realizing it, were building for us our America.

An Index of 800 Notorious Western Gunfighters

Approximately eight hundred men, between the years 1867 and 1897 crowded enough color, action and adventure into life on the western frontier that their habitat became commonly called the Wild West. It was this group of eight hundred outstanding gunmen which motivated a new way of life, a new folklore, a new type of combat and a new class of literature.

This index of western gunmen is intentionally incomplete. It omits such hunters as Buffalo Bill, such Indian fighters and scouts as Kit Carson and Jim Bridger. Stagecoach guards, such as Clark Stocking, are omitted. This list is composed of pistol men, the western gunfighters, the quickdraw artists, who could squeeze off an accurate shot while being fired on themselves.

This is not a list of men who have had a "difficulty" and killed a man. This list includes only those who, by training and mental processes, were constantly ready to do that which the ordinary man ever would avoid—kill a fellow man in the twinkling of an eye.

These men have the greatest appeal to the writers of western fiction, and to the millions of their readers. The quickdraw man has attracted an aura of glamour to him, for he was the supreme gambler, and he gambled fairly and courageously. He risked his life daily, for any unknown might create a reputation by outdrawing and outshooting one of the notorious fraternity.

The era of the quick-draw-and-shoot combat was merely an extension of the period of duelling. As one ended, the other began. The western type of combat carried more suddenness, yet more suspense and excitement than duels, for the lack of formalities introduced more imponderables.

Some of these eight hundred are heroes, some are murderers and bandits. There is not a coward in the list. Each man is the subject for a book, and indeed, many of these biographies have been written already; a few have been done several times.

The purpose of indexing them is not to provide a biography of each. It serves merely as a quick reference, a method of identifying a large number of men with their locale, whose names frequently appear in print. That old frontier revolver with the shortened barrel probably was carried by a quickdraw man. He was torn between the desire for a long barrel with its greater accuracy and a shorter barrel for its quick holster clearance. If most of his anticipated drawing was to be done indoors, you can bet he shortened the barrel.

May this list identify the initials you find cut into that old .44!

[Editor's Note: In the list of gunmen to follow, corrections have been made to enhance Mr. Holloway's original text. Many entries could not be improved upon and appear just as they did in the 1951 edition. When necessary, however, inaccuracies have been corrected.]

Ake, Jefferson—Texas gunman, outlaw and feudist.

Albro, Thomas—A tough but honest Wyoming cowboy and gambler. He killed Ted Rutledge and was killed by Big Nosed George at South Pass.

Allen, Buck—A south Texas gunman & cohort of Pink Higgins.

Allen, Jack—Marshal of Dodge, Kansas, and later a gambler and gunman of the Colorado mining camps.

Allen, William—"Billy" was a fast gun wielder in Deadwood.

Alley, James—Sheriff of Hardeman County, Texas.

Allison, Bill—A member of the dread Kimble County, Texas gang.

Allison, Clay—One of the most legendary gunfighters of the entire West, was from the Texas Panhandle. He boasted twenty-six credits, and would challenge other notorious gunmen merely to prove his own superiority.

Alvord, Burton—A cowboy from the Slaughter Ranch in Texas who became a deputy sheriff only to turn train robber.

Anderson, Hamilton—"Ham" was a member of Wes Hardin's gang in Texas. He was slain by Texas Rangers.

Anderson, William—"Bill" was a gunman around Tascosa. He saw service with the Texas Rangers and was also an outlaw, for a time, in Indian Territory.

Anglin, Abraham—Texas Ranger, selected as an outstanding enlisted man.

Armstrong, John—Texas Ranger who won a lieutenant's commission for his field service. He was truly a man after McNelly's own heart.

Arnett, George—Texas Ranger, was cited for his proficiency in arms.

Arrington, G. W.—One of the greats in the Texas Ranger hall of fame.

Aten, E. D.—Wore his guns on the side of law and order, was at one time a Texas Ranger.

Aten, Ira—Sergeant of Texas Rangers. He distinguished himself in lone-wolf assignments against outlaws. Later, he was protection man for the XIT Ranch.

Augustine, David—A gunman who fought in the DeWitt County, Texas war.

B

Bailey, D. W. H.—Noted Texas Ranger during the outlaw era.

Baker, Charles—With his brother, Frank, headed a gang of rustlers and robbers in New Mexico. Entering Texas on a foray, they were captured by Ranger Gillett, and went to prison for twenty-five years each.

Baker, Cullen M.—Chieftain of a band of outlaws and killers in East Texas during the Reconstruction era. He is credited with being the first to perfect the quickdraw technique.

Baker, Frank—Brother of Charles, see above. Frank was a friend of Billy the Kid.

Banister, John—And his brother Bill, were such outstanding riders and shots that the Rangers solicited their memberships, an unusual procedure. The brothers served with distinction.

Banister, William—Brother of John, see above.

Barker, Dudley—Texas Ranger who served under Bill McDonald.

Barnes, John—A desperado of Arizona, ran with Curley Bill's gang.

Barnes, Seaborn—"Sebe," a member of the Sam Bass gang

of bank and train robbers in Texas. He was killed by Ranger Dick Ware in Round Rock, and lies beside his chief, Sam Bass, in the old stagecoach stop cemetery.

Barrett, Thomas—A carefree kid of a cowboy, showed Wyoming its slickest sixshooterology when he killed Black Sam McCleed.

Barrickman, Alexander—A member of the desperate Wes Hardin gang, was slain by Texas Rangers.

Barton, Jerry—Constable in Cochise County, Arizona, and a deadly gunman.

Bass, Sam—Member of the Collins gang and later the leader of his own gang of train robbers in north Texas. Sam was killed by Ranger George Harrell during an attempted bank robbery at Round Rock.

Bassett, Charles—A Dodge gunman, was friend and consort of the Mastersons and Earps, and one time Marshal of Dodge.

Baylor, George W.—Captain of Texas Rangers, ex-Confederate officer, was utterly fearless and his marksmanship was amazing, even to the Rangers.

Beadsale, James—Was wanted, dead or alive, on the Texas-Mexico border, but evaded capture for seventeen eventful years.

Bean, Edward—A Smith County Texas, outlaw who was killed in Wise County while resisting arrest.

Bean, James—Brother of Ed, see above. Jim was killed in the same gunfight.

Beard, John—Brother of Moze, fought in the cattle war of Mason County, Texas, fleeing to Arizona from the Rangers.

Beard, Moze—Was rated one of the most skilled gunmen in the Texas hill country until he was killed by Rangers during the Mason County War.

Beekham, Joe—Sheriff of Motley County, Texas, who absconded with county funds and then shot his successor to death. He was killed by the Rangers.

Behan, John—A successful deputy sheriff in Pima County, Arizona, became the first sheriff of tough Cochise County.

Bell, James W.—A New Mexico lawman. He was serving as jailer of Billy the Kid, when the Kid killed him in an escape.

Bell, Joseph W.—One of the crack shots of the Texas Rangers.

Bell, Thomas—Sheriff of Bell County, Texas.

Bernard, Hiram—A Wyoming deputy sheriff who was lightning on the draw. He never honored the other man's drop, but drew against it.

Berry, James—Texas cowboy who joined the Joel Collins gang of outlaws in Kansas. He robbed trains from the Dakotas to Texas before being killed resisting arrest.

Berry, James—An Arizona stagecoach robber and gunslick, was killed by a load of buckshot in Deadwood.

Biedler, John X.—A famous Montana law officer.

Bingham, George—Texas Ranger who was killed in action in a fight with outlaws.

Bird, Allen—A Texas rustler who went to Wyoming for his health. In a battle with possemen there, he shot three, but died in the penitentiary.

Bishop, John—Efficient Texas Ranger during the outlaw era.

Black, Ike—A member of the Doolin gang of Oklahoma.

Blackburn, Duncan—Deadwood outlaw who went to prison for a long list of major crimes.

Blake, Jack—"Tulsa" was an Indian Territory outlaw who was killed by Chris Madsen and his posse.

Blue Duck—A half-breed member of Belle Starr's gang, went to prison for a long term.

Bogan, Daniel—An outlaw and gunman from Texas, who ranged the West as far as Montana.

Bond, Jack—San Simon Valley rustler who enlisted in the Texas Rangers for the purpose of spying. He was dismissed from the service by Captain Baylor and Ranger Sergeant Gillett broke up his gang. Bond fled to New Mexico where he was killed by Dan Tucker in Deming.

Bonnell, Edward—A New Mexican gunman and posseman, who fought Billy the Kid's gang.

Bonney, William—"Billy the Kid," New Mexico feudist and leader of a gang of desperados. He is known to have killed ten men, and reputed to have killed twenty-one before he was slain by Sheriff Pat Garrett of Lincoln County.

Boswell, Nathaniel K.—Deputy U. S. Marshal at Laramie, who was a fearless officer and a dead shot. His was a fine record.

Bousman, Louis—A protection man for George Littlefield, fought Billy the Kid.

Bowdre, Charles—A member of Billy the Kid's desperate gang, who was killed by a sheriff's posse.

Bowen, Brown—Brother-in-law of Wes Hardin, and just as wild, was hanged for murder.

Bowen, William—"Bill," a member of that tough, fighting Horrell gang, went with them from Lampasas, Texas, to Lincoln County, New Mexico.

Bowles, Thomas—Fought a gun battle with Wild Bill Hickok. While both men were highly skilled gunmen, only a bystander was hit during their duel.

Boyce, Reuben—Accused of being a member of the Kimble County gang, was imprisoned, but made a daring escape.

Bracken, John—A Texas Ranger who saw much action.

Brady, William—Sheriff of Lincoln County, New Mexico, was killed in the Murphy-McSween Feud.

Breakenridge, William M.—An Arizona lawman who made a brilliant record in coping with hardcase killers.

Brent, James—One of the cowboys, all picked gunmen, selected to hunt Billy the Kid to his death.

Brewer, Richard—"Dick," leader of a war party in the Lincoln County, New Mexico, feud. He was killed by Buckshot Roberts.

Bridges, Jack—A buffalo hunter and scout, who held his own in the pistol game. He became Marshal of Dodge.

Brittian, J. M.—Was a sergeant of Texas Rangers, and a distinguished officer of the law.

Broadwell, Richard—"Dick," a member of the Doolin gang of outlaws of the Indian Territory, was killed in a bank robbery at Coffeyville, Kansas.

Brocius, William—"Curly Bill," kingpin of the Tombstone rustlers, was a partner of John Ringo. He once attended church, upon which the entire congregation became frightened and left the service. Wyatt Earp claimed to have killed him with a shotgun.

Brook, Billy—Marshal of Dodge, had killed some fifteen men and was riding high, wide and handsome, until suddenly, his nerve left him. A buffalo hunter chased him out of town.

Brooks, J. B.—A Texas Ranger and peace officer.

Brooken, Bood—Brother of, and member of the gang of Bill Brooken.

Brooken, William—Leader of a south Texas gang of rustlers and gunmen. He was sentenced to 127 years in prison.

Brown, Charles—A boomtown gambler and gunman, killed Happy Jack Marco.

Brown, Henry—A tough gunman from New Mexico, and former member of Billy the Kid's gang. Became constable of Tascosa, and later was made City Marshal of Caldwell, Kansas. Shielded by his office, he organized a vicious bandit gang. He was killed by a mob.

Brown, James—Sheriff of Lee County, Texas, was a gun-fighter with several notches. He hanged Bill Longley for the third and final time.

Brown, James J.—Sheriff of Cameron County, Texas, was a tough hombre in a tough spot.

Brown, Sam—"Red," a Nevadian and Arizonian gunman and desperado who boasted seventeen credits. Finally, he lost his nerve, and was killed by Dutch Van Sickles.

Bruton, William C.—A Goliad County, Texas, cattle rustler.

Bryant, Charles—A member of the Doolin gang, was killed by Ed Short, a fighting Marshal.

Bryant, R. E.—Deputy sheriff in El Paso, that eight-barreled stingaree of a border town.

Bull, John—A noted gunfighter of Deadwood.

Bullock, Seth—The sheriff of Deadwood during the Smoky Seventies.

Bunton, Bill—Lieutenant of Henry Plummer's gang of outlaws at Bannack.

Burdette, Joe—An old Indian fighter, trail driver and Texas Ranger.

Burk, James—Sheriff of Goliad County, Texas.

Burke, Stephen—A deputy U. S. Marshal in the Indian Territory.

Burns, Dick—A member of the Peyton Jones gang, was hanged by a posse.

Burns, George—"Doc," was a noted Colorado sheriff.

Burrows, William—"Bill," was deputy to Milt Mast. He helped capture Bill Longley.

Burson, Lon—U. S. deputy Marshal and a friend of Bill Mc-Donald, with whom he worked.

Burton, Jerry—Constable in Cochise County, Arizona, and an adept gunman.

C

Cabell, Ben E.—Sheriff of Dallas County, Texas, when Big D stood for "dangerous."

Cain, Luke—Rowdy and too quick with the sixes for his native East Texas, moved on west. Who knows his later history?

Cain, Neil—Texas trail driver turned gambler and gunman in Kansas, made all the hot spots. Neil frequently dealt monte in Ben Thompson's resorts.

Calloway, Columbus—A Texas Ranger of wide experience in the profession of gunfighting.

Callicot, William—One of the aces of the border section of the Texas Rangers in the seventies.

Campbell, Daniel—Along with his brother Bob, were Oklahoma train robbers with a price on their heads. They were captured by Ranger Bill McDonald.

Campbell, George—Peace officer in Young County, Texas, and later Marshal of El Paso.

Campbell, Malcolm—A Montana sheriff who had a cattle war on his hands.

Campbell, Robert—"Bob," brother of Daniel Campbell.

Campbell, William—A New Mexico gunman who killed a prominent lawyer because he wouldn't dance with Campbell's guns barking at his feet.

Canton, Frank M.—Noted Wyoming sheriff, and Indian Territory lawman, helped break up the Dalton gang.

Carr, Ace—An outlaw who ranged both New Mexico and Texas.

Carroll, John—Deputy sheriff of Denton County, Texas.

Carson, Thomas—Deputy Marshal of Abilene, Kansas, under Wild Bill Hickok. Wes Hardin once got the drop on Carson and took Carson's trousers, forcing the officer to return to Abilene sans prisoner and trousers. It took a brave man to live that down, but Carson was a brave man, and a good officer.

Carter, Alexander—A desperado of the Montana mining camps.

Carter, Benjamin—A Texas Ranger who constantly studied and practiced the gun dealing art.

Carter, Dock—Like his brother Ben, was a fighting Ranger.

Carver, William—A member of the Hole In the Wall gang, he and Kid Curry killed the famous George Scarborough while evading a posse. Carver was killed resisting arrest.

Castello, Felix—One of Pink Higgins' gunmen from south Texas.

Cavin, William T.—"Bill" was a lawman who worked as a lone spy against the King Fisher gang. Later he became a successful cattleman.

Chacon, Augustine—Leader of a terrible bandit gang on the Mexican border. Reputed to have killed twenty-eight men, he was captured by the Arizona Rangers, and was hanged.

Chadwell, William—"Bill" was a member of Jesse James' robber gang. He was killed in the Northfield, Minnesota bank robbery.

Chambers, Lon—A gunfighting cowboy who was sent to stop the depredations of Billy the Kid's gang in Texas. Lon served as a Special Texas Ranger in Tascosa.

Champion, Nathan D.—A Montana cowman who was bold and speedy with the sixes, but died a cattle rustler in Wyoming.

Cherokee Bill—An Oklahoma half-breed outlaw who killed thirteen men before he was hanged.

Chiles, Bill—A member of the Cole Younger gang of outlaws.

Chilton, Fred—A Tascosa gun thrower, who died there with his boots on, his slayer unknown.

Chinn, G. K.—Sergeant of Texas Rangers. The non-coms of this outfit were sometimes limited in formal education, but they were uniformly superior in nerve and gun talent.

Clanton, Phineas—With Billy and Ike, were sons of an Arizona rancher who was dry-gulched. Phin and Billy were rated first class fighting men, but accused of cattle rustling.

Clanton, William—"Billy" was a brother of Phin, see above.

Clark, Hualpai—An Arizona scout, trailer and lawman. He killed the Apache Kid.

Clark, Tom—A Tascosa gambler and gunman who was killed in a shootout with Jim East.

Claybourn, William—"Billy" was a noted Arizona gunman who died at the hands of Buckskin Frank Leslie.

Clayton, Jep—One of Toyah, Texas' top gunmen.

Clements, Gipp—A brother of Manning, see below.

Clements, James—A brother of Manning, see below.

Clements, Joe—Also a brother of Manning, see below.

Clements, Manning—With his brothers, Gipp, James & Joe were leaders of a large clan of cousins who ranched together, drove to market together and fought together against the world. Wes Hardin was a member of the clan. All the Clements had a wide reputation, particularly Manning, who was considered equal to the best in the entire country in gun skill. Manning killed Joe and Dolph Shadden in a classic gunfight, but was himself killed in the same manner at a later date.

Cleveland, Jack—A Montana badman and bully was killed by Henry Plummer.

Clifton, Charles—A deadly gunman of the Dakotas.

Clifton, Daniel—"Dynamite Dick," a member of the Oklahoma Doolin gang.

Clum, John P.—A Tombstone, Arizona, editor and mayor. Clum was a colorful frontier fighter.

Coe, George—A New Mexican gunman, participated in the Lincoln County War of New Mexico.

Coe, Frank—A gambler and gunman, brother of George. Frank also fought in the Lincoln feud.

Coffee, Charles—A professional gunman from Texas, served as protection man and a trail driver for big cattle outfits.

Coffer, Dick—Sheriff of Hardeman County, Texas.

Coldwell, Neil—A captain of Texas Rangers.

Collier, Tom—Deputy sheriff to Wallace in Young County, Texas.

Collins, Henry—A brother of Joel, was an outlaw, also. He was killed by a posse in '78.

Collins, Joel—A Texas saloon keeper turned stage robber and desperado to recoup gambling losses, was killed resisting arrest following a $60,000 train holdup in Kansas.

Collins, John—A south Texas outlaw.

Collins, Williams—"Bill," another brother of Joel's, and a gunman in his own right.

Connell, Edward—A Texas Ranger, and later, a protection man for the XIT Ranch.

Connelly, Charles T.—A brave Marshal of Coffeyville. He was killed by the Daltons.

Connor, L. W.—Another of those ever-ready non-coms of the Texas Rangers.

Cook, James H.—A Texas man turned scout and lawman, operated in the northwest.

Cook, Thalis T.—The best rifle shot in the Texas Rangers, was also quite salty with the sixes. He became a peace officer of El Paso when his Ranger days were over.

Cook, William—"Bill" was the leader of a desperate gang of train robbers operating out of the Indian Territory. The Rangers got them while they were on a Texas raid.

Cooley, Scott—Trail driver, Texas Ranger, gunman, feudist and outlaw, precipitated the Mason County War by gunning two men.

Cooper, John—Mining camp bandit of Idaho and Montana.

Copeland, John—Feudist in the Lincoln trouble of New Mexico, was unlawfully "elected" sheriff during the disorder.

Corn, Lee—A Texas Ranger of the draw-and-shoot days.

Corwin, Dennis—Sheriff of Travis County, Texas.

Costello, Robert—A Deadwood gambler and gunman.

Courtright, James—Indian scout, Marshal of Fort Worth, Marshal of Lake Valley, New Mexico, and professional gambler, his gun was for hire. Rated one of the world's best professional gunmen, Luke Short outdrew him, and Jim died in Fort Worth.

Cox, William—"Will" was a DeWitt County feudist and badman.

Coy, Jacob—Gunman for Joe Foster's gambling emporium in San Antonio. Reputedly he was holding Ben Thompson's gun arm, when Ben and King Fisher were shot down.

Crane, James—"Jim," hardcase gunman around Tombstone, who was wanted for rustling, murder and stage robbery.

Cravens, Benjamin—A proddish outlaw who ranged from Texas to Kansas.

Crawford, Edward—Tough assistant marshal of Ellsworth and Abilene, Kansas, killed capable Cad Pierce only a month before his own death in a gunfight.

Crawford, Henry—A rough and tough Montana sheriff.

Crump, Silas B.—A Texas Ranger whose name appears many times in records of dangerous and critical situations.

Cruz, Florentino—"Indian Charley," a half-breed member of Curly Bill's gang in Arizona. He was killed by Wyatt Earp.

Culp, John—Texas protection man, trail driver and cowboy.

Cupps, John—Another dangerous and capable Texas Ranger. He served by the side of Si Crump.

Curry, George—"Flat Nose," a member of the Hole In the Wall gang, was killed in Utah while resisting arrest.

Curry, Kid—see Harvey Logan.

Curtis, Burt—A train robber who operated in New Mexico and Texas. He was captured by Tom Horn and Doc Shores.

D

Daniels, Benjamin—A famous gunfighter who operated all over the West, once served as Marshal of Dodge. He also served as a U. S. Marshal. President Teddy Roosevelt said Daniels was the bravest man he had ever known.

Dalton, Grattan—One of the brothers in the famous Dalton gang of bank robbers. He was killed in the Coffeyville raid.

Dalton, Robert—"Bob" was leader of the Dalton gang which had a long list of desperate raids to its discredit.

Dalton, Emmett—Another of the Dalton brothers. When Grat was shot down in Coffeyville, Emmett attempted to rescue him, which resulted in Emmett's capture.

Dalton, William—"Bill" joined the Doolin gang after the Dalton gang was broken. Bill died with his boots on.

Dalton, Frank—The fifth brother of that notorious family. Frank stayed on the side of the law. He became a deputy U. S. Marshal, and was killed in action.

Davidson, John—Oklahoma and Texas outlaw, reformed and became a peace officer of Wilbarger County, Texas.

Davis, George— New Mexican gunman, fought in the Lincoln County War.

Davis, Jack—A Texas cowboy who joined both Joel Collins' and Sam Bass' gangs of train robbers. He was not captured, and is reputed to have gone to South America.

Davis, Scott—Freighter, fighter, man-trailer and lawman in Arizona, Colorado, Wyoming and the Dakotas.

Day, James—A Texas Ranger who fought both Indians and outlaws.

Deal, J. D.—"Pony" was a Tombstone gunman and desperado of Curly Bill's gang.

Deaver, Joe—A Texas Ranger in the El Paso district.

Delaney, William—A member of the Heath gang of bandits, was hanged in Arizona.

Derrick, William—"Bill" was one of the star enlisted men of the Texas Rangers.

Devine, Netteville—Cowboy and posseman, trailed the Sam Bass gang.

Dibrell, C. M.—Was another ace of the Texas Rangers.

Dickson, George and Thomas—Brothers who were key members of the dread Hole In the Wall gang.

Dixon, Simpson—East Texan, who with Wes Hardin, killed two soldiers. He was shot to death by a posse.

Dixon, Thomas—"Tom" was a cousin of Wes Hardin and a member of his gang. Tom was hanged by a mob.

Dixon, Bud—Like his brother Tom, was a member of Wes Hardin's gang. Bud and Wes killed sheriff Charley Webb. Bud was also hanged.

Dobbs, Kid—Deputy sheriff in Tascosa.

Dolan, Pat—Captain of the Texas Rangers.

Donnelly, Edward—"Ed," was a Texas Ranger in the finest tradition.

Donnelly, Nick—Another Ranger and a fine fighting man.

Doolin, William—"Bill" was leader of a desperate gang of robbers in the Indian Territory. All of the Doolin gang were killed. Bill was killed by Marshal Heck Thomas.

Dorsey, W. G.—A fighting cowman who enlisted against Billy the Kid's gang.

Dosier, Thomas—A Deadwood gunman of wide repute.

Dowd, Daniel—A member of the dread Heath gang in Arizona. He was hanged.

Driscoll, William—"Bill" was a Kansas killer with five credits. He practiced continually with his .45, was surly, treacherous and very dangerous.

Dublin, Dell—A member of the Kimble County gang of outlaws. He and his brother Role were captured by the Rangers.

Dublin, Richard—"Dick" was also a member of the Kimble County gang, had a price on his head when he was killed by Ranger Jim Gillett.

Dublin, Role—Brother of Dell and also a member of the Kimble County gang. Was badly wounded during a shootout with Rangers.

Duesha, Charles—A famous gunman who was imported for duty on the Graham side during the Tewksbury feud.

Duffield, Milton—U. S. Marshal, gambler, gunfighter, was active in California and Arizona. Credited with thirteen notches, was killed in Tombstone. He was said to be the only man in the west nervy enough to wear a plug hat!

Duncan, Jack—A Special Texas Ranger on the trail of Wes Hardin.

Dunlap, John—"Three Fingered Jack," was the leader of an Arizona train robber gang.

Durbin, Walter—A Texas cowman who was especially handy with the sixes.

Durham, George—A Georgian serving in the Texas Rangers. His nonchalant smoking of cigarettes during the heat of a gun battle excited the envy of his comrades.

Durham, Paul—A Texas Ranger on border service.

E

Eaker, J. P.—A fighting New Mexican who tangled with Billy the Kid.

Earp, James—Brother of the famous Wyatt, was a saloon keeper and deputy peace officer. After a fine record in Kansas the brothers became embroiled in some killings in Arizona which forced their departure from that state. They went to Colorado and thence to California.

Earp, Morgan—Another brother of Wyatt's. He was killed at Tombstone in Bob Hatch's pool hall.

Earp, Virgil—Another of the brothers, was Marshal of Tombstone and a hard-eyed fighting man.

Earp, Warren—Another brother of this gunman family. Warren was a gambler by trade. He was killed by Burt Alvord, the train robber.

Earp, Wyatt—The most notorious of the family, and their moral leader. Wyatt made a wonderful record in Kansas which was largely dissipated in Tombstone, Arizona. Wyatt was a teamster, peace officer and gambler.

East, James H.—A protection man, a posseman against Billy the Kid. Jim made a name in the Panhandle and was elected sheriff of Oldham County.

Edmundson, J. F.—A member of the noted Cole Younger gang.

Edwards, Buck—A member of Billy the Kid's gang.

Edwards, Forest—Wore the guns of the Texas Rangers.

Egan, W. F.—"Dad," sheriff of Denton County, Texas, and a rough, tough old lawman.

Ellis, Jack—An American who joined Mexican bandits terrorizing the border. He was killed by Rangers in 1875.

Emory, Charles—A fighting cowboy from the Panhandle.

Emory, Thomas—A protection man for Littlefield, and one of the gunmen sent after Billy the Kid.

Evans, Daniel—Member of Belle Starr's gang. Was hanged.

Evans, Jesse—Childhood friend of Billy the Kid in Silver City where they rode and rustled together to manhood. They fought on opposite sides in the Lincoln War, but later resumed friendship. Jesse was considered the best pistol shot in New Mexico, but was killed while robbing a lowly peddler.

Everheart, W. C.—Was sheriff of Grayson County, Texas.

F

Fallon, "Rattlesnake Jake"—A Montana rustler and gunman who was killed in Lewiston.

Fetherstun, John—One of the bravest and ablest of Montana officers.

Fisher, King—A fabulous outlaw chieftain with twenty-six credits who controlled seven counties with a private army of bravos. He reformed and became a peace officer, but was killed with Ben Thompson, in San Antonio.

Fitch, James—"Jim" was a Texas Ranger serving in the North Texas cattle country.

Flannery, Ike—A member of Peyton Jones' gang of train robbers.

Forbes, Charles—A member of Jesse James' gang, died by his own hand.

Forbes, Charles—A California gambler and gunman who served as court clerk in Virginia City by day, but rode with Henry Plummer's gang of bandits by night.

Ford, John Salmon—"Rip" was captain of Texas Rangers, an officer in the Mexican War, commanded the Confederates in the last battle of the Civil War and was one of the most famous pistol men of Texas. He and McNelly owned the first Colt revolvers sent to Texas.

Ford, Robert—A member of Jesse James' gang, killed Jesse for the reward. Bob was killed in Colorado.

Foster, Joe—Nervy little gambler in old San Antone, was involved in the killings of Ben Thompson and King Fisher.

Fox, J. M.—A Montana sheriff who rode herd on some wild mining camps. He handled the deadliest gunmen with calmness and confidence.

Frazer, Bud—Served as sheriff in both Reeves and Pecos counties of Texas, was killed by Jim Miller, the outlaw.

French, James—A member of the Belle Starr gang in the Indian Territory and Dallas, Texas. Was killed while resisting arrest.

French, James—One of Billy the Kid's gunmen in the Lincoln County War.

Friar, Arthur—With his brother, Jube, were Texas outlaws. Both were killed by Rangers.

Friar, Jube—Brother of Arthur, see above.

G

Gabriel, Peter—Former sheriff of Pinal County, Arizona, killed that unusual gunman, Joe Phy, in as savage a gunfight as the West ever witnessed.

Gallagher, Jack—One of the old masters of gunplay, served as an officer in Virginia City, but engaged in outlawry on the side.

Gallagher, John—"Bittercreek," gained a dozen notches in the northwest, but fell before Texas' John Slaughter in an Arizona gunfight.

Garfias, Henry—An Arizona sheriff who enjoyed a big reputation.

Garrett, Pat—Sheriff of Lincoln County, New Mexico, protection man, captain of Texas Rangers, won fame for killing Billy the Kid.

Gatlin, William—"Bill," was a Tascosa cowboy of the hardcase crowd.

Gerren, Thomas—A deputy sheriff of Denton County, Texas, who was accused of being in league with Sam Bass, the train robber.

Gholston, Sam—A big, dark and dangerous Texas two-gun man.

Gildea, A. M.—"Gus," was a scout, Texas Ranger and U. S. Deputy Marshal.

Gillespie, Tom—A Texas Ranger who achieved especial distinction.

Gillett, James B.—As Sergeant of Texas Rangers served under Reynolds, Coldwell and Baylor. The fame he won enabled him to become Marshal of El Paso.

Gladden, George—A cowboy gunman of Mason, Texas, was imprisoned for his part in the Mason County War.

Glass, W. A.—A Texas Ranger under Cap Stevens.

Good, John—a Texas trail driver who was a ringleader in shooting up the Kansas railheads. Wyatt Earp quieted him. John said, "Sure, I only want fun, and killing the Marshal is serious." But John could be serious when more than fun was involved.

Goodin, Warren—A Jefferson, Texas, killer who was stopped by the Rangers.

Gordon, James A.—A mining engineer who turned killer. He operated in Colorado and Oklahoma until he was hanged.

Gosling, Harold—A U. S. Marshal serving in Texas.

Graham, Sam—A Texas Ranger who was a better gunman than any outlaw he met.

Grant, Joe—A Texas badman with several notches, who overmatched himself in New Mexico. Billy the Kid killed him.

Graves, William—"Whiskey Bill," was a Virginia City desperado.

Gray, John—A Texas killer who was taken in by the Rangers.

Green, Charles—Gunfighting east Texan from Henderson.

Green, James—A Texas Ranger who fought with Bill McDonald and J. M. Brittian against the cream of Oklahoma Territory outlaws.

Greenwood, Bill—A member of Jesse James' outlaw band.

Griffin, Felix—A member of Belle Starr's gang. He died with his boots on.

Griffin, Thomas—A Texas Ranger schooled in gunfighting by the great John Hughes.

Griner, Samuel—A gunman from Uvalde, where all draws were fast.

Grounds, Billy—An Arizona rustler and gunman who was wanted for robbery and murder. He was killed by a posse.

Gunn, Charles S.—A Texas Ranger who migrated to Wyoming and became a famous law officer there. He was killed by Dan Bogan.

H

Hainer, Al—Partner of Butch Cassidy, leader of the "Wild Bunch," in his early escapades.

Hale, John—Manager of the Manning ranch near El Paso, and possessor of several credits. Was killed by Dallas Stoudenmire.

Haley, H. H.—A peace officer of Grayson County, Texas.

Hall, George—Sergeant of Texas Rangers, who won a commission in the field and reached a captain's rank.

Hall, Leigh—"Lee," Texas Ranger, soldier, stock detective, train guard and professional fighter, served against Billy the Kid, broke up the Taylor-Sutton Feud and served notably otherwise.

Hall, Richard—"Dick," brother of the famous Lee, and also a gunman.

Halsey, William S.—Sheriff of Nueces County, Texas.

Hamilton, Jack—Sheriff of Bandera County, Texas.

Hanks, O. Camella—A colorful member of the Hole in the Wall gang. Was killed in San Antonio while resisting arrest.

Hanrahan, James—Scout, hunter and gunman of Kansas, Nebraska, Wyoming and the Dakotas.

Hardin, Joe—Brother of Wes, see below, was hanged by a mob.

Hardin, John Wesley—The master gunman of them all, is credited with forty notches in single combat. His credits are probably magnified but his accountable victims number more than those of any other. After serving a long prison term, he emerged a has-been and was killed by John Selman in El Paso.

Hardwick, Tom—One of the better gun artists of Deadwood.

Hardy, S. N.—Texas Ranger and outlaw hunter.

Harkness, J. C. B.—Sheriff of Frio County, Texas.

Harold, George—Indian scout and Texas Ranger on the far western frontier.

Harris, Jack—A one-armed gambler and gunman of San Antonio. Was killed by Ben Thompson.

Harris, W. H.—A noted gunfighter who served as Marshal of Dodge.

Harrell, George—Texas Ranger who killed Sam Bass in Round Rock.

Harrison, Charles—A Colorado saloon owner and gun-fighter who was rated the quickest draw in the West. His accuracy did not match his speed, and Jim Levy killed him in a middle-of-the-street shootout.

Harrison, Dick—A Texas Ranger who saw protracted service against the outlaws.

Harwell, Jack—Another Texas Ranger of the Bill McDonald school.

Hawkins, James—A tough sergeant of Texas Rangers.

Hays, John Coffee—"Jack," was probably the first man in Texas to own a Colt revolver. He was a captain of Texas Rangers, colonel in the Mexican War, and later, the reigning pistoleer of California.

Head, Harry—A hardcase around Tombstone who was accused of stage robbery. He ran with the Clantons.

Head, Richard—"Dick," one of the Texas Ranger aces under Baylor.

Heath, John—Leader of a gang of rustlers and bandits in Arizona.

Heister, Frank—A DeWitt County, Texas, gunman who fought in the Taylor-Sutton Feud.

Heffridge, Bill—Member of the Joel Collins gang of train robbers. Was killed resisting arrest.

Helm, Boone—A Virginia City outlaw and gunman.

Helms, Jack—Marshal of rugged Cuero, sheriff of DeWitt County and deputy U. S. Marshal, was killed by Wes Hardin.

Herndon, Albert—A member of the Sam Bass gang, was captured by Texas Rangers.

Henry, Dutch—The most noted and desperate outlaw of Kansas, was shot six times by a posse, recovered and reformed.

Hickok, James Butler—"Wild Bill," the most publicized of

all gunfighters although his actual record was relatively un-impressive. As he possessed all the qualifications essential to the gunfighter, he was feared and respected as Marshal of Abilene, Kansas. He was killed by a drunken bum, Jack McCall, who shot Hickok in the back during a Deadwood poker game.

Hicks, Milton—Arizonian gunman and desperado.

Hicks, William—Brother of Milton. Both of them rode with Ringo's gang.

Higgins, John Pinckney—Rancher, trail driver, stock detective and feudist, was a relentless killer with twenty credits. He generally was on the side of the law.

Hill, Frank—A Texas Ranger in Hughes' hot outfit.

Hill, Gail—A professional gunfighter in the Deadwood country, was deputy sheriff, stage guard, train guard and was involved in many bloody battles.

Hill, Joe—An outlaw and one of Arizona's tough gunmen.

Hill, Thomas—A New Mexican desperado, fought in the Lincoln County War, and later was killed with his own rifle while robbing a peddler's wagon.

Hillman, Bill—A talented gunman, made the Northwest mining camps.

Hindman, George—A peace officer in Lincoln County, New Mexico, became involved in that war and was killed by the Kid's gang.

Hinds, Benjamin—A Texas desperado and gambler.

Hogue, Edward—Assistant Marshal of both Abilene and Ellsworth, Kansas, when those were cattle-railroad boom towns.

Holcomb, John—Dismissed from the Texas Rangers for his over-inclination to fight, turned outlaw in New Mexico. Returning to Texas, he was captured by Rangers, but broke jail only to be killed while rustling cattle.

Holliday, John H.—"Doc," a consumptive dentist who went to Dallas for his health, and there turned gambler and gunfighter. Under the influence of the Earps, he cut a wide swath through Arizona until all were forced out of that state. Doc died in Colorado.

Horn, Thomas—Indian scout, army officer, stock detective, deputy sheriff and killer, operated over the entire west. He was hanged for murder.

Horner, Joe—The leader of a band of Texas stage robbers.

Horrell, Benjamin—One of six brothers who became involved in a cattle war in Lampasas, Texas. At length, they moved their ranch to New Mexico, but started a war there that is reputed to have cost fifty lives. Ben was killed in Lincoln, where the Horrells shot up the town, killing three men.

Horrell, John—Along with his brothers, after shooting up two towns in New Mexico and killing seven men, returned to Lampasas, Texas.

Horrell, Mart—With his brother Tom, were leaders of the Horrell faction. On returning to Lampasas, they again became involved in violence. A mob hanged Mart and Tom.

Horrell, Merritt—Killed by Pink Higgins in Jerry Scott's saloon.

Horrell, Thomas—Leader of the Horrells in their fierce war against Pink Higgins and his cohorts.

Horrell, William—"Bill," the sixth of the deadly Horrell brothers.

Howard, James—A member of the Heath gang of Arizona, was hanged with four companions in Cochise County.

Howie, Neil—A Montana lawman who matched the outlaw killers with gun magic.

Hudgens, John—Brother of William, both were gunmen in New Mexico and participated in the fight against Billy the Kid.

Hudgens, William—Brother of John, see above.

Hughes, George—"Hog," was one of the colorful members of the Rangers.

Hughes, James—Arizona desperado active in Tombstone.

Hughes, John R.—Famous captain of the famous Company D, Texas Rangers.

Hughes, Lowe—Another ace of the Texas Rangers, sometimes confused with John.

Hume, James—Chief protection man for the Wells Fargo Express Company.

Hunt, Zwing—An Arizona rustler who was killed by Indians while evading a posse.

Hunter, Thomas—Wyoming cowboy, was no killer but had the nerve and mechanical skill to match the best.

Hunter, William—A Montana bandit who ran with Henry Plummer's crew.

I

Ives, George—A Montana road agent and henchman of Henry Plummer. He was hanged for murder.

J

Jackman, S. D.—A U. S. Marshal of the Western District of Texas.

Jackman, W. T.—Sheriff of Hays County, Texas.

Jackson, Frank—"Blocky," was a member of the Sam Bass gang who won the admiration of the Texas Rangers by his bravery.

Jackson, Teton—Of Jackson's Hole, was the bold leader of a Wyoming gang of rustlers. He was killed while escaping his captors.

Jacobs, William—An Arizona gunman who was ambushed and killed during the Tonto Basin War.

James, Franklin Alexander—"Frank," was a brother of Jesse and a member of the most notorious gang. He was pardoned by Governor Crittenden of Texas.

James, Jesse Woodson—"Dingus," the most famous outlaw of the West, headed a desperate gang of desperados until he was killed by Bob Ford, a member of the gang.

Jennings, Al—An Oklahoma train robber credited with leading the dread Jennings gang. Little Dick West may have been the actual leader. Al was courageous and an ace with weapons, but vicious as a mad wolf.

Jennings, Frank—Brother of Al, and also a member of that gang.

Jennings, N. A.—A Philadelphia journalist who went to Texas to learn sixshooterology. After serving in the Texas Rangers, he returned east to write of his experiences.

Johnson, Arkansas—The trusted lieutenant of Sam Bass. He was killed by June Peak and his Rangers in the Salt Creek Fight.

Johnson, Edward W.—Deputy U. S. Marshal who lost one hand in a gunfight and then became very proficient with his other hand.

Johnson, Jack—"Turkey Creek," was one of the most redoubtable pistol men of the Dakotas.

Johnson, William—"Bill," deputy sheriff of Young County, Texas, and first Marshal of El Paso. He was killed by Dallas Stoudenmire.

Johnson, William—"Rattlesnake Bill," a rustler and bandit of Cochise County, Arizona.

Jones, Frank—Captain of Texas Rangers.

Jones, John B.—Major of Texas Rangers, and one of that body's immortals. This able leader was killed on duty.

Jones, Peyton—Ex-guerrilla and outlaw leader, was one of the first bank robbers, having inaugurated this type of crime before the James gang took it up.

Jones, Walter—Deputy Marshal of El Paso under the noted Stoudenmire.

K

Kane, Neil—A Texas trail driver who abandoned cattle for Kansas gambling and gunthrowing.

Karl, William—"Buckskin Bill," notorious Denver gunman.

Kean, Jack—A member of the Cole Younger gang.

Kelly, Charles—A gunman of New Mexico who fought the Kid's gang.

Kelly, Daniel—An Arizona outlaw and member of the Heath gang. He was hanged by Sheriff Ward of Cochise County.

Kennedy, Young—A Texas rider and Dodge gunman, was slain by a posse.

Kerry, Hobbs—A member of the Jesse James gang of train robbers, was imprisoned.

Ketchum, Jack—"Black Jack," leader of a New Mexican outlaw gang, was hanged for robbing a train in New Mexico.

Ketchum, Samuel—Arizona desperado and killer, was a brother of Black Jack.

Ketchum, Thomas—Another brother of Black Jack, who was slain in New Mexico.

Ketchum, William—Another brother of Black Jack, who was killed by a sheriff's posse.

Killeen, Mike—A Tombstone gunman who was outdrawn and killed by Buckskin Frank Leslie.

Kilpatrick, Ben—A member of the Wild Bunch, was killed during a train robbery.

Kilpatrick, George—A member of Ketchum's gang, was killed in a train robbery at Folsom, New Mexico.

Kimbrell, George—As sheriff of Lincoln County, New Mexico, captured and jailed Billy the Kid but the Kid escaped.

Kimbrough, William—Texas Ranger and buddy of those masterful Maltimores.

King, Edward—Appointed Special Texas Ranger at Tascosa, was a cowboy and trail driver, and especially fast with the sixes.

King, Luther—An Arizona outlaw wanted for rustling, murder and stage robbery.

King, Roger—A professional gunman of Tombstone.

Kinney, John—A hard drinking, hard shooting ex-soldier who lived in Mexico and led a murderous gang of border bandits.

Kirchner, Karl—Texas Ranger who fought outlaws and feudists.

Kitchen, Peter—An Arizona rancher, Indian fighter and gunman.

Knight, George A.—The U. S. Marshal in Dallas who was charged with cleaning up the southern district of Oklahoma Territory.

Krimpkau, Augustus—"Gus," Texas Ranger who was killed by the fast-drawing Johnny Hale.

L

La Fors, Joe—Deputy U. S. Marshal in Wyoming.

Lamb, Frank—A Wyoming stagecoach robber and hardcase killer.

Lang, John—One of Tascosa's slick gunmen who were appointed Special Texas Rangers.

Lant, David—A Wyoming gunman and member of the Wild Bunch.

Lankford, Ace—A member of the Kimble County gang.

Larn, John—Simultaneously cattle rustler and sheriff of Shackelford County, Texas. Killed in his jail cell by a mob while awaiting hanging.

Lathrop, George—"Big Nosed," a Texas killer with a long string of credits, many of them plain murders. He had a $5,000 price on his head in Wyoming. Bob Rankin captured him and he was lynched at Rawlins.

Lawson, Pat—A professional gunman of Wyoming, served as stock inspector and railroad guard.

Lay, Elza—Alias Bob McGinnis, was a member of Black Jack Ketchum's gang. Lay served twenty years for train robbery.

Ledbetter, Bud—Famous Oklahoma peace officer who was both game and a gunman.

Lee, Robert—"Bob," a member of the Hole in the Wall Gang. Aerved a long prison term for train robbery.

Leigh, Fred—One of the better pistol shots of Texas, was killed by Cape Willingham in Tascosa.

Leonard, Billy—A Tombstone gunfighter wanted for murder and stage robbery. He was a friend of Doc Holliday.

Leslie, "Buckskin Frank"—A Tombstone bartender and probably the most efficient gunfighter in Arizona history. Reputed to have killed more than a dozen men in single combat, Frank went to prison for murdering a woman.

Levy, James—"Jim," was rated among the top twenty gunmen of the entire west. Ranged from Arizona to Wyoming.

Lewis, Del—Sheriff of Cochise County, Arizona.

Lewis, James—A south Texas cattle rustler and badman.

Lewis, Kid—An Oklahoma bank robber and member of the Beckham gang. He was lynched for murder.

Ligon, David—A distinguished Texas Ranger.

Liddel, Richard—"Little Dick," a member of the Jesse James gang.

Linn, Charles N.—A notorious El Paso gunman who was killed by an amateur.

Loftus, Hill—A member of the Beckham gang of Oklahoma bank robbers.

Logan, Harvey—"Kid Curry," with Butch Cassidy, led the dreaded Hole in the Wall Gang, also called the Wild Bunch, over Wyoming, Montana, Nevada, Utah, Idaho, Oklahoma, Texas and New Mexico. He committed suicide when cornered by a posse.

Logan, John—Brother of Harvey, and a member of the gang, was killed in a gunfight.

Logan, Lonny—A second brother of Harvey, also a member of the gang. He was killed resisting arrest.

Long, Dock—A Texas Ranger serving on border details.

Long, Ira—Captain of Texas Rangers who won a special commendation for his fighting qualities.

Longabaugh, Harry—"The Sundance Kid," a member of the Hole in the Wall Gang, took his own life to avoid arrest.

Longley, William P.—"Bill," notorious Texas gunman and outlaw who ranged the entire West, reputedly killing thirty-two men before being hanged at Giddings, Texas, in 1878.

Love, Harry—A California pistol man with a West-wide reputation.

Loving, Frank—Texas trail driver, professional gambler and cool gunfighter, participated in many gunfights. His most notable victim was Levi Richardson.

Lowe, "Rowdy Joe"—A honky-tonk operator and gunman who made the Kansas boomtowns.

Loyd, George—Corporal of Texas Rangers and an outstanding peace officer.

Lucy, James—Cowboy and Texas Ranger, was a cool and quick weapons man.

Lyle, Edward—A member of Curly Bill's gang in Arizona.

Lyle, John—A brother of Ed, and also an outlaw.

Lynch, Mike—One of the few oldsters in the Texas Rangers, was crafty and his wide experience rendered him very valuable.

Lyons, Hayes—A Virginia City badman and robber.

M

Maben, H.—A Texas Ranger and friend of Mac McMurray.

Mabry, Seth—Texas cattleman and consort of the fast set, from Rio to Kansas.

Madsen, Chris—Distinguished Oklahoma peace officer, liquidated many outlaws such as Tulsa Jack. Chris, Heck Thomas and Billy Tilghman were called the "Three Guardsmen."

Maley, John—Tough gunman who ranged New Mexico and the Texas Panhandle.

Maltimore, Henry—With his brother Kit, made gun history with the Texas Rangers.

Maltimore, Kit—A veteran Texas Ranger and brother of the noted Henry.

Marlow, Alfred—With his brothers, George, Charles, Lewellyn and Boone, were Texas outlaws. While being transferred from one jail to another, they were attacked by a mob and Alf and Lewellyn (called Ep), were killed. Obtaining guns from their guards, the remaining brothers shot five of their assailants.

Marlow, Boone—See Alfred Marlow. Boone killed Marion D. Wallace, a Texas sheriff, and a good one.

Marlow, Charles—see above.

Marlow, George—see above.

Marlow, Lewellyn—"Ep," see above.

Marshall, James—"Jim," an ex-officer of the law from Cripple Creek who was extremely fast and accurate. He reputedly ran Bat Masterson out of Denver.

Martin, Jack—"Society Jack," a star Texas Ranger and friend of Wild Bill Hickok, Wyatt Earp and Jack Gallagher.

Martin, James—A cocky cowboy from Helena, Texas, was killed in Newton, Kansas.

Mason, Barney—Brother-in-law of Pat Garrett, also was a gunman and man-trailer. Barney was prominent around Tascosa.

Mason, Jim Pope—A longriding Texas outlaw.

Mast, Milton—Sheriff of Nacogdoches County, Texas, and one of the most famous peace officers of the state, helped capture Bill Longley.

Masterson, Edward—Younger brother of the famous Bat, was killed by Al Walker and Jack Wagner.

Masterson, William Barclay—"Bat." Hunter, scout, trader, gambler, sheriff of Ford County, Kansas, deputy U. S. Marshal and Marshal of Dodge, rated six tough credits.

Mathers, David—"Mysterious Dave," frontier gunman, one-time Marshal of Dodge, once killed four men in one night.

Mathews, Billy—A gunman of New Mexico who fought in the Lincoln War.

Mathews, John Pierce—Known as John Pierce rather than Mathews, was a Louisiana killer before becoming sheriff of Childress County, Texas. He was killed by Bill McDonald in a fierce gunfight.

May, Boone—A famous Deadwood peace officer.

McCampbell, Joe—The leader of a rustler band at Carrizo Springs. Texas Rangers captured the entire gang.

McCarthy, Timothy—A Texas Ranger. Was killed on duty.

McCarty, Fred—A Utah bank and train robber, and son of Bill McCarty.

McCarty, George—Brother of Bill and Tom, and member of the same Utah gang of robbers.

McCarty, Thomas—Leader of that gang of outlaws in Utah known as the McCarty Gang.

McCarty, William—"Bill," brother of Tom and George and father of Fred, all members of the same gang.

McCauley, W. J.—Sergeant of Texas Rangers, and nephew of Bill McDonald, received excellent training in the art of draw-and-shoot.

McCleed, Samuel—"Black Sam," a Wyoming killer and outlaw, died in a trail-camp gunfight, killed by Tom Barrett.

McClure, Robert—"Bob," a Texas Ranger noted for action against the Cook-Skeeter gang.

McCoy, Arthur—An outlaw who was part-time member of the Jesse James gang.

McCoy, Bill—The name Dan Bogan wore in Wyoming.

McCullar, Henry—A Tascosa hardcase, was killed by Mexican Frank.

McDaniels, Bud—A member of the Younger gang who was killed while resisting arrest.

McDaniels, Tomlinson—Brother of Bud, and a member of the same gang, was killed during a holdup.

McDonald, William—"Bill," the most famous of all Texas Rangers, was the nemesis of literally hundreds of outlaws.

McGee, Henry W.—An outstanding Texas Ranger, was made sergeant, and later became Marshal of Waco.

McGuire, Andrew—"Andy," a member of the Jesse James gang, was captured and hanged.

McIntire, James—A Texas Panhandle gunman, former Texas Ranger and protection man, went to New Mexico with Jim Courtright to fight homesteaders for large cattle interests.

McKay, Bill—The most handsome and dashing of Texas Rangers.

McKidrict, Joe—A fine Texas Ranger who died at the hands of a drunken comrade.

McKinney, C. B.—Texas Ranger, cattleman and sheriff of La Salle County, Texas.

McKinney, T. P.—"Tip," deputy sheriff of Lincoln County, New Mexico.

McKowen, Johnson—An associate of Blasting Bill Longley, never ran from trouble.

McLean, Frank—Deputy marshal of Dodge under Wyatt Earp.

McLowry, Frank—With his brother, Tom, sided with the Clantons against the Earps. In a Tombstone battle, the Earps and Doc Holliday killed both McLowry boys and two of the Clantons.

McLowry, Thomas—Brother of Frank, see above.

McMahan, Frank—Deputy U. S. Marshal in El Paso, when that town was running with its bit in its teeth.

McMasters, Sherman—Like Doc Holliday, was an outlaw gunman who sometimes fought on the side of the law through a peculiar friendship with Wyatt Earp.

McMurray, Frank—An outlaw killer and the leader of a desperate rustler gang of Oklahoma Territory.

McMurray, S. A.—Captain of Texas Rangers, commanded Company B. Mac rose from the ranks, and what better praise?

McNab, Frank—A vicious killer in New Mexico's Lincoln War. He was killed by Sheriff Peppin's posse.

McNelly, John—A Texas Ranger and the nephew of the immortal L. H. McNelly.

McNelly, L. H.—Captain of Texas Rangers, is called the first great captain, as he set the pattern for those following him. His outstanding feats are legion, yet he died in 1877, when only thirty-three.

Mead, Thomas—A Texas Ranger in that fast shooting Company D.

Meador, William—"Bill," City Marshal of Cuero, Texas, killed a number of men, and it has been whispered that not all were justified.

Meggeson, Thomas—Professional gunman of Wyoming, served as railroad guard, stock detective and protection man.

Meyers, Albert—A Philadelphian turned Texan who was potentially a stingaree until a woman tamed him.

Meyers, Charles—A fine peace officer who helped Bill McDonald break the Sand Creek gang.

Middleton, John—A New Mexican gunman who was shot by Buckskin Roberts.

Middaugh, W. H.—A brilliant officer of the law in Denver, when that city was a raw mining town. He was killed in an ambush.

Miller, Clell—A colorful old outlaw of the early West, often raided with the Jesse James gang.

Miller, Clem—A member of the Younger gang, was killed following a bank robbery.

Miller, James—Texas and New Mexican gunman, was part-time lawman, part-time outlaw, but full-time killer.

Milton, Jeff—Texas Ranger, Deputy U. S. Marshal, and El Paso chief of police. His famous quote, "I never killed a man who didn't need killing."

Mitchell, A. T.—Texas trail driver and cattleman.

Mitchell, R. A.—One of Pink Higgins' cowmen, and a handy man with the irons.

Monroe, Thomas—A Texas cowboy who carried the .44 gospel into Kansas.

Moon, James—An outlaw who headed a sixteen-man gang of desperados near Fort Ewall, Texas.

Moore, Morris—A peace officer of Travis County, Texas.

Moore, M. F.—Lieutenant of Texas Rangers.

Moore, W. C.—"Outlaw Bill," ran the LX outfit in the Panhandle when life was a constant battle with rustlers.

Morco, John—"Happy Jack," of California, assistant marshal of Ellsworth, Kansas, boasted a dozen notches when killed by Charley Brown.

Morgan, Billy—A New Mexican outlaw who raided Texas with the Baker gang. He was captured by Ranger Jim Gillett and imprisoned.

Morris, Harvey—One of Billy the Kid's gunmen in the Lincoln County War. He was killed trying to escape a surrounded house.

Morrison, Edward—A Texas cowboy who became a professional gunman.

Morton, Billy—A New Mexican gunman who was shot by Billy the Kid, for the murder of Tunstall.

Mossby, John—A New Mexican fireball who fought the Kid and his gang.

Mossman, Burton C.—Organized the Arizona State Ranger Force. He broke the Pete Smith gang, killed Salivaras in a gunfight and captured the deadly Chacon.

Mourland, Milliard—One of the stars of the Texas Rangers.

Moyer, Ace—Gunman and desperado who, with his brother, Con, was hanged by Wyoming vigilantes.

Moyer, Conrad—Saloon owner, thug and gunman. Brother of Ace Moyer. Was hanged in Wyoming.

Mulqueen, Thomas—Was considered one of the most outstanding pistol men of the Dakotas.

Murphy, James—Member of the Sam Bass gang of train robbers, who, to secure the release of his father, betrayed his comrades to their death. Murphy killed himself the following year.

Murry, "Plunk"—A laughing, fighting Texas Ranger.

N

Neagle, David—A deputy sheriff of Cochise County, Arizona, became Marshal of Tombstone.

Neil, Edgar—Texas Ranger under Bill McDonald, and later the sheriff of boisterous San Saba County, Texas.

Nevill, Charles L.—One of the stars of the Texas Rangers, rose from the ranks to become a captain. Later he was sheriff of Presidio County.

Newcomb, George—"Bitter Creek," was a member of the Doolin gang. He died resisting arrest.

Nixon, T. C.—Marshal of boomtown Dodge, Kansas.

Norton, J. W.—"Brocky Jack," a famous gunfighter, and Marshal of Ellsworth, Kansas.

Norwood, Edward—A Texas and New Mexican gunman.

O

Oakes, George—A scout and gunfighter who achieved fame on the frontier.

O'Day, Thomas—"Peep," a member of the Hole in the Wall Gang.

O'Folliard, Thomas—A Texas cowboy who joined Billy the Kid's gang. His bravery won the plaudits of friend and foe. He was killed by a posse.

Ogg, William—"Billy," a noted gunfighter of the early northwest mining camps.

Oglesby, James—Texas cowman, trail driver and gunslick.

Oglesby, T. L.—A sergeant of Texas Rangers who won a commission in the field.

O'Keefe, Thomas—A notorious gunman of Montana and Wyoming.

Olive, John T.—"Jack," sheriff of Williamson County, Texas, was cool and deadly.

Ollinger, Robert—"Bob," a New Mexican two-gunman who participated in the Lincoln War. While serving as jailer of the Kid, Billy killed Bob with a shotgun and escaped.

O'Neil, William—"Bucky," one of the most colorful peace officers of Arizona, was killed in action in the Cuban war.

Orell, George—Texas Ranger who saw service with George Hall.

O'Schaughnessy, Joseph—a U. S. Marshal serving in Texas.

Outlaw, Bass—Made one of the few blots on the record of the Texas Rangers. Bass was a sergeant who was dismissed for drunkenness, but was reinstated after satisfactorily serving a term as deputy U. S. Marshal. But he resumed his excessive drinking. Bass was a marvel with a gun and a fine man when sober, but mean and quarrelsome when drunk. After killing a comrade while "likkered up," he was killed by John Selman in El Paso.

Owen, William—"Bill," a Montana rustler and gunfighter.

Owens, John—A Wyoming peace officer, gambler and Indian fighter, had a dangerous reputation over the entire West.

Owens, Perry—An Arizona sheriff and westerner of the old school.

Owens, Peter—Texas cowman, soldier and trail driver, was killed in a trail fight.

Owens, Thomas—A desperate Kansas outlaw.

Oyster, John—One of the most respected of the Deadwood gunslicks.

P

Paddock, Richard—"Dick," a Virginia City gunman.

Pannell, Dudley—A wild rooter-tooter of old Tascosa.

Parker, George Leroy—"Butch Cassidy," co-leader with Harvey Logan of the Wild Bunch, a desperate gang of outlaws. Butch killed himself to avoid arrest, as did two other members of this gang.

Parker, John—A Texas Ranger who was as fast as any.

Parrotte, "Big Nosed George"—Leader of a Deadwood gang of stage robbers.

Patterson, Frank—An Arizona outlaw and Tombstone gunman.

Paul, Robert—"Bob," shotgun guard, deputy sheriff of Cochise County, Arizona, sheriff of Pima County, and Deputy U. S. Marshal in Arizona.

Peak, Junius—"June," Captain of Texas Rangers and the slayer of Arkansas Johnson.

Peck, Pete—Texas gunfighter and trail driver.

Peel, Langford—"Farmer," was a particularly poisonous killer who ranged Nevada, Colorado, Oklahoma and Montana. He was killed in the latter state.

Peppin, George W.—"Dad," was appointed sheriff of Lincoln County, New Mexico, during the famous feud. He participated in an era of violence.

Perkins, Jack—Texas cowboy and killer with several credits.

Perry, Albert E.—Sergeant of Texas Rangers serving in the Panhandle.

Perry, Ollie—Texas Ranger, and later, a peace officer in San Saba County, Texas.

Peshaur, George—A professional gunfighter from Texas who sided Ben Thompson during the Kansas booms.

Peterson, Len—A Texas Ranger who turned to cattle rustling in New Mexico. He joined Frank Stevenson's gang.

Phelps, Burton—A shy and deceptively green-appearing youth who could outdraw anyone he met. He avoided the limelight, but his gun fame spread, nevertheless. Burt's friend betrayed him to his death at the hands of Bill Driscoll.

Phy, Joe—An unusual gunman. He neither drank nor smoked, a fact which spread his fame over the West almost as rapidly as did his gun skill.

Pickett, Thomas—A member of Billy the Kid's gang of outlaws.

Pierce, Cad—Trail driving Texan who turned gunfighter in Kansas. He was killed by Ed Crawford.

Pierce, Charles—A member of the Doolin gang of desperados, was killed while resisting arrest.

Pierce, Elliot—"Doc," a Deadwood undertaker and friend of Wild Bill Hickok.

Pierce, John—See Mathews, John Pierce.

Pierce, L. C.—Deputy sheriff to Jim East in Oldham County, Texas, and one of the finest peace officers.

Pierce, Shanghai—Six feet and four inches of scrapping cattleman, was a northerner who fought in the Confederate Army and became a very dangerous man. He was a large scale rancher who fought in the Taylor-Sutton Feud.

Pipes, Samuel—A member of the Sam Bass gang of train robbers, was captured by Texas Rangers.

Pitts, Charles—A member of the Jesse James gang, died with his boots on.

Pitts, Edward—A fine Texas Ranger of the Shootin' Seventies.

Platt, John—Texas Ranger and member of a famous family of peace officers.

Platt, Sam—A Texas Ranger who had four brothers also serving on the force.

Platt, Thomas—Texas Ranger and brother of Sam and John, above.

Plummer, Henry—A Nevada sheriff who organized a band of bandits for wholesale robberies in the mining towns. He was deadly on the draw, but was hanged by vigilantes.

Poe, John W.—Of the Panhandle, was a stock detective and peace officer, serving as deputy sheriff and later sheriff in Lincoln County, New Mexico, and as Marshal of Fort Griffin, Texas.

Polk, Cal—A Texas gunman sent by ranchers to stop Billy the Kid's depredations in the Panhandle.

Pool, James—Deputy sheriff of Presidio County, Texas.

Poston, Charles D.—Was an outstanding peace officer of Arizona.

Potter, Andrew J.—"Jack," was a reformed desperado who turned to preaching, but he never pulled off his gun. It was said that he was equally ready to preach, pray or perforate.

Potter, Mack—A member of the Kimble County gang of Texas outlaws, who was captured by Rangers and went to prison.

Powers, William—"Bill," a member of the Doolin gang, was killed in a Kansas bank raid.

R

Rae, Nick—A longrider accused of rustling. Was killed by a posse in Wyoming.

Raidler, William—"Bill," a member of the Doolin gang, was killed by Billy Tilghman.

Rankin, Bob—A U. S. Marshal in Wyoming who captured many outlaws. Among them was "Big Nosed George."

Ray, Ned—A Virginia City law officer who played the middle against both ends. He belonged to a robber gang which terrorized the town.

Rayner, William P.—El Paso's flashy two-gun man who was killed by Bob Rennick.

Reagan, Richard—"Dick," Sheriff of Anderson County, Texas, once captured Wes Hardin. Outlaws feared him.

Reasor, Charles—A member of the Jesse James gang.

Reasor, Charles—Appointed Special Texas Ranger at Tascosa.

Reed, James—A member of the Jesse James gang, was the first husband of Belle Starr. Jim was killed in Texas for the reward on his head.

Rennick, Robert—A gunfighter out El Paso way.

Reynolds, Glenn—Sheriff of Gila County Arizona, commanded unusual respect for his gunskill. He was killed by the Apache Kid.

Reynolds, N. O.—"Mage," a lieutenant of Texas Rangers who commanded a company. Many credit him with being the best Ranger of all time.

Reynolds, Starke—A Texas outlaw and member of the Kimble County gang. He was ambushed and killed while out on bond.

Rhodes, John—An Arizona gunman, fought for the Tewksbury clan during the Graham feud.

Rich, Charles—A Deadwood gunman of wide notoriety.

Richardson, Levi—Hunter, scout and gunman, was killed by Frank Loving in Dodge. He was considered one of the West's outstanding pistol men.

Riley, Benjamin F.—A Texas Ranger of wide repute.

Ringer, James Gladden—Texas outlaw and associate of Wes Hardin.

Ringgold, John—A Texas gunman of wide fame, fought in the Mason County War. Later, known as John Ringo, he was feared as the fastest and deadliest shot in Arizona. John was murdered in his sleep while alone on the desert, and a dozen men claimed the "credit."

Rivers, Frank—A New Mexican gunman who fought in the Lincoln County War.

Rivers, William—"Billy," a Kansas hunter and fighter who won fame as a peace officer.

Roarke, Mike—A Texas trail driver and gunman who joined Billy the Kid, after a career of crime in Kansas.

Roberts, Daniel W.—Captain of Texas Rangers and son of Buck Roberts.

Roberts, Hawk—A Texas Ranger with an Indian and outlaw fighting background.

Roberts, James—A protection man for the Three D Ranch.

Roberts, "Buckshot"—An old soldier and gunfighter who was a mass of wounds and scars. Alone, he fought Billy the Kid, and twelve others, killing one and wounding four before his death.

Robinson, George—Lieutenant of Texas Rangers.

Robinson, Robert—Protection man for George Littlefield in Texas.

Rodgers, Norman—Texas Ranger on the Mexican border patrol.

Rogers, J. H.—A Texas Ranger on outlaw detail.

Rudabaugh, David—An outlaw leader in Kansas and New Mexico, later joined Billy the Kid.

Rudd, W. L.—"Colorado Chico," a Texas Ranger who was born in England.

Rutherford, William—"Bill," a Texas Ranger who poked law into the border with a gun barrel.

Ryan, Jacob—A Texas gunman and feudist from DeWitt County.

Ryan, William—"Bill," was a member of the Jesse James gang.

Rynning, Thomas H.—Captain of Arizona State Rangers.

S

Sample, Omer W.—"Red," a member of the Heath gang of Arizona, was hanged in Cochise County.

Sandoval, Jesus—The most cunning and brutal of Texas Rangers. He was dismissed from the force for allegedly murdering prisoners.

Saunders, J. Wood—Texas Ranger and later, protection man for the XIT Ranch.

Scarborough, George—A deputy U. S. Marshal, carried a big pistol reputation out El Paso way. He killed John Selman and in turn was killed by Will Carver and Kid Curry.

Scoggins, Jake—A New Mexican gunfighter who was active in Lincoln County.

Scott, Jerry—A Texas saloon keeper and gunman of wide reputation.

Scott, John—Got mean enough to fight three Texas Rangers.

Scott, William—A Texas outlaw, and one-time member of Sam Bass' gang.

Scott, William—Captain of Texas Rangers.

Seaborn, John—One of those quiet and determined non-coms of the Texas Rangers.

Seiker, Edward—With his brother, L. P., who due to long service and dependability, were two of the most prominent Texas Rangers. They won promotions for gallant service.

Seiker, L. P.—Brother of Ed, above.

Selman, John—A brave and efficient Marshal of El Paso. He had fourteen credits when killed by George Scarborough.

Shadden, Adolph—A tough gunman of the Texas cattle country.

Shadden, Joe—Brother of Dolph, and also a gunman of note. Manning Clements killed both these brothers.

Shears, George—A desperate Montana outlaw.

Shepherd, George—A member of the Cole Younger gang, was imprisoned.

Shepherd, Olle—Brother of George, and also a member of the Younger gang, was killed by a posse.

Shivers, Dock—A smart and fast Texas Ranger.

Shoenfield, Lew—A noted gunman of Montana, Wyoming and the Dakotas.

Shores, C. W.—"Doc," a peace officer of Texas, Colorado and New Mexico, was a tenacious man-trailer. Served as sheriff of Gunnison County.

Short, Edward—A fighting Marshal of Kansas and Oklahoma Territory, helped break many gangs, including the Daltons.

Short, Luke—An underrated gunman who killed such headliners as Charley Storms and Jim Courtright. He served as Marshal of Dodge and was also a professional gambler. He died in bed at age thirty-nine.

Sippy, Benjamin—An eminent Marshal of Tombstone.

Siringo, Charles A.—A stove-up cowpoke who became a Pinkerton agent. Represented Panhandle ranchers in their war against the Kid.

Sitterlie, Joe—Peace officer of DeWitt County, Texas, was taken in by the Rangers for being too handy with his cutters.

Skinner, Cyrus—Robber, gambler and gunman of Virginia City.

Skurlock, Dock—A gunman of the Panhandle and New Mexico, fought in the Lincoln County War.

Slade, Joseph A.—An official of the Pony Express with twenty-six notches. His reputation as a gunman, and his weakness for drink ruined him and he was hanged in Montana.

Slaughter, John—A Texas cattleman and fighter who became sheriff of tough Cochise County, Arizona.

Small, Augustus—"Gus," a noted Texas Ranger of the outlaw era.

Small, William—Member of the Hole In The Wall Gang. Reformed in Wyoming and became sheriff of Valley County.

Smith, Eugene—Of Wyoming and the Dakotas, was a fearless gunman on the side of the law.

Smith, Jack—"Dogface," a Texas cowboy who was sudden with the .45.

Smith, L. B. —A Texas Ranger, was killed in action on the Mexican border.

Smith, Thomas—Marshal of Taylor, Texas, U. S. Deputy Marshal and Wyoming stock detective. Killed by an outlaw in 1892. Other Tom Smiths achieved wide frontier reputations. Tom Smith, a peace officer of Abilene, Texas, was a famous pistol man. Tom Smith, Marshal of Abilene, Kansas, was even more famous, for he went unarmed. He served only six months before he was killed by a farmer. No member of the gunfighting fraternity had given him any trouble.

Smith, William—Arizona killer and outlaw leader who moved to New Mexico for his health.

Sowell, A. J.—A Texas Ranger from Seguin, a town which bred some smart and tricky gunmen.

Spaniard, Jack—Half-breed lover of Belle Starr, and member of her gang. He was hanged.

Sparks, John C.—Captain of Texas Rangers.

Sparks, Thomas M.—Sergeant of Texas Rangers.

Spence, Peter—An Arizona gunman and outlaw, was slain by the Earps as a suspect for the killing of Morgan Earp.

Spotswood, Thomas—Member of the Texas gang headed by Sam Bass.

Stallings, James—A Texas Ranger who abandoned a fine record to turn outlaw.

Standard, Jesse—A keen-eyed Texas cowboy, lean, lank and dangerous.

Standifer, B. Y.—"Bill," sheriff of Crosby County, Texas, served the Spur Ranch as protection man. He was killed by Pink Higgins.

Starr, Belle—The widow of Jim Reed, married Sam Starr and became the leader of a desperado gang based at Younger's Bend in Oklahoma Territory. She was killed by Edgar Watson.

Starr, Edward—Wyoming cowman and feudist, was accused of cattle rustling.

Starr, Samuel—Second husband of Belle Starr, who like her first husband, was an outlaw who died with his boots on.

Steele, George—A gunman and desperado of Colorado.

Stephen, Steve—A New Mexican gunfighter, participated in the Lincoln War.

Stevens, George—"Big Nose," a Wyoming badman.

Stevens, G. W.—Captain of Texas Rangers.

Stevenson, Frank—New Mexican and Texan cattle rustler whose Canutillo gang was broken by Jim Gillett, and Frank was imprisoned.

Stiles, Billy—An Arizona train robber who turned state's evidence against his gang. He later joined the Arizona Rangers.

Stilwell, Frank—An ex-peace-officer and hardcase around Tombstone, was shotgunned by the Earps while awaiting trial for stage robbery.

Stinson, Buck—A deputy of Henry Plummer at Virginia City, was an outlaw operating behind his badge.

Stockton, Ike—A gunman in the Lincoln County War, was a gambler and a killer, but as brave as they come.

Stoker, John—Deputy Sheriff of Tarrant County when Fort Worth was rough and ready.

Storms, Charles—A bad man around Dodge and Abilene. He was killed by Luke Short in Tombstone.

Stoudenmire, Dallas—Marshal of El Paso at its worst, was the gunfighter personified, once killing three gunmen within a few seconds. He became deputy U. S. Marshal before he was killed by Jim Manning.

Strawhan, Jake—Hays City gunman who was killed by Wild Bill Hickok.

Stringer, Jake—Leader of a Montana gang of desperados.

Sughrue, Bud—Marshal of Dodge and a craftsman at gunplay.

Sughrue, Pat—One of the famous peace officers of the West, operated in Kansas and Wyoming.

Sullivan, John—Sergeant of Texas Rangers who was always busy. He helped break the Cook-Skeeter gang of Oklahoma train robbers.

Sullivan, W. J.—A Texas Ranger of that tough Company B.

Sutton, Fred—Claimed to have been sent by Texas ranchers to aid Pat Garrett in cornering Billy the Kid in New Mexico.

Swilling, Henry—An outlaw and rustler of Cochise, Arizona.

Swilling, Thomas—One of those hard and fast Texas Ranger sergeants.

T

Talley, George—Dismissed from the Rangers and charged with murder for killing an unarmed man, fled to Mexico and remained on the dodge for forty years.

Taylor, Buck—Brother of Scrap and Will, cousins of a large clan of Taylors and Hardins who were troublemakers from Texas to Kansas. Buck was from Clinton, fought in the DeWitt County war and was killed at a dance.

Taylor, James—Cousin of Wes Hardin, fought in the Taylor-Sutton Feud of Cuero.

Taylor, Scrap—Another member of the large Taylor clan, was hanged by a mob.

Taylor, Tom—Brother of Jim, also fought in the DeWitt war.

Taylor, William—One of the leaders of the Taylor clan, was a dandy in dress, but had a true fighting man's temperament. The more angry he became, the cooler he was. A hard-eyed killer, he was an associate of Wes Hardin and King Fisher.

Terwiliger, William—"Bill," a member of the Plummer gang in Bannock and Virginia City.

Tewksbury, Edward—One of the fighting sheepmen of the Tonto Basin War. He was accused of killing John Graham, the last of the Graham brothers, in the Graham-Tewksbury Feud.

Tewksbury, James—His anxious trigger finger precipitated a fight in which two Hashknife men were killed and Tom Tucker was shot five times.

Tewksbury, John—Killed in an ambush. He was one of the leaders of his faction in the Graham-Tewksbury Feud.

Thomas, Heck—A U. S. Marshal, was one of the most noted of all Oklahoma peace officers. He killed or captured many outlaws. Among them was Bill Doolin, whom Heck killed in a gun battle.

Thomas, Henry—One of the outstanding men of the Texas Rangers.

Thomas, John—Another brave and skillful gunfighter of the Ranger force.

Thompkins, Bill—A Texas Ranger who accepted the dangerous assignment of joining Bill Taylor's Cuero gang for securing inside information.

Thompson, Ben—One of the most noted gunmen Texas produced. Marshal of Austin, a professional gambler, proprietor of the Bullhead Saloon in roaring Abilene, Kansas. After an eventful career, he was killed in San Antonio.

Thompson, Hill—"Smokey," a gunman of the Texas and New Mexico ranges who cut a swath in Kansas.

Thompson, Bill—Brother of the famous Ben, was a gunman in his own right, though somewhat unpredictable and flighty.

Tilghman, William—"Billy," has been called the West's greatest peace officer. He rode herd on Oklahoma for fifty years before he was killed in action.

Tipton, Daniel—A gunfighter known throughout Kansas and Texas. He stayed on the side of the law.

Towle, Frank—Stagecoach robber and associate of Sam Bass in South Dakota.

Tracy, Harry—A psychopathic killer who terrorized the northwest.

Trout, James—Fought outlaws with the authority of his Texas Ranger badge.

Tucker, F. F.—Another Texas Ranger on outlaw detail.

Tucker, Thomas—Fighting leader of the Hashknife outfit who became a peace officer in Santa Fe.

Tumlinson, Joe—Generalissimo of the Suttons in the De-Witt County, Texas, war. He organized two hundred gunmen to prosecute this feud.

Turner, Benjamin—A member of the Horrell gang from Texas, was killed in a New Mexican fight.

Turner, "Bull"—A member of the Brooken gang who quit them and tried to go straight. The gang, distrusting his intentions, killed him.

Turner, Thomas—Sheriff of Santa Cruz County, Arizona.

U

Underwood, Henry—Brother of "Old Dad," was a member of the Sam Bass gang of train robbers.

Underwood, John—"Old Dad," a Texan trail driver who joined the Joel Collins gang of bandits.

Utter, Charles—"Colorado Charley," one of the famous gunmen who ranged from Texas to the Dakotas in the Smoky Seventies.

V

Valley, Frank—A Tascosa gunman who was killed by Len Woodruff.

Vandenberg, Robert—Peace officer of Ford County, Kansas, and later, Marshal of Dodge.

Vaughn, John—A Texas desperado whom the Rangers captured with Ham White.

Vermillion, John—"Texas Jack," a gunman sidekick of Wyatt Earp.

W

Waddill, H. B.—Coldly impersonal and methodical Texas Ranger.

Waightman, Red Buck—An Oklahoma half-breed, one of the most colorful members of the dreaded Bill Doolin gang, was killed by a posse.

Waite, Fred—A New Mexican gunman who fought in the Lincoln County War.

Wagner, Jack—A gunman of the Kansas cattle-railhead boomtowns, was killed by Bat Masterson over the death of Ed, Bat's brother.

Wagner, John—"Dutch," a desperate Montana outlaw and killer.

Walde, Edward—Stage driver, Indian fighter and Texas Ranger.

Walker, Alfred—Killed Ed Masterson and was in turn killed by Bat, Ed's brother.

Wall, John—A Deadwood outlaw and Wyoming stage robber, was shot three times by Scott Davis, but lived to serve a prison term.

Wallace, Marion D.—A Texas sheriff who was slain by Boone Marlow, the leader of the notorious Marlow gang.

Ward, J. L.—A Cochise County, Arizona sheriff who hanged five men on one gallows.

Ware, Richard—"Dick," the Texas Ranger who killed Sebe Barnes, became the first sheriff of Mitchell County, and later a U. S. Marshal.

Warner, Matt—A famous Utah outlaw who became a good peace officer.

Warren, J. W.—Another of those Texas Ranger non-coms, who were the best in the business.

Warren, Thomas—A noted Denver, Colorado, gunman.

Watkins, Eugene—Gambler and gunman from Texas, was slain as he killed two others over a monte game.

Watson, "Pegleg"—A train robber who operated in Texas and New Mexico.

Watts, James—One of New Mexico's better pistol men who fought the Kid.

Webb, Charles—Deputy sheriff of Brown County, Texas, who was killed by Wes Hardin…he of the forty notches.

Webb, Joshua—One of the famous badman marshals of the midwestern cowtowns.

Wesley, John—A member of the Henry Brown gang, who was hanged for a murder committed during a bank robbery.

West, Edward—A Texas cowboy who joined Billy the Kid in New Mexico.

West, John—"Jack." A Texas "hogleg" man of wide repute.

West, Richard—"Little Dick," a member of the Doolin and Jennings gangs, was killed by Heck Thomas.

Wheeler, Benjamin—Deputy Marshal to Henry Brown in Caldwell, joined Brown's outlaw gang when the latter turned to lawlessness. Ben was hanged for murder committed during a bank robbery.

Wheeler, Harry—Soldier, ranger, peace officer and one of the finest shots in the West. Was a noted leader of men in Arizona.

Whipple, George—Sheriff of Route County, Colorado.

White, Hamilton—Texas stagecoach robber and killer, was captured by Texas Rangers after a sixty-mile chase.

White, James—A member of Jesse James' gang.

White, John—Brother of Jim, and also a member of the James gang.

Whitehead, Robert—Texas trail driver and gunfighter.

Whitney, Chauncey B.—Indian scout and Ellsworth Marshal, was killed by the drunken Bill Thompson.

Williams, Benjamin—Deputy U. S. Marshal of the Indian Territory, and a fearless manhunter.

Williams, George—A protection man for the Littlefield ranch, served against Billy the Kid.

Willingham, Cape S.—The first sheriff of Oldham County, Texas, when Tascosa was yet a wild and wicked town.

Wilson, Andrew—"Andy," a wizened and shrewd old Texas Ranger who had seen it all.

Wilson, Bone—A Texas outlaw who was killed by Rangers.

Wilson, John—Brother-in-law of Bill Longley, and a "tough customer."

Wilson, Vernon—Texas Ranger and sidekick of Mage Reynolds.

Wilson, William—"Bill," a Texan on the dodge, joined Billy the Kid's gang in New Mexico.

Wixon, Eli—A Texas badman who was captured by Rangers in Kerr County.

Wolforth, Patrick—A Texas lawman, helped break the vicious Brooken gang.

Woodring, Sidney—A wary old Oklahoma rustler and outlaw who raided Texas and fell to the Rangers.

Woods, Harry—Deputy sheriff of Cochise County, Arizona.

Woods, Powell—A fighting cowman, was an associate of Pink Higgins.

Woods, Wade—A hardcase around Tascosa.

Worley, John—Deputy sheriff of Mason County, was killed by that ace gunman, Scott Cooley.

Wyatt, John—"Texas Jack," a Kansas gambler and gunman who was killed in Fort Worth.

Y

Yager, Erastus—A Montana boomtown badman.

Yandell, William—"Bill," a quickdraw artist of Tascosa.

Young, John—A Texas Ranger "guide." He was too young to take the Ranger oath, but served as a regular and drew regular pay.

Younger, Bruce—Uncle of the noted Younger brothers. Belonged to the gang headed by his nephew, Cole.

Younger, James—Died a suicide after serving twenty-five years in prison for the depredations of the Younger gang.

Younger, John—Another of the brothers who was killed by a detective who also died at John's hand in a doubly fatal shootout.

Younger, Thomas Coleman—Leader of the Younger gang of train and bank robbers. The Younger gang often joined forces with the Jesse James gang.

Younger, Robert—"Bob," died in prison for his part in the Younger gang activities.

Yountis, Oliver—Member of the Dalton gang of bank robbers, was killed by a posse headed by Chris Madsen and Heck Thomas.

Z

Zachary, Robert—"Bob," a Montana gunman who was associated with the Henry Plummer combine.

www.ingramcontent.com/pod-product-compliance
Lightning Source LLC
Chambersburg PA
CBHW020338100426
42812CB00029B/3169/J